Memory Thinking for C & C++ Windows Diagnostics

Slides with Descriptions and Source Code Illustrations

Second Edition

Dmitry Vostokov
Software Diagnostics Services

OpenTask

Memory Thinking for C & C++ Windows Diagnostics: Slides with Descriptions and Source Code Illustrations, Second Edition

Published by OpenTask, Republic of Ireland

OpenTask books are available through booksellers and distributors worldwide. For further information or comments, send requests to press@opentask.com.

A CIP catalog record for this book is available from the British Library.

ISBN-13: 978-1912636617 (Paperback)

Revision 2.06 (May 2025)

Table of Contents

Preface

This full-color reference book is a part of the Accelerated C & C++ for Windows Diagnostics training course organized by Software Diagnostics Services (www.patterndiagnostics.com). The text contains slides, brief notes highlighting particular points, and illustrative source code fragments. The second edition added 45 Visual Studio projects with more than 5,500 lines of code. The book's detailed Table of Contents makes the usual Index redundant. We hope this reference is helpful for the following audiences:

- C and C++ developers who want to deepen their knowledge;
- Software engineers developing and maintaining products on Windows platforms;
- Technical support, escalation, DevSecOps, cloud and site reliability engineers dealing with complex software issues;
- Quality assurance engineers who test software on Windows platforms;
- Security and vulnerability researchers, reverse engineers, malware and memory forensics analysts.

If you encounter any error, please use the contact form on the Software Diagnostics Services web site or, alternatively, via Twitter @DumpAnalysis.

Facebook group:

http://www.facebook.com/groups/dumpanalysis

LinkedIn page and group:

https://www.linkedin.com/company/software-diagnostics-institute/
https://www.linkedin.com/groups/8473045/

About the Author

Dmitry Vostokov is an internationally recognized expert, speaker, educator, scientist, inventor, and author. He founded the pattern-oriented software diagnostics, forensics, and prognostics discipline (Systematic Software Diagnostics) and Software Diagnostics Institute (DA+TA: DumpAnalysis.org + TraceAnalysis.org). Vostokov has also authored over 50 books on software diagnostics, anomaly detection and analysis, software and memory forensics, root cause analysis and problem solving, memory dump analysis, debugging, software trace and log analysis, reverse engineering, and malware analysis. He has over 30 years of experience in software architecture, design, development, and maintenance in various industries, including leadership, technical, and people management roles. Dmitry founded OpenTask Iterative and Incremental Publishing (OpenTask.com) and Software Diagnostics Technology and Services (former Memory Dump Analysis Services) PatternDiagnostics.com. In his spare time, he explores Software Narratology and Quantum Software Diagnostics. His interest areas are theoretical software diagnostics and its mathematical and computer science foundations, application of formal logic, semiotics, artificial intelligence, machine learning, and data mining to diagnostics and anomaly detection, software diagnostics engineering and diagnostics-driven development, diagnostics workflow and interaction. Recent interest areas also include functional programming, cloud native computing, monitoring, observability, visualization, security, automation, applications of category theory to software diagnostics, development and big data, and diagnostics of artificial intelligence.

Introduction

Original Training Course Name

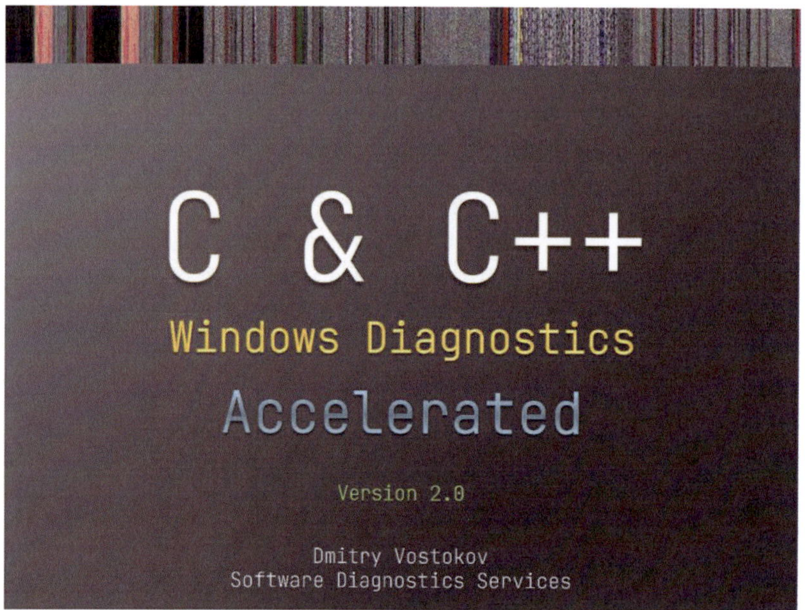

Prerequisites

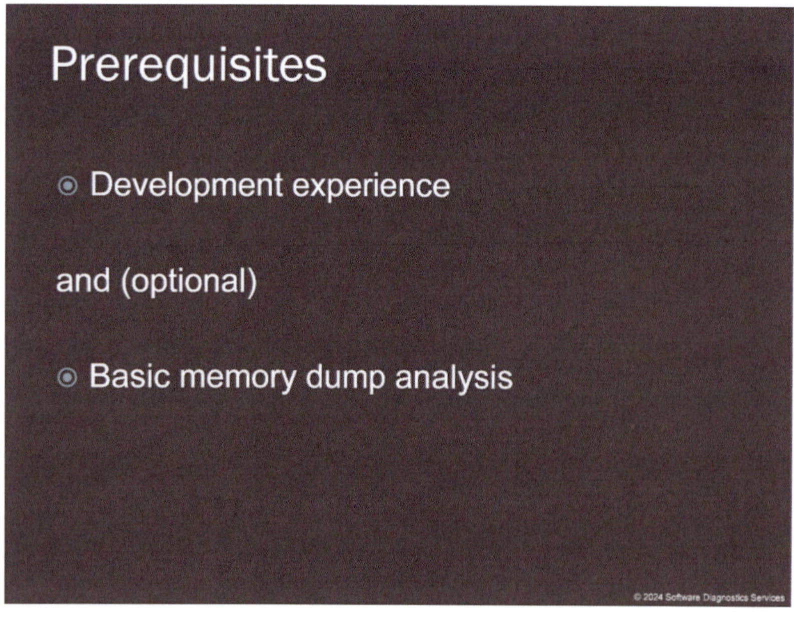

To get most of this training, you are expected to have basic development experience in a programming language other than C or C++ and optional basic memory dump analysis experience. I also included the necessary x64 review for some topics.

Training Goals

Training Goals

- Review common fundamentals of C and C++
- Review C++ specifics
- Use WinDbg for learning C and C++ internals
- See how C and C++ knowledge is used during diagnostics and debugging

Our primary goal is to learn C and C++ and its internals in an accelerated fashion. First, we review common C and C++ fundamentals necessary for software diagnostics. Then, we learn various C and C++ features with a focus on memory and internals. We also see examples of how the knowledge of C and C++ helps in diagnostics and debugging.

Training Principles

Training Principles

- Talk only about what I can show
- Lots of pictures
- Lots of examples
- Original content and examples

There were many training formats to consider, and I decided that the best way is to concentrate on slides and code examples you can verify.

Schedule

Schedule

```
std::vector<Session> sessions;
assert(sessions.size() == 6);
assert(sessions.capacity() > 6);
```

© 2024 Software Diagnostics Services

I originally planned the training to have only 5 one-hour sessions, but I gradually extended it to 12 sessions to fit all necessary material in sufficient detail in the first version, and then fit it into 5 90-minute sessions. For the second edition I plan 6 2-hour sessions.

Training Idea

Training Idea

- Reading Windows-based Code training
- Memory dump analysis training
- Reversing training
- Windows API training

© 2024 Software Diagnostics Services

For years, people asked me to resume my very old training in reading Windows-based code (see the References part). Finally, I gave in. Attendees of memory dump analysis and reversing training courses asked questions related to C and C++, and I realized that they would have also benefitted if they had this training. This training may also fill some gaps between these courses. Finally, I recently developed the **Accelerated Windows API** training course (see the References section at the end of the book), where solid knowledge of classic C and C++ is assumed, and the current C and C++ course may provide such knowledge.

Version 2.0 Idea

Version 2.0 Idea

- Missing topics
- Missing source code projects
- Memory Thinking for Rust training

Unfortunately, the first version didn't include some important topics and source code projects were not included too. After I developed the **Memory Thinking for Rust** training with extensive source code support, I realized that a similar project structure would benefit C and C++ training.

General C & C++ Aspects

General C & C++ Aspects

- Philosophy of pointers
- Structures, classes, and objects
- Promotions and conversions
- Macros, types, and synonyms
- Source code organization, PImpl
- Pointer dereference walkthrough
- Functions and function pointers
- Inheritance
- Operators, function objects
- Destructors, virtual destructors
- Local stack variables and values
- Memory operators and expressions
- Alignment
- Slicing
- Iterators as pointers
- Lambdas and their internals
- Threads and synchronization
- Deleted and default members
- Unions
- Variadic functions and templates
- Memory and pointers
- Basic types
- Memory and structures
- Uniform initialization
- Memory storage
- Values, lvalues, rvalues
- References (lvalue and rvalue)
- Constant values and expressions
- Namespaces
- Constructors, copy, move, assignment
- Virtual functions, pure methods
- VTBL and VPTR
- Access levels
- Overloading, overriding
- Templates
- Memory ownership, RAII
- Smart pointers
- Conversion constructors
- Enumerations

The general C and C++ aspects that we discuss in this course:

- Philosophy of pointers
- Structures, classes, and objects
- Promotions and conversions
- Macros, types, and synonyms
- Source code organization, PImpl
- Pointer dereference walkthrough
- Functions and function pointers
- Inheritance
- Operators, function objects
- Destructors, virtual destructors
- Local stack variables and values
- Memory operators and expressions

- Alignment
- Slicing
- Iterators as pointers
- Lambdas and their internals
- Threads and synchronization
- Memory and pointers
- Basic types
- Memory and structures
- Uniform initialization
- Memory storage
- References (lvalues and rvalues)
- Values, lvalues, rvalues
- Constant values and expressions
- Namespaces
- Constructors, copy, move, assignment
- Virtual functions, pure methods
- VTBL and VPTR
- Access levels
- Overloading, overriding
- Templates
- Memory ownership, RAII
- Smart pointers
- Deleted and default members
- Unions
- Conversion constructors
- Variadic functions and templates
- Enumerations

Highlighted topics are new to this edition.

What We Do Not Cover

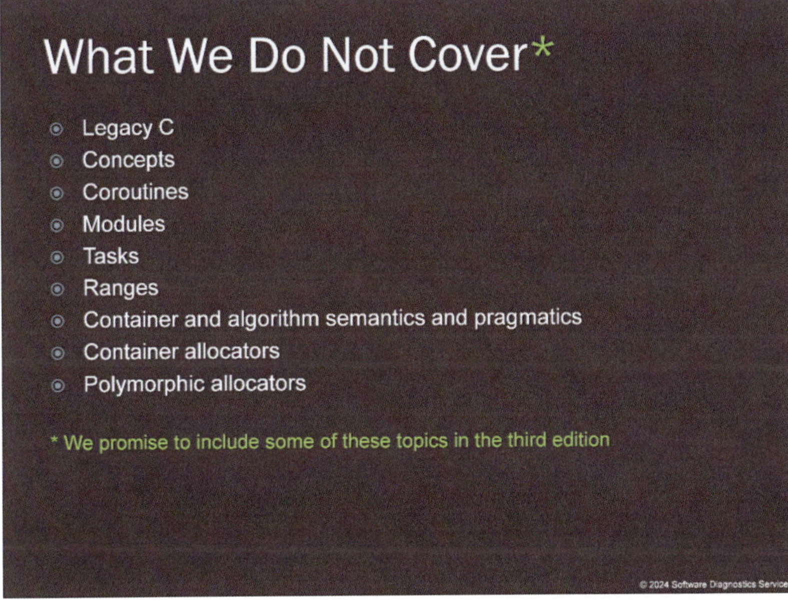

There are some C++ topics that we did not include in the first edition but promised to include in the second edition:

- Legacy C
- Concepts
- Coroutines
- Modules
- Tasks
- Ranges
- Container and algorithm semantics and pragmatics
- Container allocators
- Polymorphic allocators

We promise to include the remaining topics in the third edition of this course.

Windows C & C++ Aspects

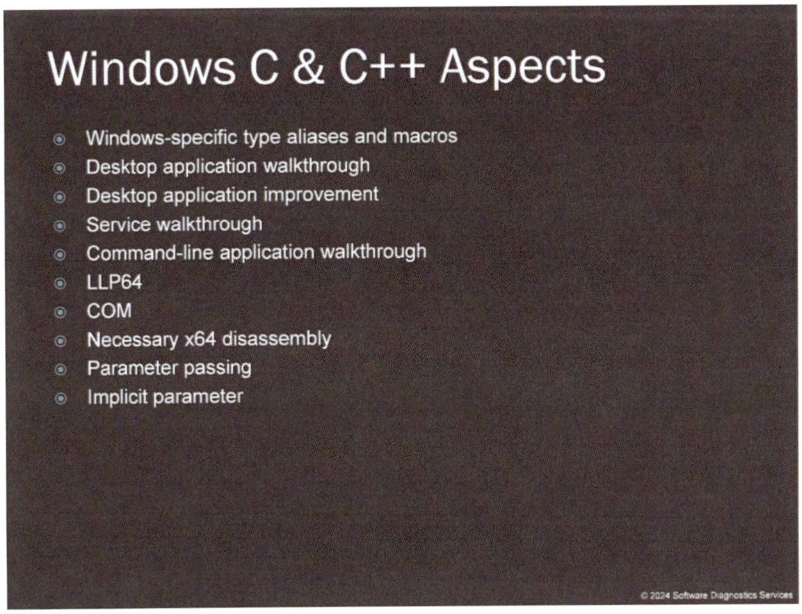

Windows C & C++ Aspects

- Windows-specific type aliases and macros
- Desktop application walkthrough
- Desktop application improvement
- Service walkthrough
- Command-line application walkthrough
- LLP64
- COM
- Necessary x64 disassembly
- Parameter passing
- Implicit parameter

© 2024 Software Diagnostics Services

In addition, we also discuss related Windows aspects, including:

- Windows-specific type aliases and macros
- LLP64
- Necessary x64 disassembly
- Parameter passing
- Implicit parameter

Why C & C++?

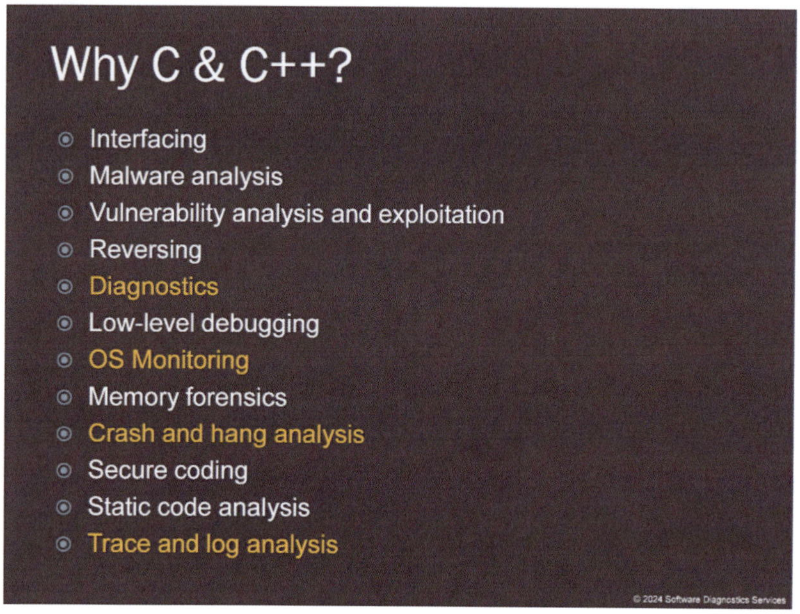

First, why did we create this course? Even if you don't develop in C and C++, the knowledge of C and C++ and their internals is necessary for many software construction and post-construction activities:

- Interfacing
- Malware analysis
- Vulnerability analysis and exploitation
- Reversing
- **Diagnostics**
- Low-level debugging
- **OS Monitoring**
- Memory forensics
- **Crash and hang analysis**
- Secure coding
- Static code analysis
- **Trace and log analysis**

In this training, we mostly look at C and C++ from a software diagnostics perspective. This perspective includes memory dump analysis and, partially, trace and log analysis. The knowledge of C and C++ is tacitly assumed in my other courses, where most abnormal software behavior modeling exercises are written in C and C++. Of course, there is an intersection of what we learn with other areas.

Which C & C++?

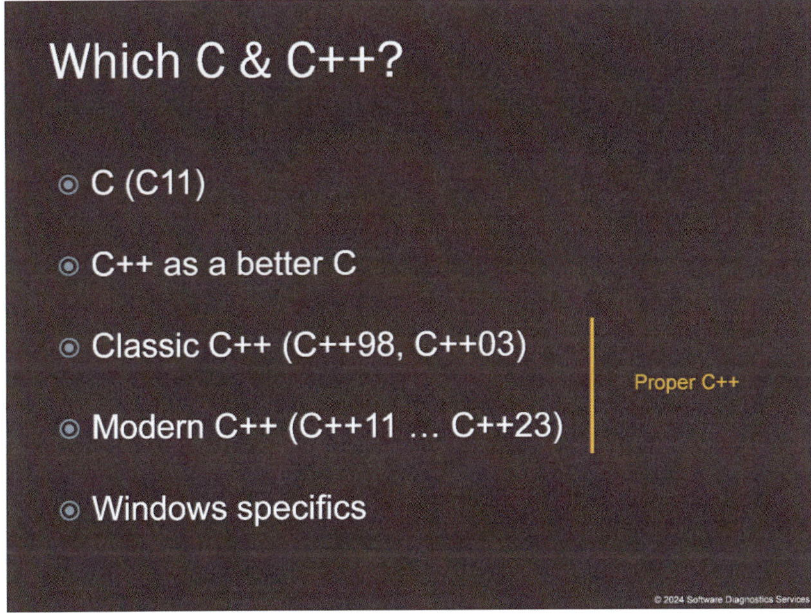

Which C and C++? We look at a unified presentation approach combining all C and C++ variants. Since this course is about diagnostics and not designing and implementing code, we generally do not make distinctions in slides. It is not possible to cover all the differ-ences in the short time that we have. We also describe things as they are in Windows programming, not as they ought to be from the latest C++ standards. However, in the second edition, we provide separate source code projects for separate categories: plain C (we choose C11 in project settings), C++ as a better C (modifi-cations needed to make C code com-pile as C++), classic C++ (before C++11), and modern C++ (mostly C++17) with some illustrated features from C++20 and C++23.

My History of C & C++

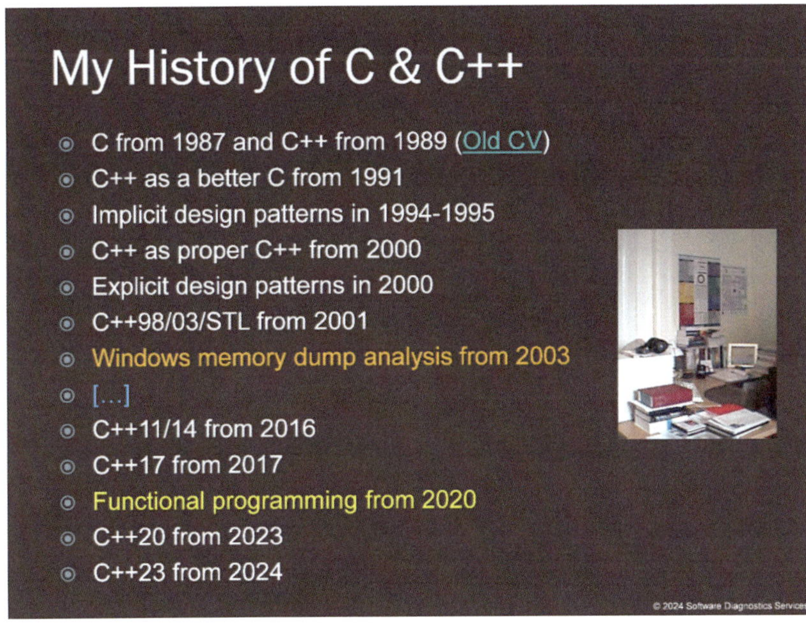

This history slide is only about C and C++ languages. Despite many years, it is still easy to recall when I started learning C. It was shortly after I started my university education. And although my first programming language was FORTRAN, I read the classic K&R book in a library. C++ is harder to recall, but most likely, it was in 1989, at least according to my old CV, which is the source of truth. I definitely started using C++ in com-mercial projects around 1991 but used it as a better C, and there was no standard template library (STL) at that time. I recall some fascinating C++ GUI frameworks for MS-DOS, like Zinc. In 1994-1995 I designed a word processor for Windows 3.1, and in the process, I implicitly used many design patterns

I later discovered in the GOF book in 2000. The authors also use a word processor for illustration. I mainly understood C++ as C++ in 2000 when I read a book about CORBA distributed object technology that used C++ and also a book about the internals of Windows COM using C++. This also greatly improved my COM programming and debugging skills – I used to debug COM and ActiveX components a lot during the years 1998 – 2000. I continued learning C++ by reading many books of that time and learned the merits of using STL and also how to use it effectively. In 2001, I joined a company that developed C++ static analysis tools, and this greatly improved my C++ knowledge up to the expert level at that time. C++03 didn't have major changes compared to C++98, and this is why I included it with C++98 for the year 2001. In 2003, things turned out unexpectedly as I moved from full-time development using C++ to full-time memory dump analysis of C++ programs. I continued using C++03 for writing diagnostic tools, though. In 2016, I learned that the language completely changed to C++11/14. I came back to full-time C++ programming in late 2017, where I also started using language features from C++17. In 2020, I moved to functional programming in Scala, which also influenced my C++ coding for new projects. I started using C++20 last year, and this year – C++23. Last year I also switched from Scala to Rust and wrote **Memory Thinking for Rust** book, which was beneficial for me to see certain C and C++ aspects in the new light.

Zinc
https://en.wikipedia.org/wiki/Zinc_Application_Framework

Old CV
https://opentask.com/Vostokov/CV.htm

C and C++ Mastery Process

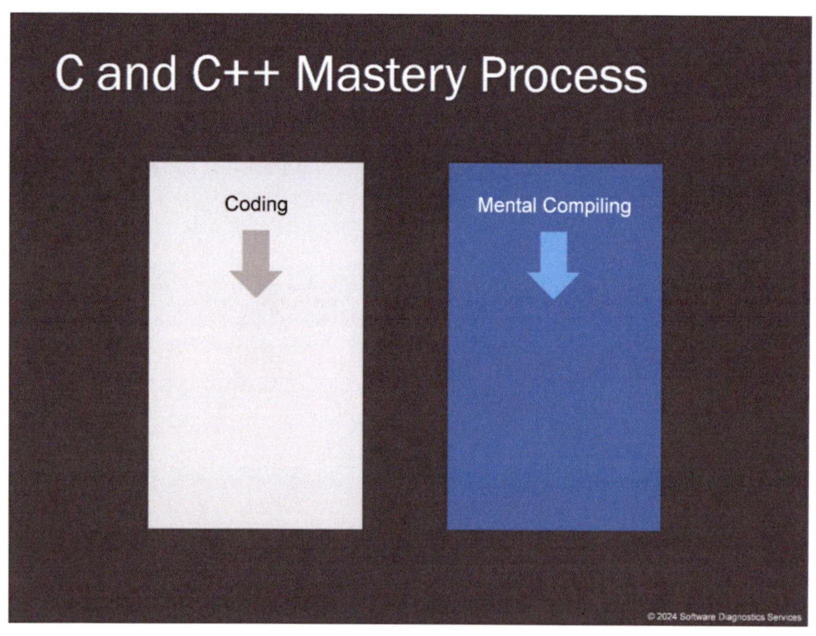

Despite high-level features in C++, there's still much low-level overlap with C, and when I program in C and C++, I mentally compile to memory. This helps when I have a doubt about whether this or that construct is safe. And I also believe that looking at how C and C++ constructs are implemented in memory greatly helps in learning these languages.

Thought Process

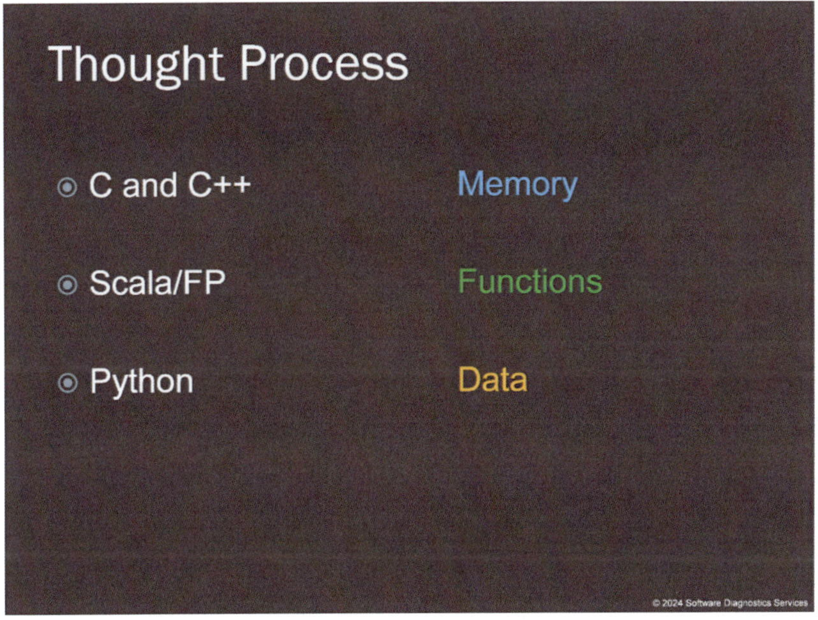

This slide about a thought process when using a programming language is perhaps controversial. With C and C++, we think about memory; with Scala/FP, we think about functions; and with Python, we think about data.

Philosophy of Pointers

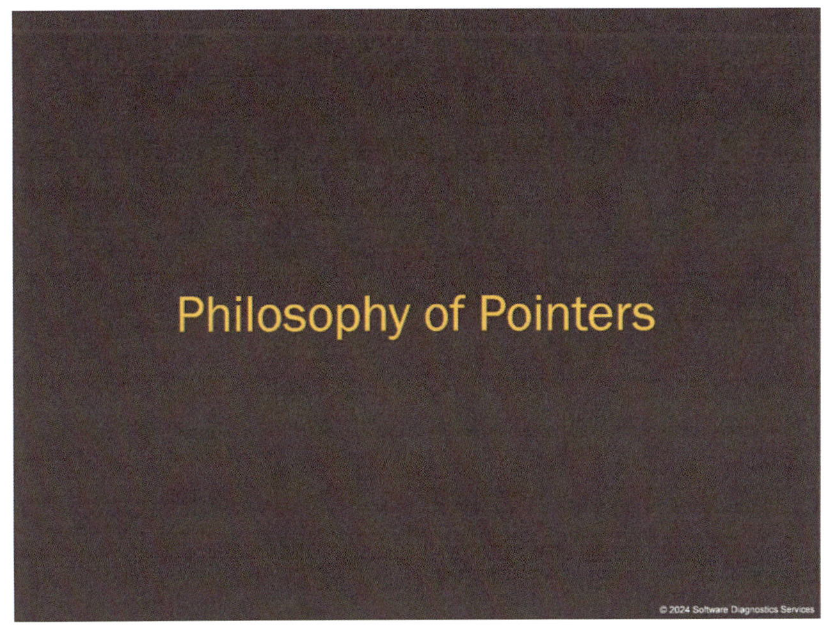

We start with pointers, the most important concept in C and also in C++. I originally created this approach in 2015 but now extended it for this training. The second edition also adds source code projects in C and several flavors of C++.

Pointer

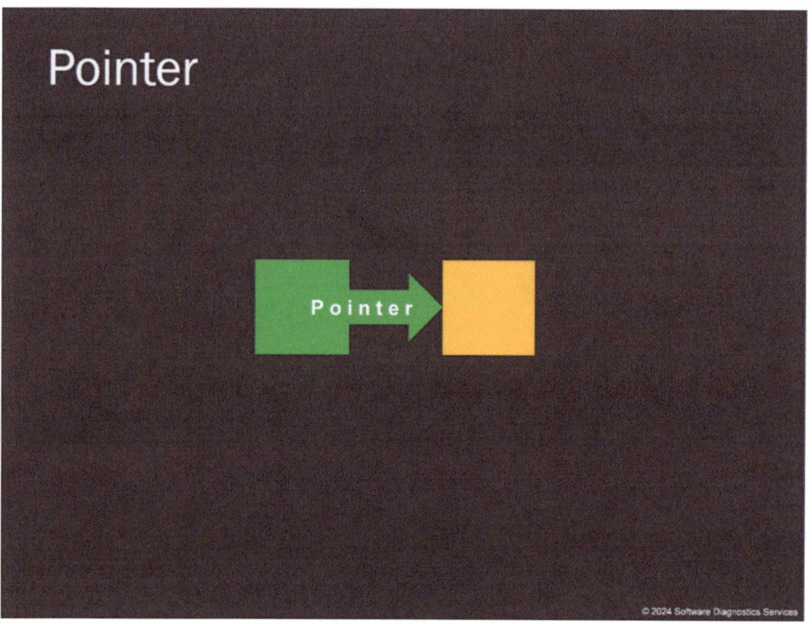

Conceptually, a pointer is an entity that refers (or points) to some other entity. We say entity, not an object, so as not to confuse it with objects in C++ or objects in object-oriented programming. This can be my finger, for example, pointing to an apple.

Pointer Dereference

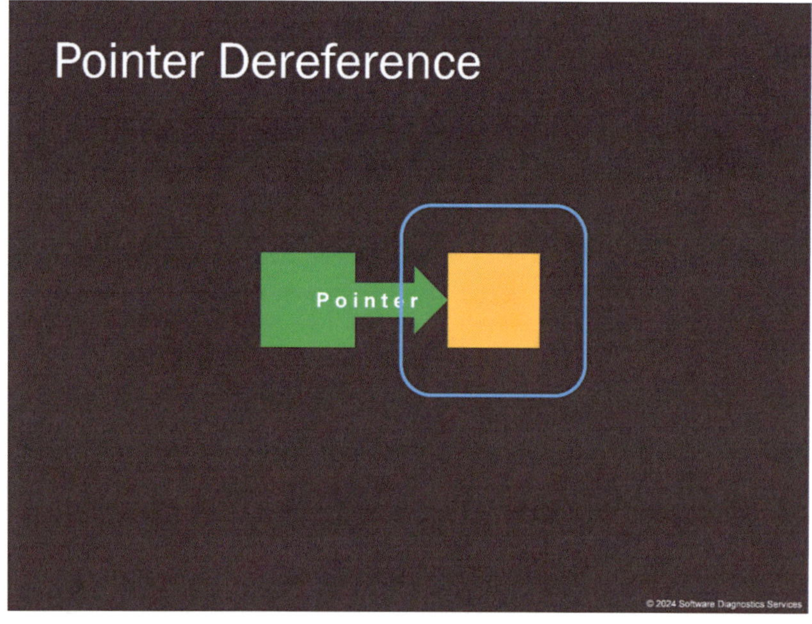

A pointer dereference is an act of getting the entity it references for further inspection or usage. Imagine I point to an apple, and you grab it to eat.

One to Many

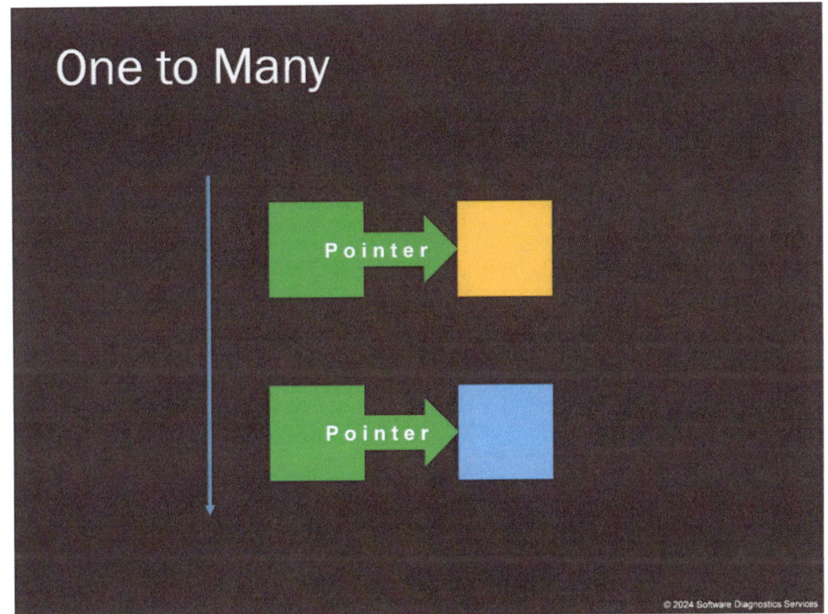

During its lifetime, a pointer may point to different entities. If no pointer points to an entity, it may become lost in certain execution scenarios, the so-called memory leak.

Many to One

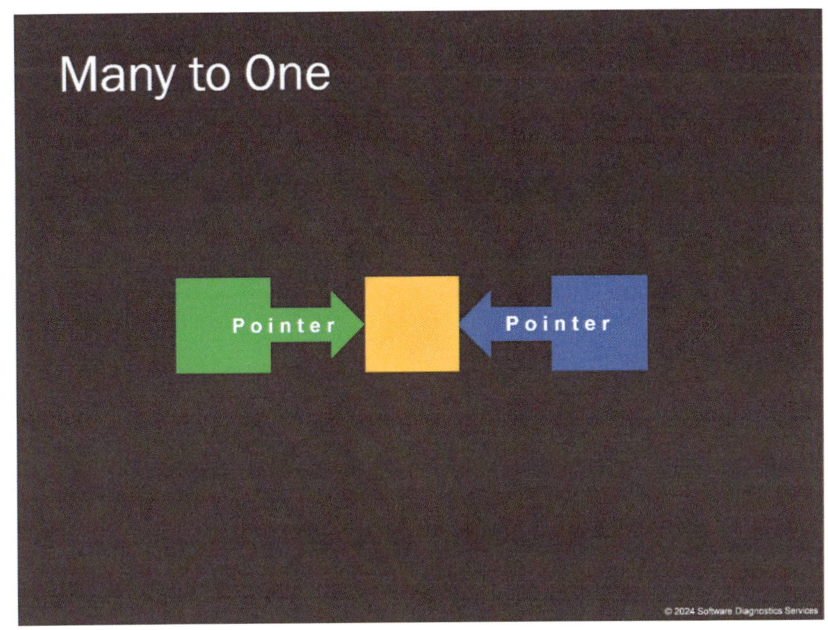

Several pointers can refer (or point) to the same entity. For example, two people are pointing to the same apple. So, conceptually, pointers are distinct from entities they point to. Should we call the latter pointees?

Many to One Dereference

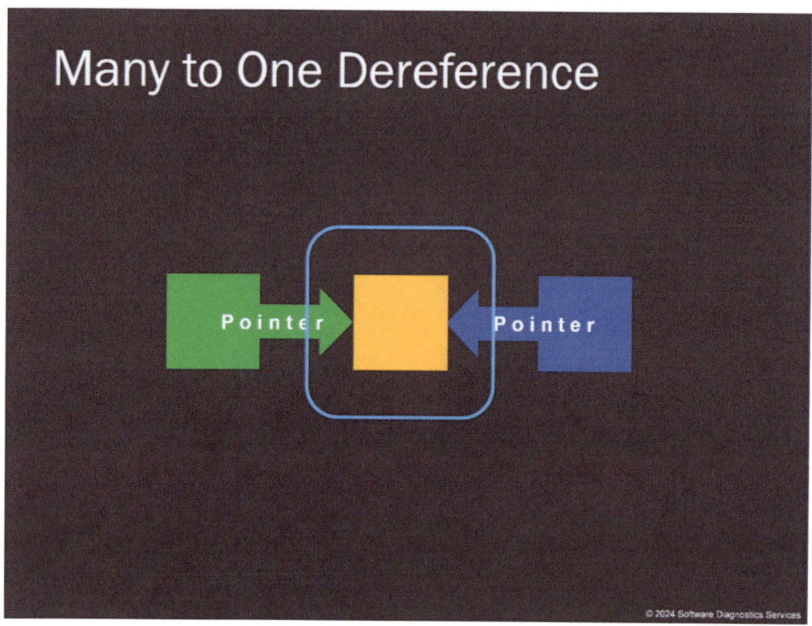

Of course, if you dereference two pointers pointing to the same entity, you get the same entity. If someone else grabs an apple, I point to, at the same time as you do, you both get the same apple.

Invalid Pointer

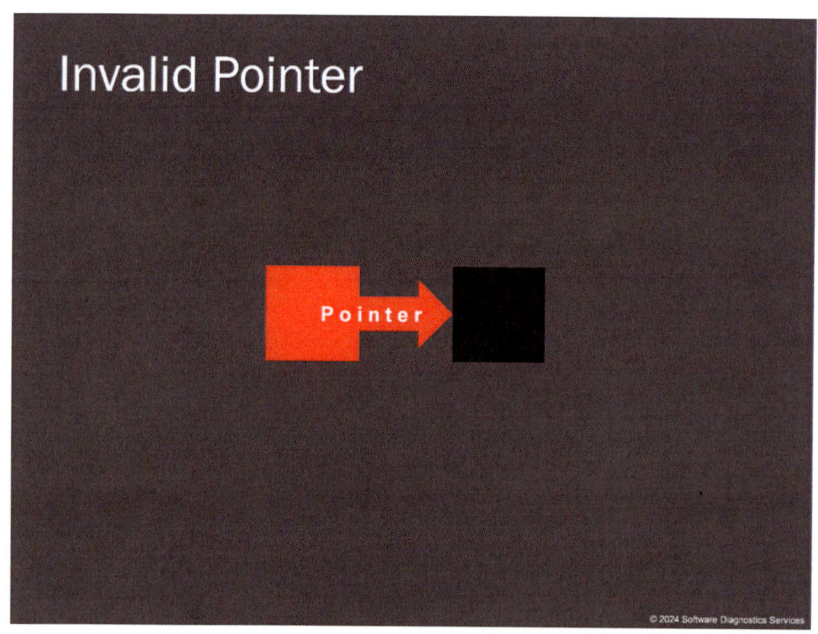

Some pointers may be invalid; for example, I may point to an imaginary apple.

Invalid Pointer Dereference

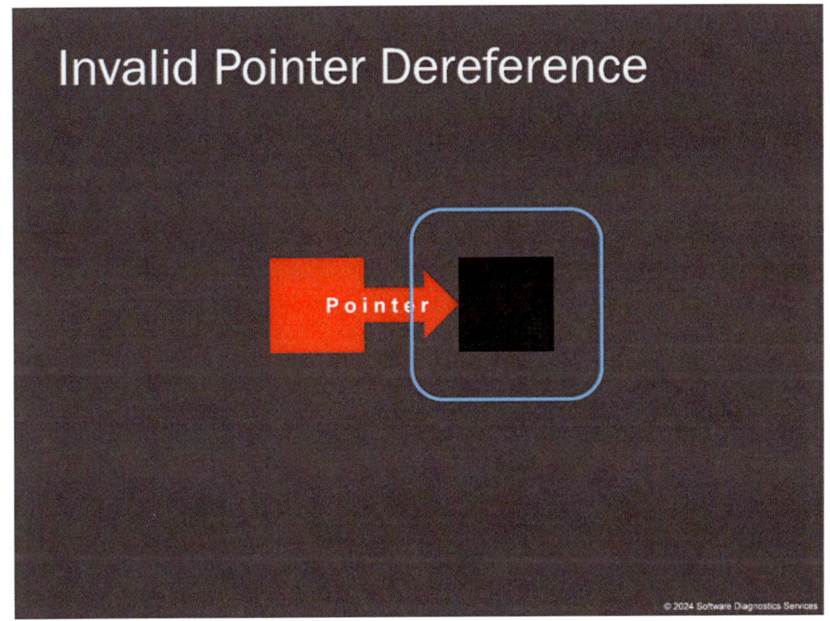

When you dereference an invalid pointer, you get a problem; for example, you fail to get an imaginary apple I point to. Or the apple can be in a cage, inaccessible.

Wild (Dangling) Pointer

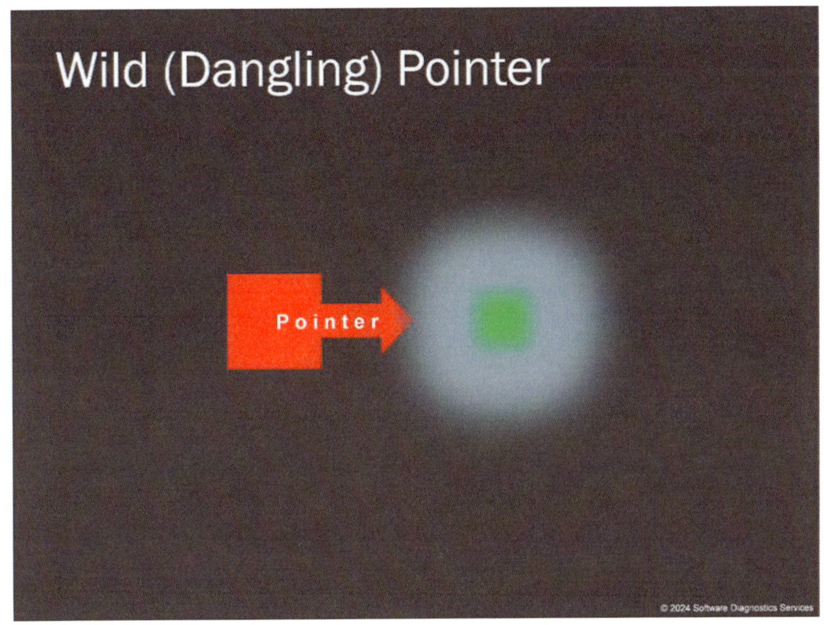

Some pointers are called dangling – they used to point to valid entities some time ago, but not anymore, so a dereference fails. You're reaching for an apple that I point to, but someone snatches it a split second ago.

Pointer to Pointer

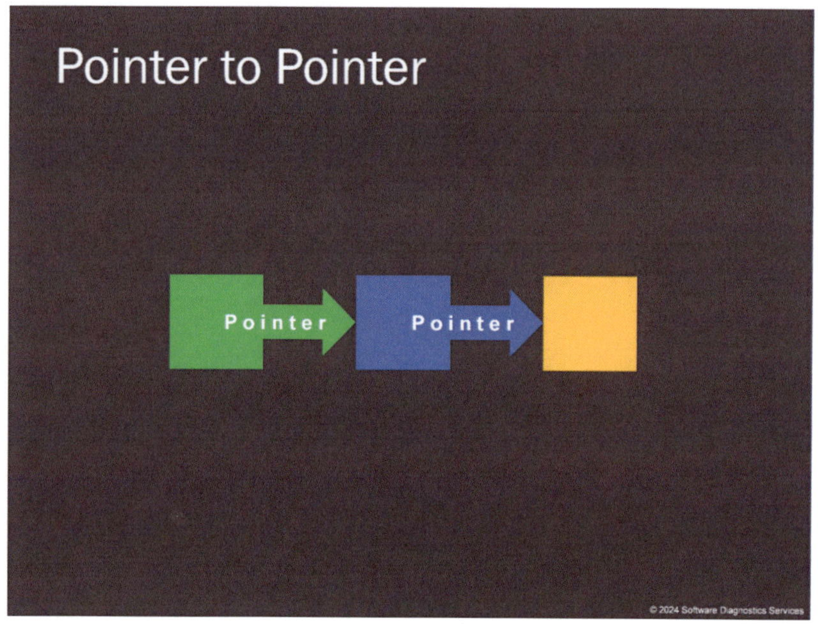

Since a pointer is also an entity that can be pointed to, there can be a chain of pointers. You point to me; I point to an apple.

Pointer to Pointer Dereference

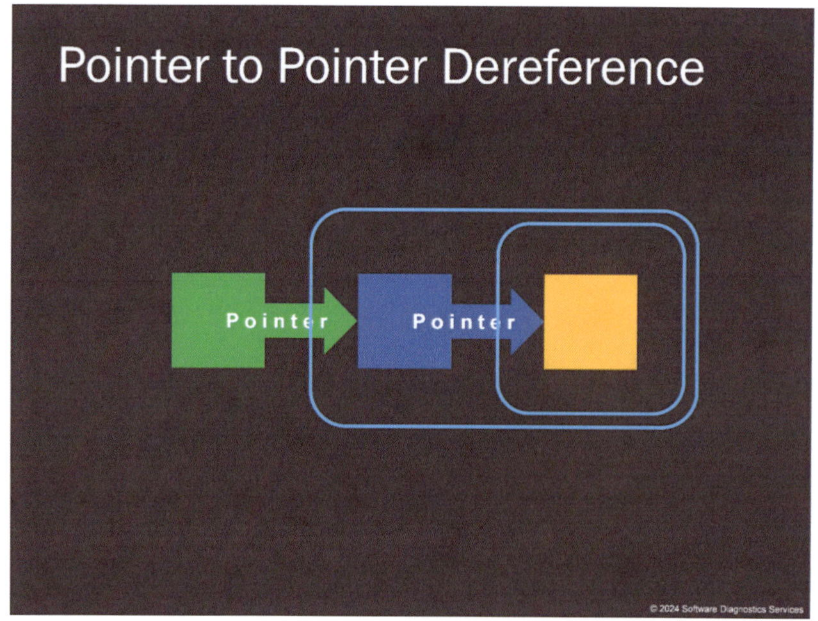

When we dereference the first pointer, we get an entity, another pointer, which we can also dereference to get the underlying entity. You point to me, but an alien snatches me with an apple I point to. Inside a ship, another alien takes an apple for analysis.

Naming Pointers and Entities

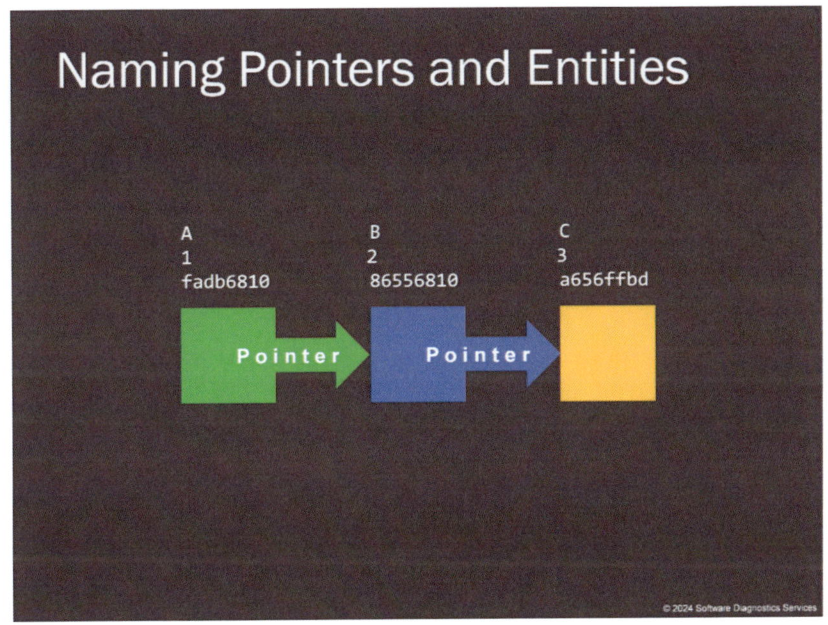

Names are distinct from entities. They can be programming language identifiers or just unique numbers or IDs.

Names as Pointer Content

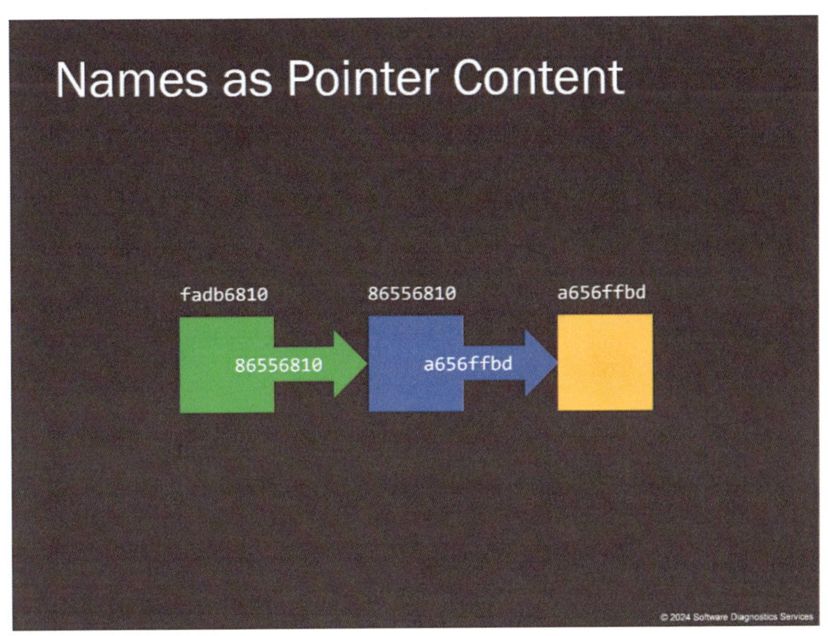

Pointers, as entities, may contain names, and these names may be names of pointers, too. If a pointer contains only a name, we say the pointer value is the name. So, the pointer value can be another pointer name, and the latter pointer value is the name of some other entity.

Pointers as Entities

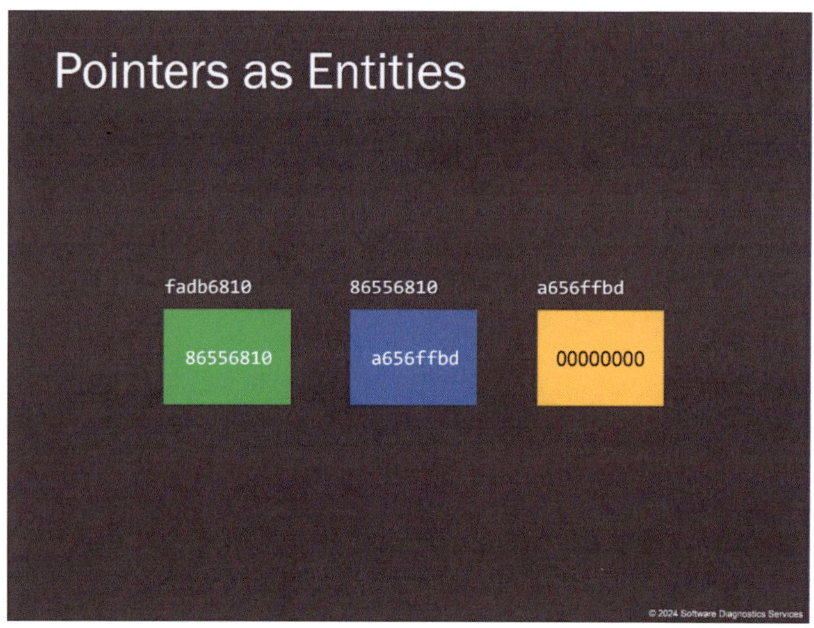

Pointer dereference is an act. If we put acts aside, pointers are just entities with some content that can be interpreted as a name if necessary. All these dereferences happen only at runtime. The pointer content (its value) may be invalid for all time without any problem until we use it.

Pointer Code Examples

The `pointers` projects:

- `pointers_c` — C
- `pointers_c_cpp` — C++ as a better C
- `pointers_classic_cpp` — Classic C++
- `pointers_modern_cpp` — Modern C++

can be found in the archive[1]. In the following slide descriptions, we only show relevant code snippets and their output.

[1] https://www.patterndiagnostics.com/Training/ACPPWD/ACPPWD.zip

Warning

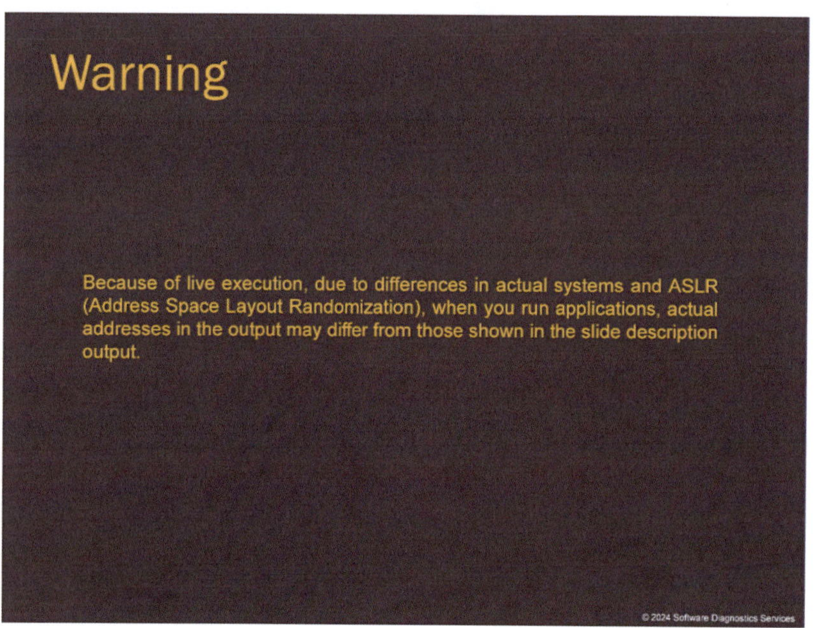

Pointer

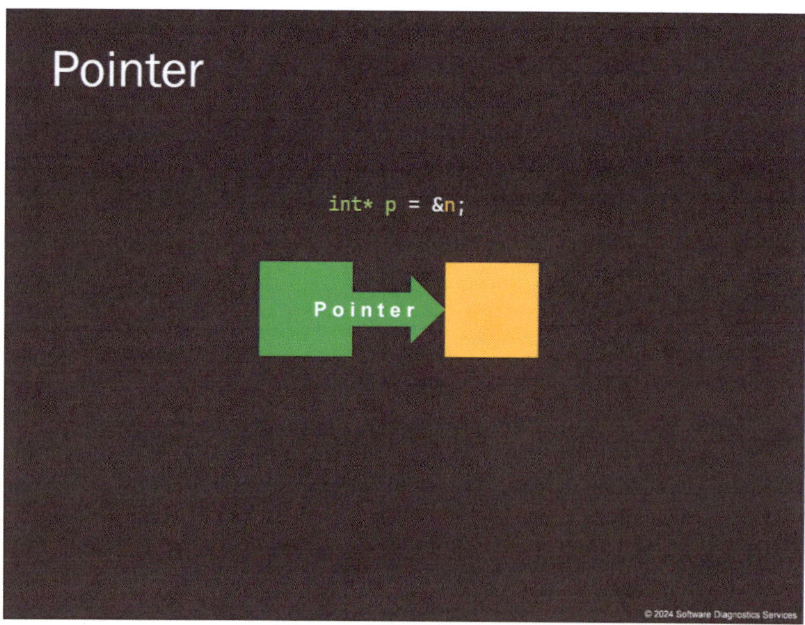

C C++ as a better C

```
puts("--- Pointer ---");
{
    int n = 0;
    int* p = &n;

    printf("n value: %d address of n: %p \n"
        "p value: %p address of p: %p \n", n, &n, p, &p);
}
```

Classic C++

```
std::cout << "--- Pointer ---" << std::endl;
{
    int n = 0;
    int* p = &n;

    std::cout << "n value: " << n << " address of n: " << &n << std::endl <<
        "p value: " << p << " address of p: " << &p << std::endl;
}
```

Modern C++

```
std::println("--- Pointer ---");
{
    int n{};
    int* p{&n};

    std::println("n value: {:d} address of n: {:016X} \n"
        "p value: {} address of p: {}",
        n, reinterpret_cast<uintptr_t>(&n), p, &p); // why we need custom formatters
}
```

Output

```
--- Pointer ---
n value: 0 address of n: 000000A15A4FE664
p value: 000000A15A4FE664 address of p: 000000A15A4FE688
```

* Placement Style

* Placement Style

```
int *p; // first edition
int* p; // second edition
int * p;
```


After writing the book on Rust, I reevaluated how I put types in source code. I used the first variant since I started programming in C almost four decades ago. The * belongs to the type, not the variable. So, in this edition, I switched to the second variant. Also, cppreference.com uses the same variant.

Pointer Dereference

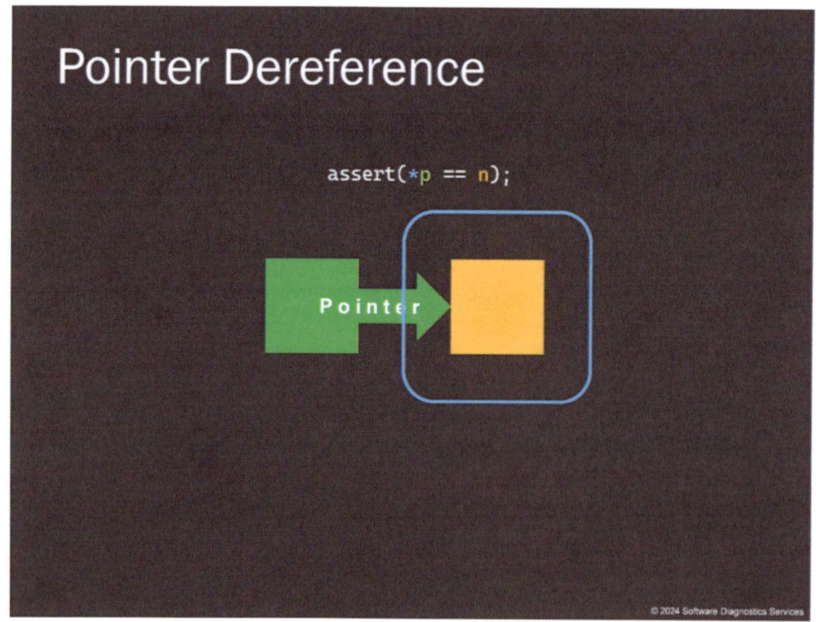

C C++ as a better C

```
puts("--- Pointer Dereference ---");
{
    int n = 0;
    int* p = &n;
    assert(*p == n);

    printf("n value: %d address of n: %p \n"
         "p value: %p dereference of p: %d address of p: %p \n",
         n, &n, p, *p, &p);
}
```

Classic C++

```
std::cout << ("--- Pointer Dereference ---") << std::endl;
{
    int n = 0;
    int* p = &n;
    assert(*p == n);

    std::cout << "n value: " << n << " address of n: " << &n << std::endl <<
        "p value: " << p << " dereference of p: " << *p << " address of p: " << &p << std::endl;
}
```

Modern C++

```
std::println("--- Pointer Dereference ---");
{
    int n{};
    int* p{&n};
    assert(*p == n);

    std::println("n value: {:d} address of n: {} \n"
        "p value: {} dereference of p: {:d} address of p: {}",
        n, &n, p, *p, &p);
}
```

Output

```
--- Pointer Dereference ---
n value: 0 address of n: 000000A15A4FE6A4
p value: 000000A15A4FE6A4 dereference of p: 0 address of p: 000000A15A4FE6C8
```

One to Many

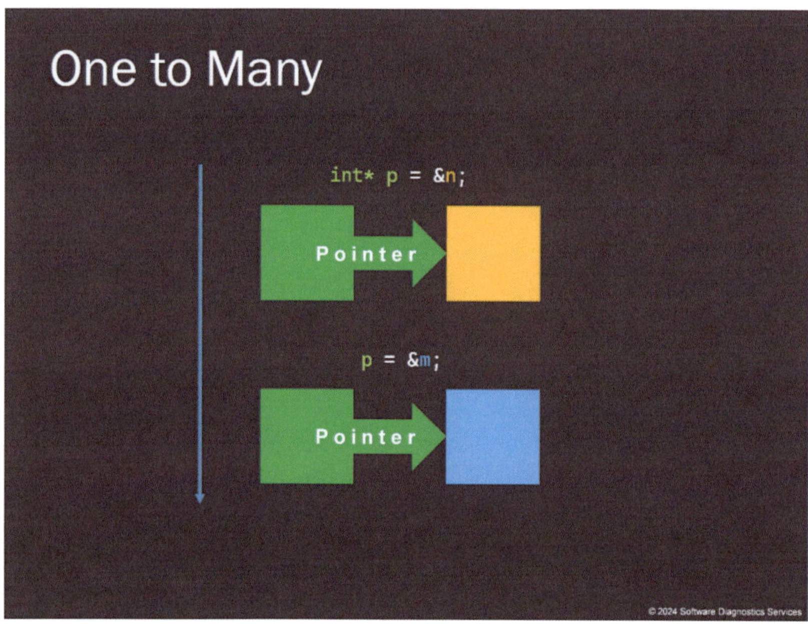

C C++ as a better C

```
puts("--- One to Many ---");
{
     int n = 0, m = 0;
    int* p = &n;

    printf("p value: %p dereference of p: %d address of p: %p \n",
        p, *p, &p);

    p = &m; // no leak

    printf("p value: %p dereference of p: %d address of p: %p \n",
        p, *p, &p);
}
```

Classic C++

```
std::cout << ("--- One to Many ---") << std::endl;
{
    int n = 0, m = 0;
    int* p = &n;

    std::cout << "p value: " << p << " dereference of p: " << *p << " address of p: " << &p <<
std::endl;

    p = &m; // no leak

    std::cout << "p value: " << p << " dereference of p: " << *p << " address of p: " << &p <<
std::endl;
}
```

Modern C++

```
std::println("--- One to Many ---");
{
    int n{}, m{};
    int* p{&n};

    std::println("p value: {} dereference of p: {:d} address of p: {}",
        p, *p, &p);

    p = &m; // no leak

    std::println("p value: {} dereference of p: {:d} address of p: {}",
        p, *p, &p);
}
```

Output

```
--- One to Many ---
p value: 000000BD2DAFE174 dereference of p: 0 address of p: 000000BD2DAFE1B8
p value: 000000BD2DAFE194 dereference of p: 0 address of p: 000000BD2DAFE1B8
```

Memory Leak

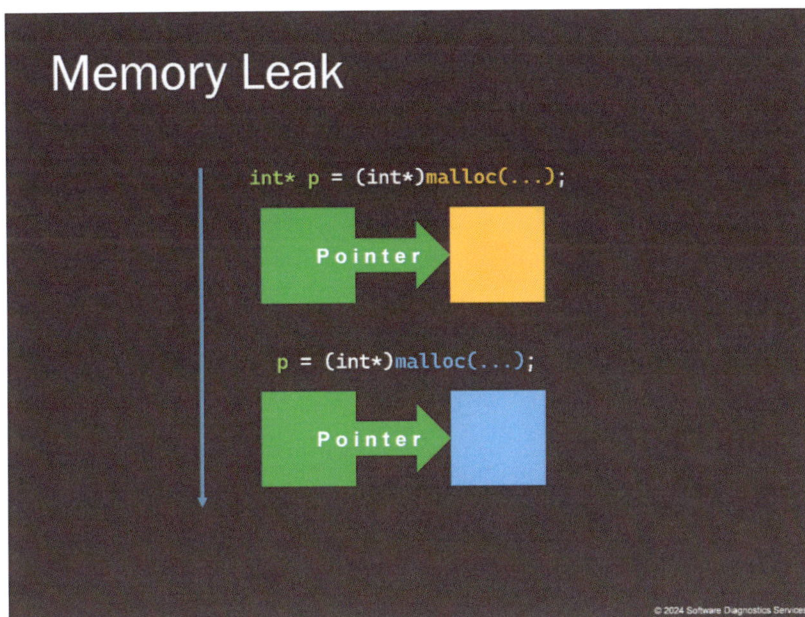

C

```
puts("--- Memory Leak ---");
{
    int* p = malloc(sizeof(int));
    if (!p) return -1;

    *p = 0;

    printf("p value: %p dereference of p: %d address of p: %p \n",
        p, *p, &p);

    p = malloc(sizeof(int)); // memory leak
    if (!p) return -1;

    *p = 0;

    printf("p value: %p dereference of p: %d address of p: %p \n",
        p, *p, &p);

    free(p);
}
```

C++ as a better C

```
puts("--- Memory Leak ---");
{
    int* p = (int*)malloc(sizeof(int)); // Needs a cast in C++
    if (!p) return -1;

    *p = 0;

    printf("p value: %p dereference of p: %d address of p: %p \n",
        p, *p, &p);

    p = (int*)malloc(sizeof(int)); // memory leak
    if (!p) return -1;

    *p = 0;

    printf("p value: %p dereference of p: %d address of p: %p \n",
        p, *p, &p);

    free(p);

}
```

Classic C++

```
std::cout << ("--- Memory Leak ---") << std::endl;
{
    int* p = new int(0);

    std::cout << "p value: " << p << " dereference of p: " << *p << " address of p: " << &p <<
std::endl;

    p = new int(0); // memory leak

    std::cout << "p value: " << p << " dereference of p: " << *p << " address of p: " << &p <<
std::endl;

    delete p;
```

```
}
```

Modern C++

```
std::println("--- Memory Leak ---");
{
    int* p{new int{}};

    std::println("p value: {} dereference of p: {:d} address of p: {}",
        p, *p, &p);

    p = new int{}; // memory leak

    std::println("p value: {} dereference of p: {:d} address of p: {}",
        p, *p, &p);

    delete p;
}
```

Output

```
--- Memory Leak ---
p value: 000001F3F7D77190 dereference of p: 0 address of p: 000000BD2DAFE1D8
p value: 000001F3F7D76F90 dereference of p: 0 address of p: 000000BD2DAFE1D8
```

Many to One

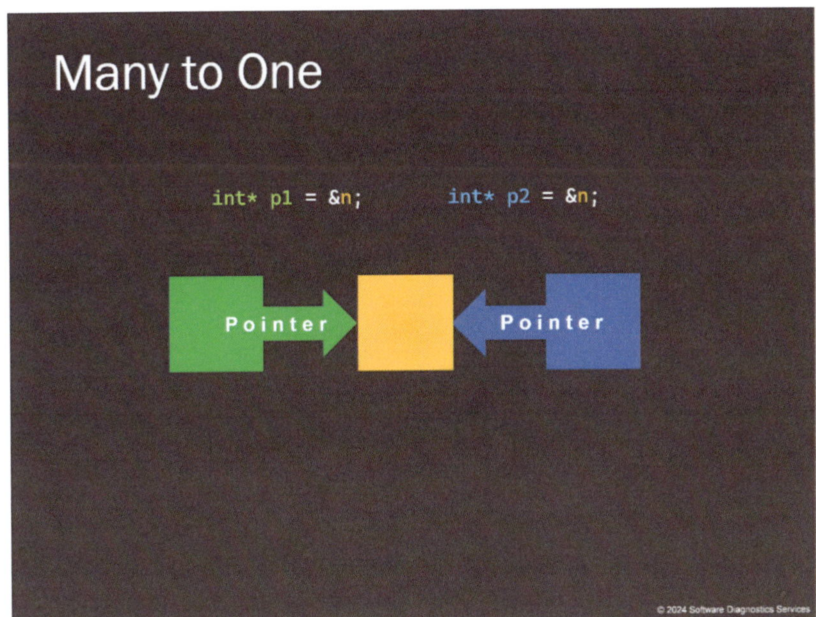

C C++ as a better C

```
puts("--- Many to One ---");
{
    int n = 0;
    int* p1 = &n;
    int* p2 = &n;
    assert(p1 == p2);

    printf("n value: %d address of n: %p \n"
        "p1 value: %p address of p1: %p \n"
        "p2 value: %p address of p2: %p \n",
        n, &n, p1, &p1, p2, &p2);
}
```

Classic C++

```
std::cout << ("--- Many to One ---") << std::endl;
{
    int n = 0;
    int* p1 = &n;
    int* p2 = &n;
    assert(p1 == p2);

    std::cout << "n value: " << n << " address of n: " << &n << std::endl <<
        "p1 value: " << p1 << " address of p1: " << &p1 << std::endl <<
        "p2 value: " << p2 << " address of p2: " << &p2 << std::endl;
}
```

Modern C++

```
std::println("--- Many to One ---");
{
    int n{};
    int* p1{&n};
    int* p2{&n};
    assert(p1 == p2);

    std::println("n value: {:d} address of n: {} \n"
        "p1 value: {} address of p1: {} \n"
        "p2 value: {} address of p2: {}",
        n, &n, p1, &p1, p2, &p2);
}
```

Output

```
--- Many to One ---
n value: 0 address of n: 000000A15A4FE744
p1 value: 000000A15A4FE744 address of p1: 000000A15A4FE768
p2 value: 000000A15A4FE744 address of p2: 000000A15A4FE788
```

Many to One Dereference

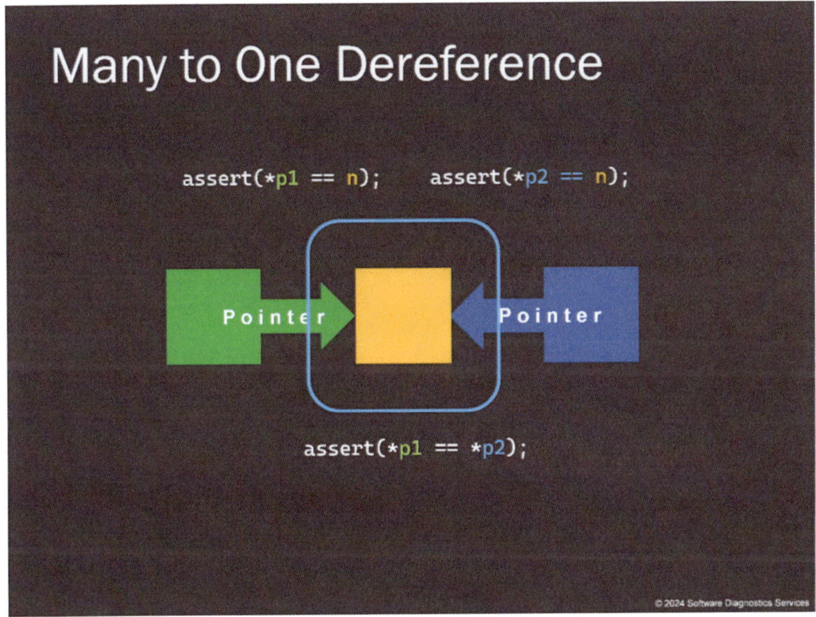

C C++ as a better C

```
puts("--- Many to One Dereference ---");
{
    int n = 0;
    int* p1 = &n;
    int* p2 = &n;
    assert(*p1 == *p2);

    printf("n value: %d address of n: %p \n"
        "p1 value: %p dereference of p1: %d address of p1: %p \n"
        "p2 value: %p dereference of p2: %d address of p2: %p \n",
        n, &n, p1, *p1, &p1, p2, *p2, &p2);
}
```

Classic C++

```
std::cout << ("--- Many to One Dereference ---") << std::endl;
{
    int n = 0;
    int* p1 = &n;
    int* p2 = &n;
    assert(*p1 == *p2);

    std::cout << "n value: " << n << " address of n: " << &n << std::endl <<
        "p1 value: " << p1 << " dereference of p1: " << *p1 << " address of p1: " << &p1 <<
std::endl <<
        "p2 value: " << p2 << " dereference of p2: " << *p2 << " address of p2: " << &p2 <<
std::endl;
}
```

Modern C++

```
std::println("--- Many to One Dereference ---");
{
    int n{};
    int* p1{&n};
    int* p2{&n};
    assert(*p1 == *p2);

    std::println("n value: {:d} address of n: {} \n"
        "p1 value: {} dereference of p1: {:d} address of p1: {} \n"
        "p2 value: {} dereference of p2: {:d} address of p2: {}",
        n, &n, p1, *p1, &p1, p2, *p2, &p2);
}
```

Output

```
--- Many to One Dereference ---
n value: 0 address of n: 000000A15A4FE7A4
p1 value: 000000A15A4FE7A4 dereference of p1: 0 address of p1: 000000A15A4FE7C8
p2 value: 000000A15A4FE7A4 dereference of p2: 0 address of p2: 000000A15A4FE7E8
```

Invalid Pointer

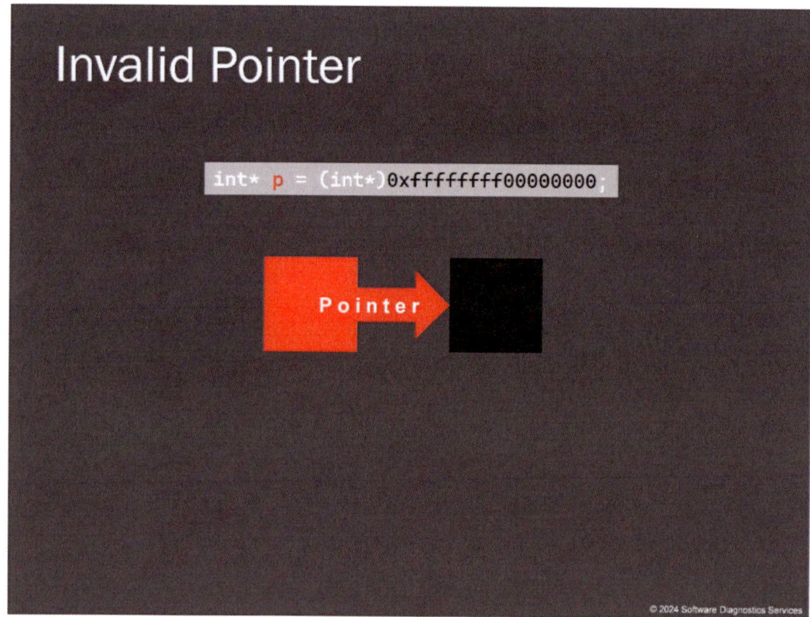

C C++ as a better C

```
puts("--- Invalid Pointer ---");
{
    int* p = (int*)0xffffffff00000000;

    printf("p value: %p address of p: %p \n", p, &p);
}
```

Classic C++

```
std::cout << ("--- Invalid Pointer ---") << std::endl;
{
    int* p = reinterpret_cast<int*>(0xffffffff00000000);

    std::cout << "p value: " << p << " address of p: " << &p << std::endl;
}
```

Modern C++

```
std::println("--- Invalid Pointer ---");
{
    int* p{reinterpret_cast<int*>(0xffffffff00000000)};

    std::println("p value: {} address of p: {}", p, &p);
}
```

Output

```
--- Invalid Pointer ---
p value: FFFFFFFF00000000 address of p: 000000A15A4FE808
```

Invalid Pointer Dereference

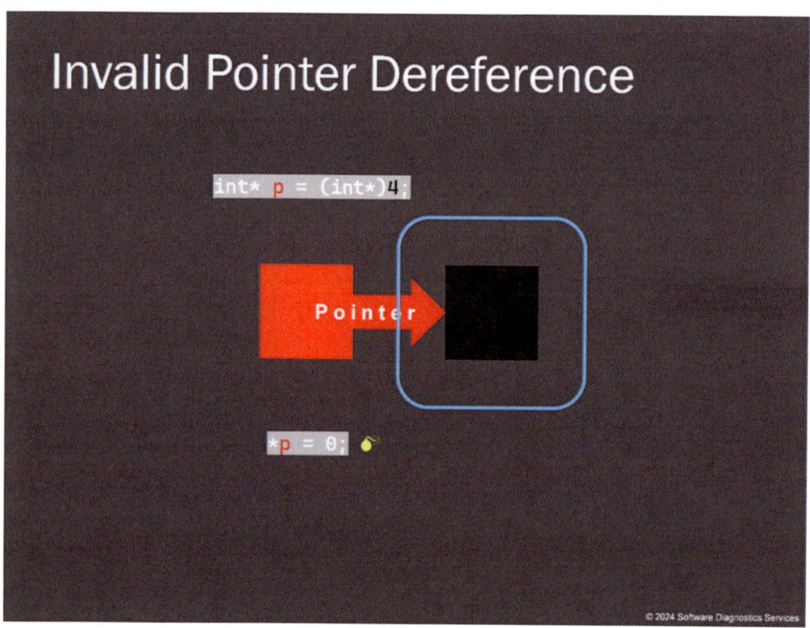

C C++ as a better C

```
puts("--- Invalid Pointer Dereference ---");
{
    int* p = (int*)4;

    printf("p value: %p address of p: %p \n", p, &p);

    // *p = 0; // crash
}
```

Classic C++

```
std::cout << ("--- Invalid Pointer Dereference ---") << std::endl;
{
    int* p = reinterpret_cast<int*>(4);

    std::cout << "p value: " << p << " address of p: " << &p << std::endl;

    // *p = 0; // crash
}
```

Modern C++

```
std::println("--- Invalid Pointer Dereference ---");
{
    int* p{reinterpret_cast<int*>(4)};

    std::println("p value: {} address of p: {}", p, &p);
```

```
    // *p = 0; // crash
}
```

Output

```
--- Invalid Pointer Dereference ---
p value: 0000000000000004 address of p: 000000A15A4FE828
```

Wild (Dangling) Pointer

Wild (Dangling) Pointer

```
int* p = (int*)malloc(...);
free(p);
```

Pointer

```
*p = 0;
```


C

```
puts("--- Wild (Dangling) Pointer ---");
{
    int* p = malloc(sizeof(int));
    if (!p) return -1;

    *p = 0;

    printf("p value: %p dereference of p: %d address of p: %p \n",
        p, *p, &p);

    free(p); // dangling pointer

    printf("p value: %p address of p: %p \n",
        p, &p);

    // printf("p value: %p dereference of p: %d address of p: %p \n",
    //     p, *p, &p);  // may crash
```

```
    // assert(*p == 0); // may crash or fail

    p = NULL; // Not dangling
}
```

C++ as a better C

```
puts("--- Wild (Dangling) Pointer ---");
{
    int* p = (int*)malloc(sizeof(int)); // needs a cast in C++
    if (!p) return -1;

    *p = 0;

    printf("p value: %p dereference of p: %d address of p: %p \n",
        p, *p, &p);

    free(p); // dangling pointer

    printf("p value: %p address of p: %p \n",
        p, &p);

    // printf("p value: %p dereference of p: %d address of p: %p \n",
    //     p, *p, &p);  // may crash

    // assert(*p == 0); // may crash or fail

    p = NULL; // Not dangling
}
```

Output

```
--- Wild (Dangling) Pointer ---
p value: 0000021602A96FD0 dereference of p: 0 address of p: 000000E5F3CFFB68
p value: 0000021602A96FD0 address of p: 000000E5F3CFFB68
```

Classic C++

```
std::cout << ("--- Wild (Dangling) Pointer ---") << std::endl;
{
    int* p = new int(0);

    std::cout << "p value: " << p << " dereference of p: " << *p << " address of p: " << &p <<
std::endl;

    delete p; // dangling pointer

    std::cout << "p value: " << p << " address of p: " << &p << std::endl;

    // std::cout << "p value: " << p << " dereference of p: " << *p << " address of p: " << &p <<
std::endl; // may crash

    // assert(*p == 0); // may crash or fail

    p = NULL; // Not dangling
}
```

Modern C++

```
std::println("--- Wild (Dangling) Pointer ---");
{
    int* p{new int{}};

    std::println("p value: {} dereference of p: {:d} address of p: {}",
        p, *p, &p);

    delete p; // dangling pointer

    std::println("p value: {} address of p: {}",
        p, &p);

    // std::println("p value: {} dereference of p: {:d} address of p: {}",
    //     p, *p, &p); // may crash

    // assert(*p == 0); // may crash or fail

    p = nullptr; // Not dangling
}
```

Output

```
--- Wild (Dangling) Pointer ---
p value: 0000020F302575D0 dereference of p: 0 address of p: 000000F7AF78E7B8
p value: 0000000000008123 address of p: 000000F7AF78E7B8
```

Pointer to Pointer

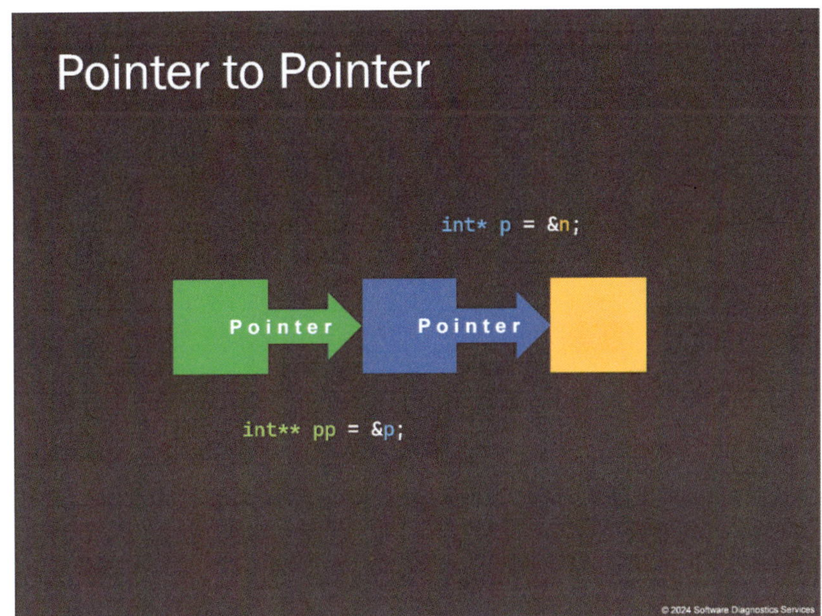

C C++ as a better C

```
puts("--- Pointer to Pointer ---");
{
    int n = 0;
    int* p = &n;
    int** pp = &p;

    printf("n value: %d address of n: %p \n"
        "p value: %p address of p: %p \n"
        "pp value: %p address of pp: %p \n",
        n, &n, p, &p, pp, &pp);
}
```

Classic C++

```
std::cout << ("--- Pointer to Pointer ---") << std::endl;
{
    int n = 0;
    int* p = &n;
    int** pp = &p;

    std::cout << "n value: " << n << " address of n: " << &n << std::endl <<
        "p value: " << p << " address of p: " << &p << std::endl <<
        "pp value: " << pp << " address of pp: " << &pp << std::endl;
}
```

Modern C++

```
std::println("--- Pointer to Pointer ---");
{
    int n{};
    int* p{&n};
    int** pp{&p};

    std::println("n value: {:d} address of n: {} \n"
        "p value: {} address of p: {} \n"
        "pp value: {} address of pp: {}",
        n, &n, p, &p, pp, &pp);
}
```

Output

```
--- Pointer to Pointer ---
n value: 0 address of n: 000000A15A4FE864
p value: 000000A15A4FE864 address of p: 000000A15A4FE888
pp value: 000000A15A4FE888 address of pp: 000000A15A4FE8A8
```

Pointer to Pointer Dereference

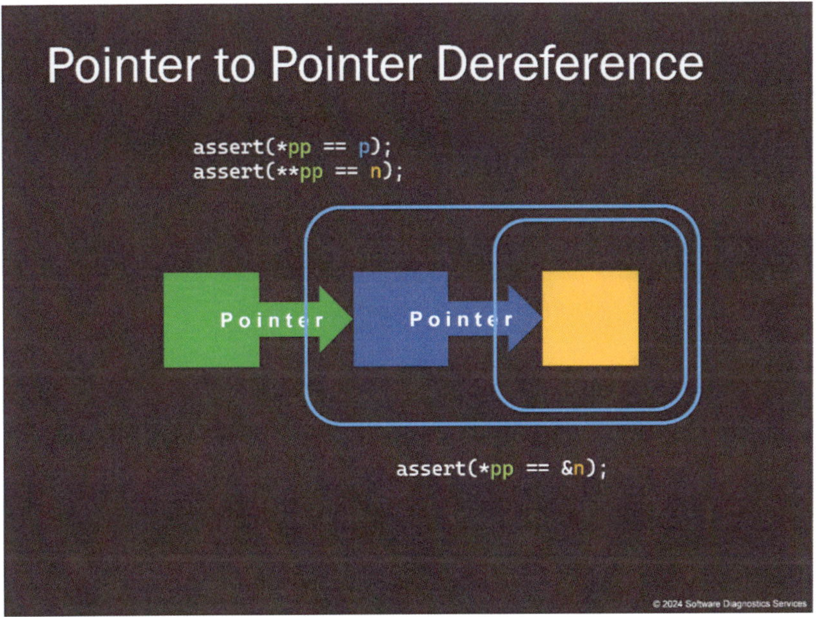

C C++ as a better C

```
puts("--- Pointer to Pointer Dereference ---");
{
    int n = 0;
    int* p = &n;
    int** pp = &p;
    assert(*pp == p);
    assert(*pp == &n);
    assert(**pp == n);

    printf("n value: %d address of n: %p \n"
        "p value: %p address of p: %p \n"
        "pp value: %p address of pp: %p \n"
        "dereference of pp: %p double dereference of pp: %d \n",
        n, &n, p, &p, pp, &pp, *pp, **pp);
}
```

Classic C++

```
std::cout << ("--- Pointer to Pointer Dereference ---") << std::endl;
{
    int n = 0;
    int* p = &n;
    int** pp = &p;
    assert(*pp == p);
    assert(*pp == &n);
    assert(**pp == n);

    std::cout << "n value: " << n << " address of n: " << &n << std::endl <<
```

```
        "p value: " << p << " address of p: " << &p << std::endl <<
        "pp value: " << pp << " address of pp: " << &pp << std::endl <<
        "dereference of pp: " << *pp << " double dereference of pp: " << **pp << std::endl;
}
```

Modern C++

```
std::println("--- Pointer to Pointer Dereference ---");
{
    int n{};
    int* p{&n};
    int** pp{&p};
    assert(*pp == p);
    assert(*pp == &n);
    assert(**pp == n);

    std::println("n value: {:d} address of n: {} \n"
        "p value: {} address of p: {} \n"
        "pp value: {} address of pp: {} \n"
        "dereference of pp: {} double dereference of pp: {:d}",
        n, &n, p, &p, pp, &pp, *pp, **pp);
}
```

Output

```
--- Pointer to Pointer Dereference ---
n value: 0 address of n: 000000A15A4FE8C4
p value: 000000A15A4FE8C4 address of p: 000000A15A4FE8E8
pp value: 000000A15A4FE8E8 address of pp: 000000A15A4FE908
dereference of pp: 000000A15A4FE8C4 double dereference of pp: 0
```

Undefined Behavior

Undefined Behavior

- OK | Corruption | Crash | Spike | Hang | Leak
- Different on different machines
- Different at different times
- Depends on compiler-generated code
- Depends on memory layout

When looking at `Wild (Dangling) Pointer` code example, you may have noticed a comment that an assertion there may crash or fail. This is an example of the undefined behavior: depending on runtime and memory layout, when we dereference a dangling pointer, its address may be valid or invalid.

Memory and Pointers

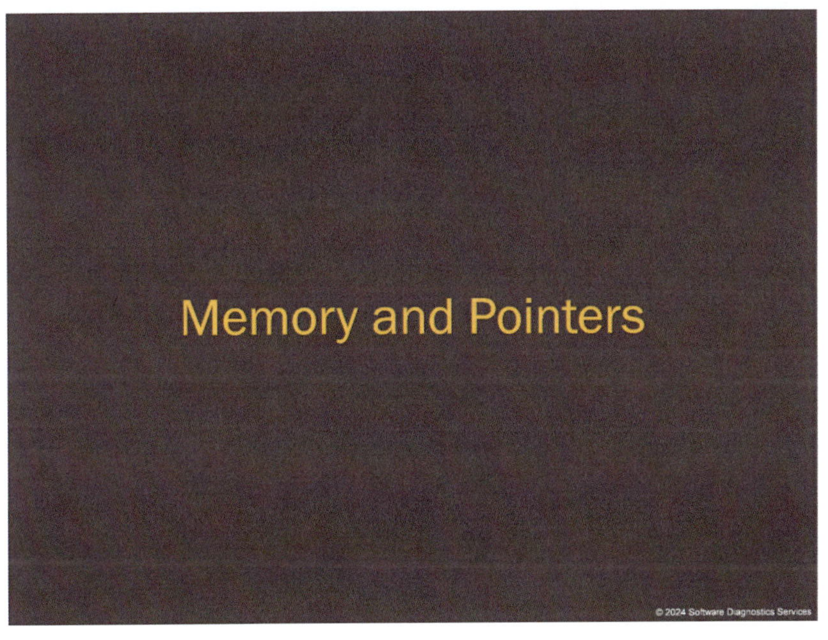

Now, we look at memory representation of pointers and entities they point to.

The `memory_and_pointers` projects:

- `memory_and_pointers_c` C
- `memory_and_pointers_c_cpp` C++ as a better C
- `memory_and_pointers_modern_cpp` Modern C++

can be found in the archive[2]. In the following slide descriptions, we only show relevant code snippets and their output.

[2] https://www.patterndiagnostics.com/Training/ACPPWD/ACPPWD.zip

Mental Exercise

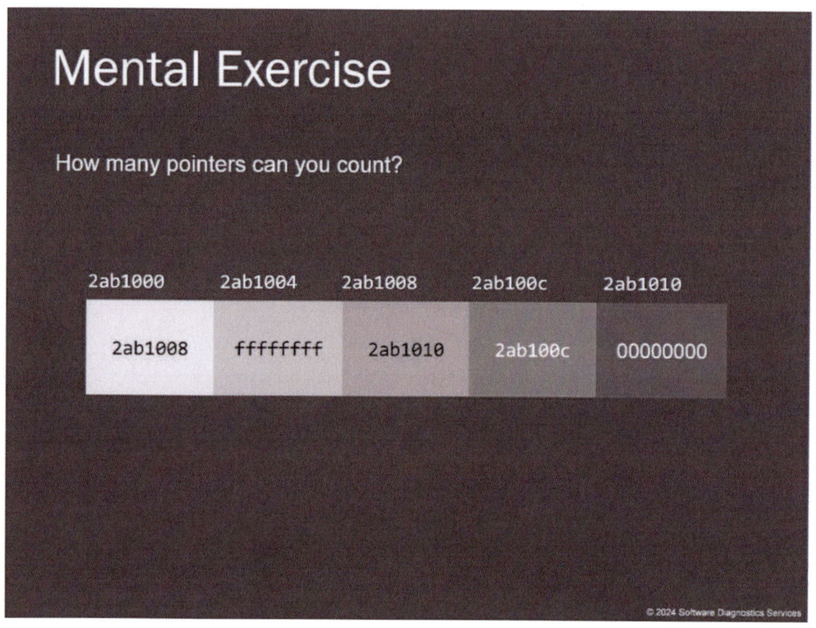

Here, in this picture, entities are the so-called memory cells. Memory cells have addresses that start from 0 and are usually incremented by the so-called pointer size, which is 4 on 32-bit systems and 8 on 64-bit systems. Here, for visual clarity, we use memory cells from a 32-bit system.

Debugger Memory Layout

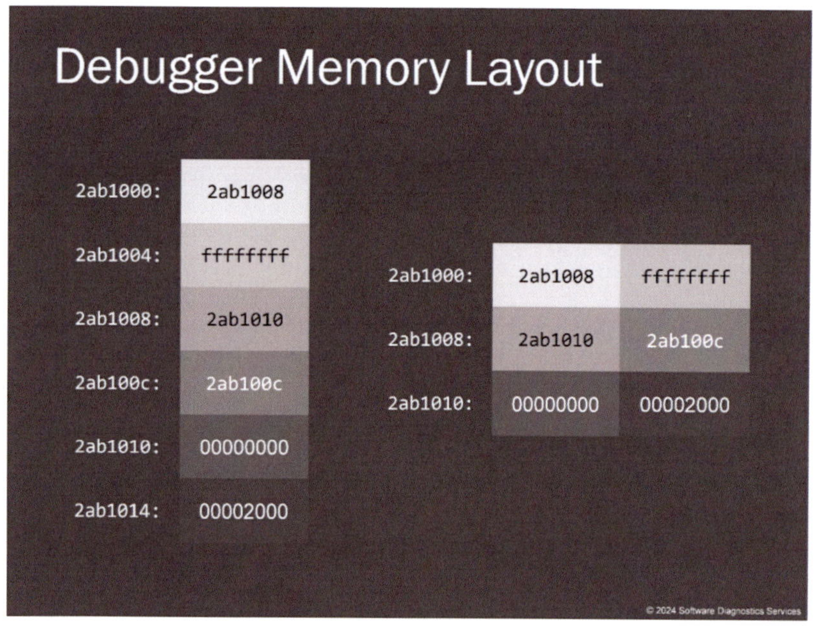

When we use a debugger, it prints memory cell addresses and their contents in a certain layout shown on this slide. Some debugger commands use 2-column and some n-column layouts to print memory.

Memory Dereference Layout

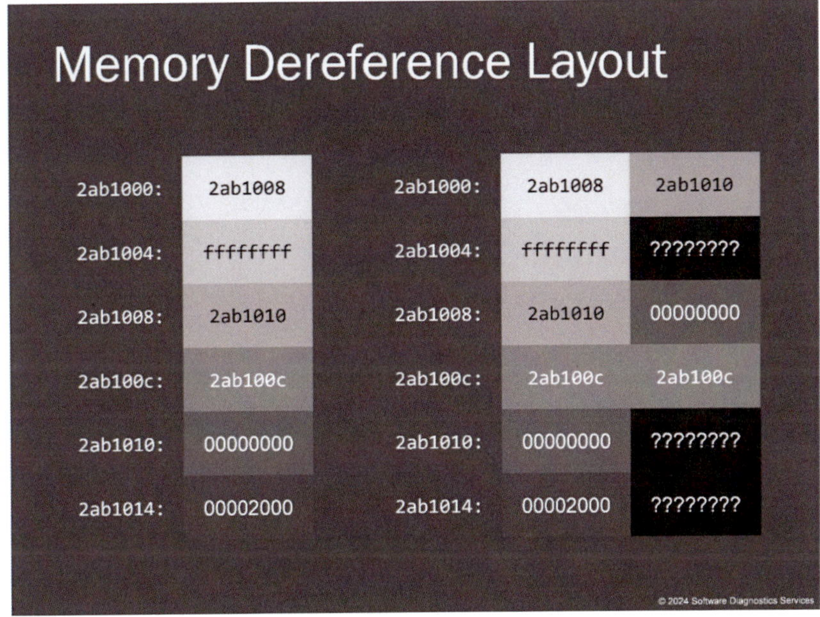

For a 2-column format, a debugger command may interpret the second column as a pointer. In such a case, the third column is a value from a pointer dereference. Also, notice a case when a pointer points to itself.

Names as Addresses

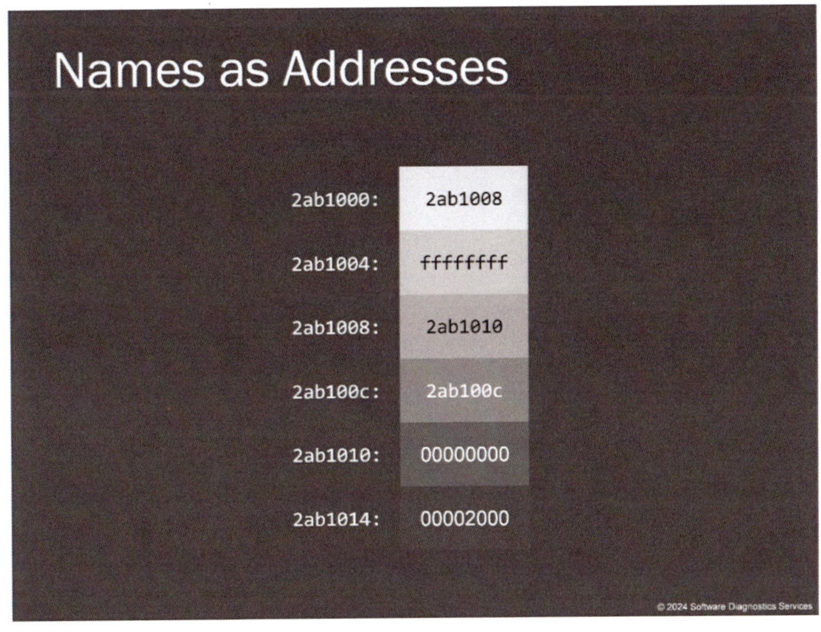

To repeat, for memory layout, names are interpreted as addresses, and memory cell content (cell value) can also be interpreted as a memory address.

Addresses and Entities

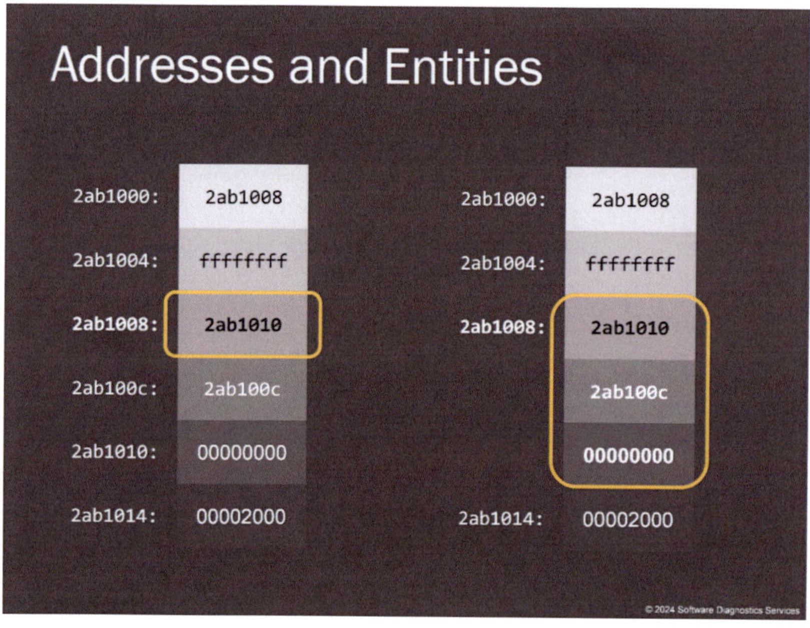

Entities can be either single cells or multicells. Each part of a multicell can be interpreted as a memory address, if necessary, even if it wasn't meant to be a memory address.

Addresses and Structures

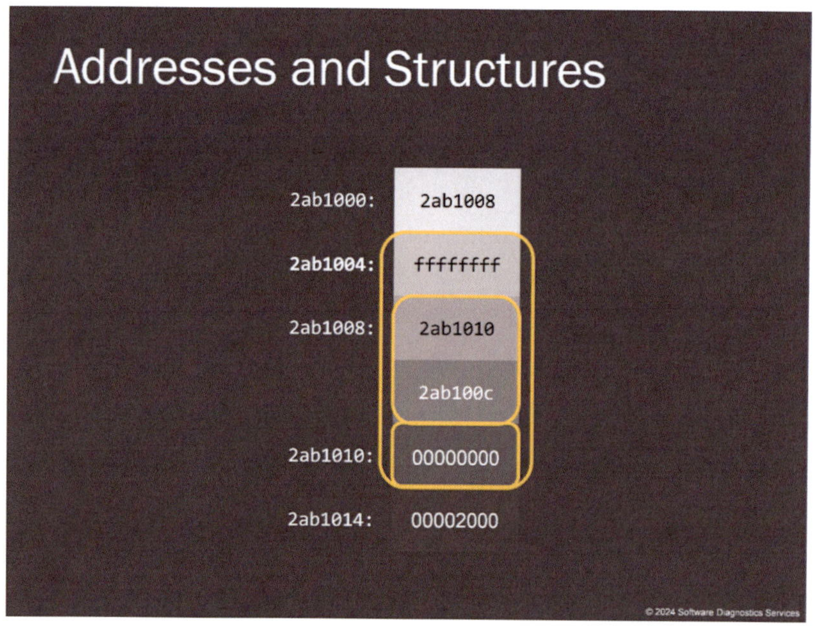

A structure in memory is a sequential collection of memory cells; some may be multicell and themselves substructures. Each part of a structure, its member, or structure field has its own address as well, in addition to the overall address of the structure.

Pointers to Structures

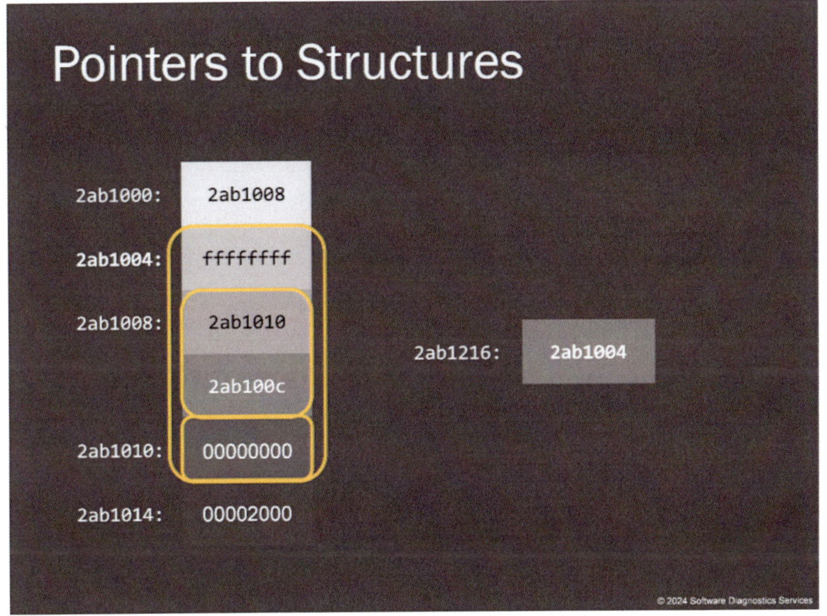

A structure has its address. A pointer to a structure is a memory cell that contains that address. It has its own address. At this point, structures are abstract collections of memory cells. We look at proper C and C++ structures and corresponding source code later.

Arrays

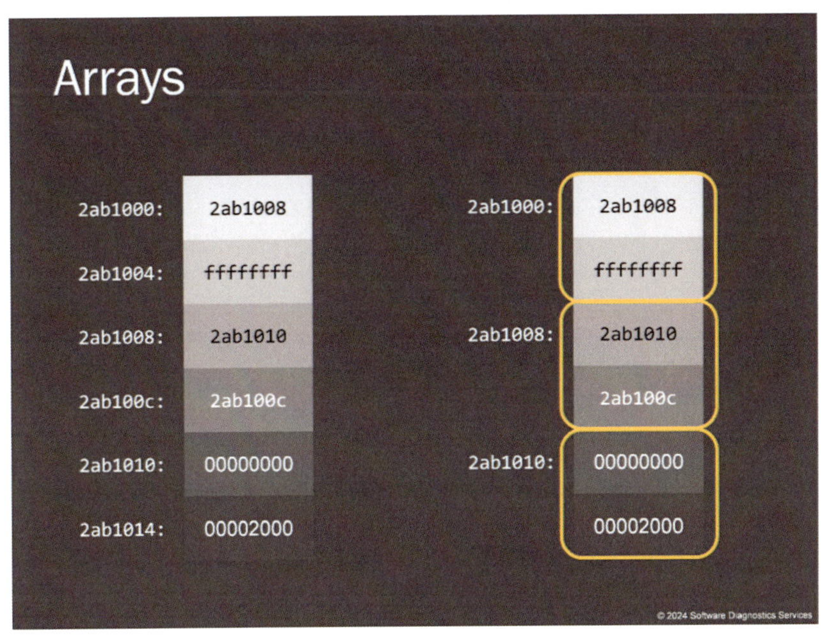

An array is a contiguous sequence of n-cells in memory called array elements. Each array element has its own address. Since the size of each array element is fixed and the same, addressing the random element is fast.

Arrays and Pointers to Arrays

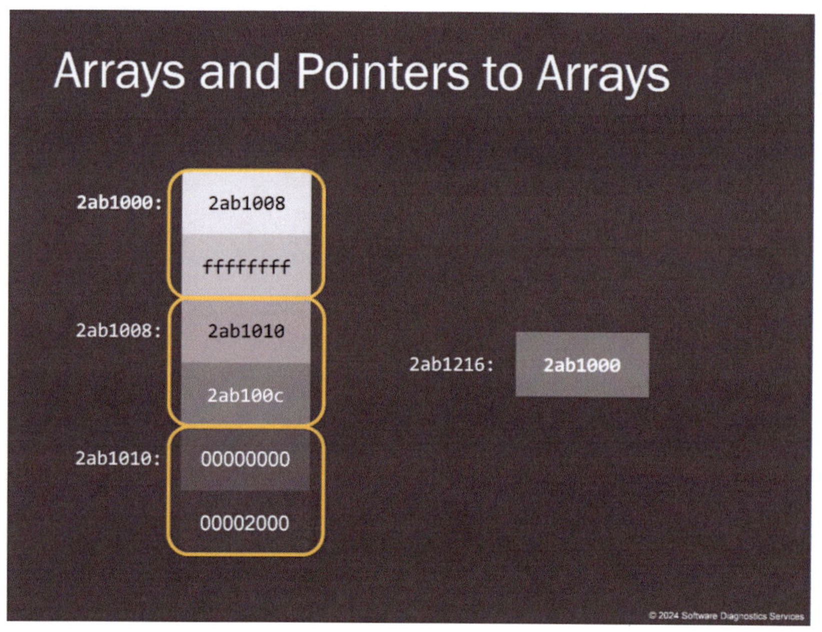

The array address is the address of its first element. But a pointer to an array is a different memory cell that contains the array address. This is similar to structures and pointers to structures. An array can be considered as a structure as well.

C C++ as a better C

```
puts("--- Arrays and Pointers to Arrays ---");
{
    int arr[10] = { 0, 1, 2, 3, 4, 5, 6, 7, 8, 9 };

    printf("address of arr: %p value of arr: %p address of the first arr element: %p \n",
        &arr, arr, &arr[0]);

    int (*parr)[10] = &arr;

    printf("address of parr: %p value of parr: %p \n",
        &parr, parr);
}
```

Modern C++

```
std::println("--- Arrays and Pointers to Arrays ---");
{
    int arr[10]{ 0, 1, 2, 3, 4, 5, 6, 7, 8, 9 };

    std::println("address of arr: {} value of arr: {} address of the first arr element: {}",
        &arr, arr, &arr[0]);

    int (*parr)[10]{&arr};

    std::println("address of parr: {} value of parr: {}",
        &parr, parr);
}
```

Output

```
--- Arrays and Pointers to Arrays ---
address of arr: 00000075BC75F468 value of arr: 00000075BC75F468 address of the first arr element:
00000075BC75F468
address of parr: 00000075BC75F4A8 value of parr: 00000075BC75F468
```

Strings and Pointers to Strings

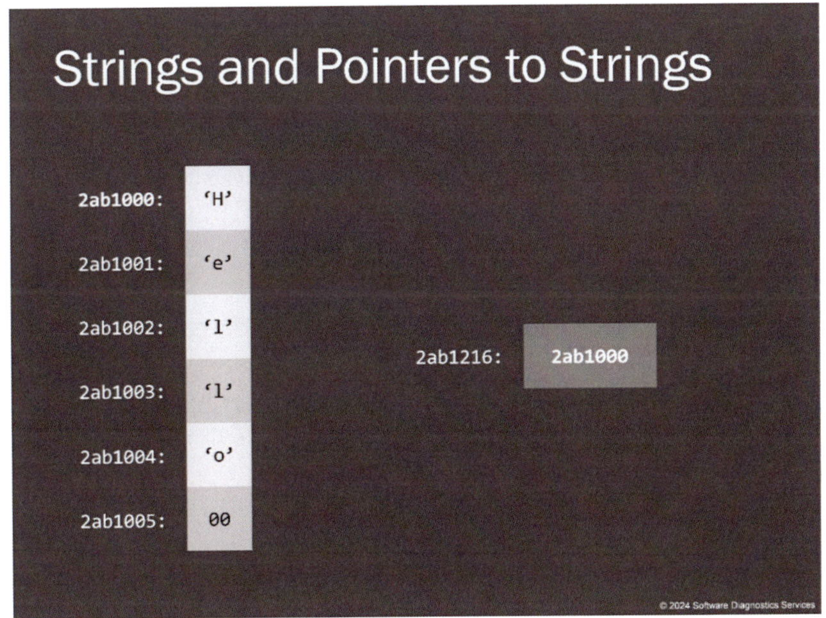

What about strings? An ASCII string is a zero-terminated array of one-byte memory cells. The address of a string is the address of its first byte. Similar to arrays, a pointer to a string is a memory cell that contains the address of the string, the address of its first element – its first character.

C

```
puts("--- Strings and Pointers to Strings ---");
{
    char* str = "Hello";

    printf("address of str: %p value of str: %p address of the first str element: %p \n"
        "address of the sixth str element: %p value of the sixth str element: %d \n",
        &str, str, &str[0], &str[5], str[5]);

    char** pstr = &str;

    printf("address of pstr: %p value of pstr: %p \n",
        &pstr, pstr);

    printf("address of the first str element: %p \n"
        "address of the sixth str element: %p value of the sixth str element: %d \n",
        &(*pstr)[0], &(*pstr)[5], (*pstr)[5]);
}
```

C++ as a better C

```
puts("--- Strings and Pointers to Strings ---");
{
    const char* str = "Hello"; // in C++ can't be char*

    printf("address of str: %p value of str: %p address of the first str element: %p \n"
        "address of the sixth str element: %p value of the sixth str element: %d \n",
        &str, str, &str[0], &str[5], str[5]);

    const char** pstr = &str;

    printf("address of pstr: %p value of pstr: %p \n",
        &pstr, pstr);

    printf("address of the first str element: %p \n"
        "address of the sixth str element: %p value of the sixth str element: %d \n",
        &(*pstr)[0], &(*pstr)[5], (*pstr)[5]);
}
```

Modern C++

```
std::println("--- Strings and Pointers to Strings ---");
{
    const char* str{"Hello"}; // str may be interpreted by template code as a value "Hello"

    std::println("address of str: {} value of str: {:016X} address of the first str element:
{:016X} \n"
        "address of the sixth str element: {:016X} value of the sixth str element: {:d}",
        &str, reinterpret_cast<uintptr_t>(str), reinterpret_cast<uintptr_t>(&str[0]),
        reinterpret_cast<uintptr_t>(&str[5]), str[5]);

    const char** pstr{&str};

    std::println("address of pstr: {} value of pstr: {}",
        &pstr, pstr);

    std::println("address of the first str element: {:016X} \n"
        "address of the sixth str element: {:016X} value of the sixth str element: {:d}",
        reinterpret_cast<uintptr_t>(&(*pstr)[0]),
        reinterpret_cast<uintptr_t>(&(*pstr)[5]), (*pstr)[5]);
}
```

Output

```
--- Strings and Pointers to Strings ---
address of str: 000000D68DD6FA58 value of str: 00007FF7251AAE90 address of the first str element:
00007FF7251AAE90
address of the sixth str element: 00007FF7251AAE95 value of the sixth str element: 0
address of pstr: 000000D68DD6FA78 value of pstr: 000000D68DD6FA58
address of the first str element: 00007FF7251AAE90
address of the sixth str element: 00007FF7251AAE95 value of the sixth str element: 0
```

Basic Types

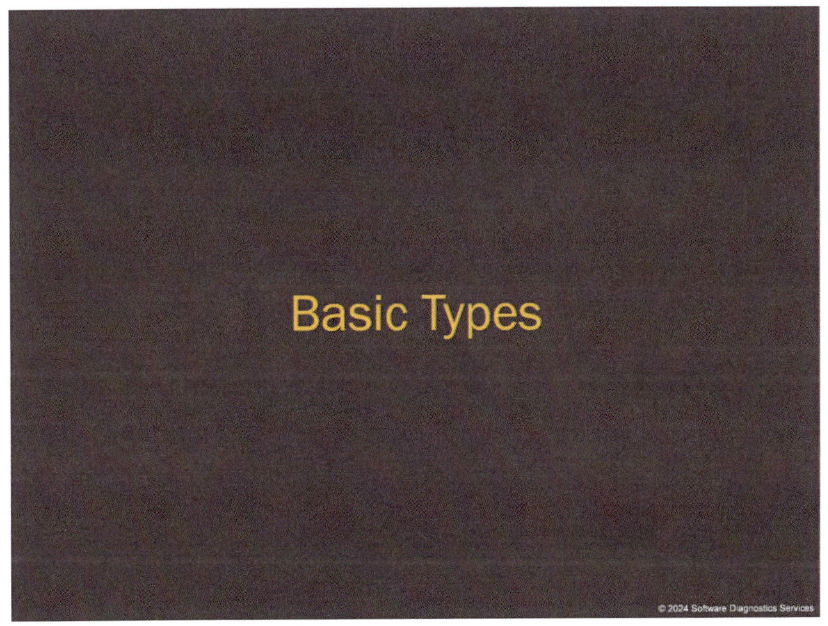

Now, we look at a few fundamental basic types.

The `basic_types` projects:

- `basic_types_c` C
- `basic_types_c_cpp` C++ as a better C
- `basic_types_modern_cpp` Modern C++

can be found in the archive[3]. In the following slide descriptions, we only show relevant code snippets and their output.

[3] https://www.patterndiagnostics.com/Training/ACPPWD/ACPPWD.zip

ASCII Characters and Pointers

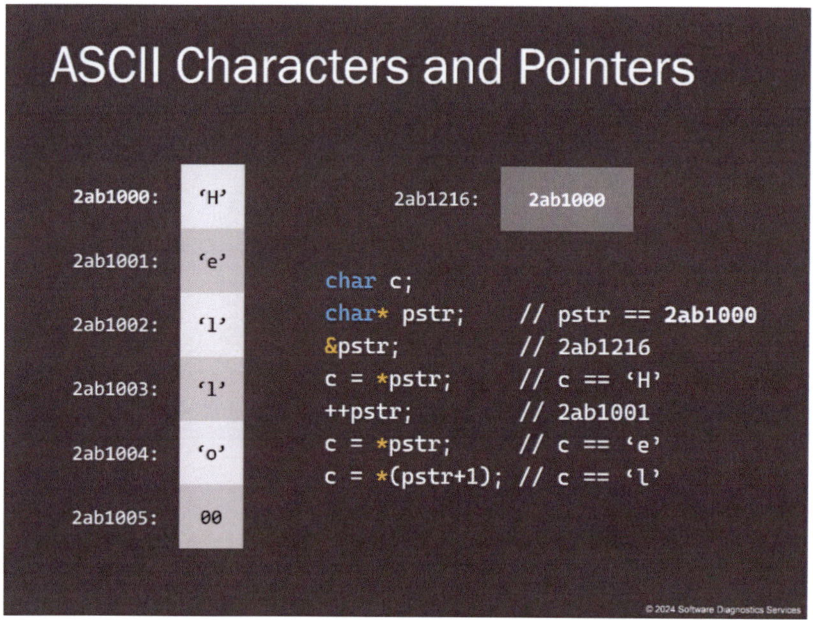

We have already looked at ASCII zero-terminated strings and pointers conceptually using memory diagrams. Here, we look at some idiomatic C and C++ code.

C C++ as a better C

```
puts("--- ASCII Characters and Pointers ---");
{
    char str[] = { 'H', 'e', 'l', 'l', 'o', 0 };

    char* pstr = str;
    printf("value of pstr: %p address of pstr: %p \n", pstr, &pstr);

    char c = *pstr;
    printf("value of c: %c \n", c);

    ++pstr;
    printf("value of pstr: %p \n", pstr);

    c = *pstr;
    printf("value of c: %c \n", c);

    c = *(pstr + 1);
    printf("value of c: %c \n", c);
}
```

Output

```
--- ASCII Characters and Pointers ---
value of pstr: 00000056FD2FC004 address of pstr: 00000056FD2FC028
value of c: H
value of pstr: 00000056FD2FC005
value of c: e
value of c: l
```

Bytes and Pointers

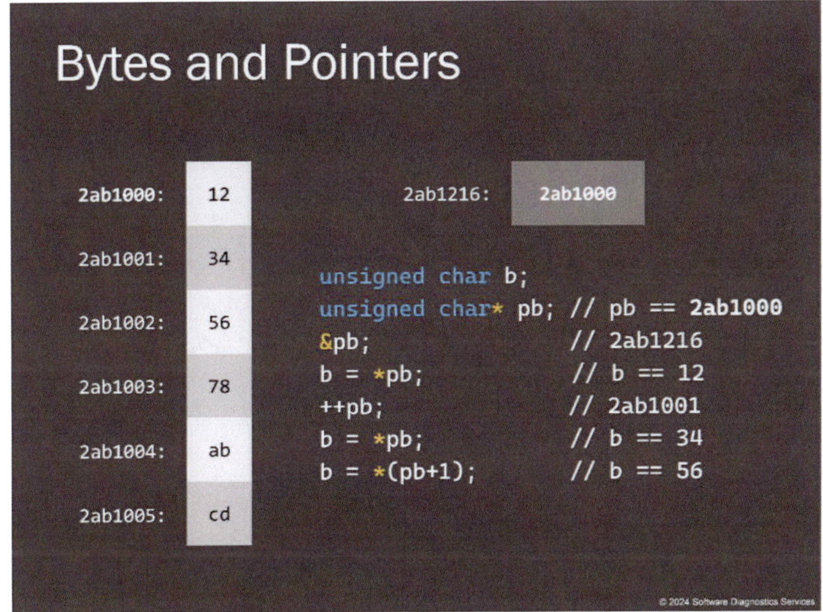

Characters are signed with small integer values from -128 to 127. But if we want to work with bytes with unsigned values from 0 to 255, we need to use unsigned characters. Later, we see what other types are available to work with bytes.

C C++ as a better C

```
puts("--- Bytes and Pointers ---");
{
    unsigned char barr[] = { 0x12, 0x34, 0x56, 0x78, 0xab, 0xcd };

    unsigned char* pb = barr;
    printf("value of pb: %p address of pb: %p \n", pb, &pb);

    unsigned char b = *pb;
    printf("value of b: %x \n", b);

    ++pb;
    printf("value of pb: %p \n", pb);

    b = *pb;
    printf("value of b: %x \n", b);

    b = *(pb + 1);
    printf("value of b: %x \n", b);
}
```

Output

```
--- Bytes and Pointers ---
value of pb: 00000056FD2FC064 address of pb: 00000056FD2FC088
value of b: 12
value of pb: 00000056FD2FC065
value of b: 34
value of b: 56
```

Wide Characters and Pointers

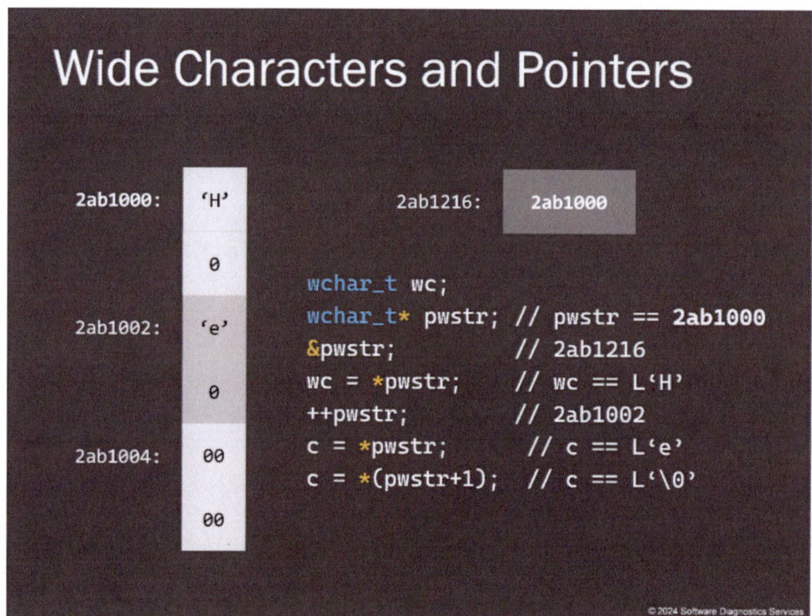

Native Windows strings are UNICODE, and it is natural to use wide characters that occupy two bytes each.

C C++ as a better C

```
puts("--- Wide Characters and Pointers ---");
{
    wchar_t wstr[] = { L'H', L'e', L'l', L'l', L'o', 0 };

    wchar_t* pwstr = wstr;
    printf("value of pwstr: %p address of pwstr: %p \n", pwstr, &pwstr);

    wchar_t wc = *pwstr;
    printf("value of wc: %lc \n", wc);

    ++pwstr;
    printf("value of pwstr: %p \n", pwstr);

    wc = *pwstr;
    printf("value of wc: %lc \n", wc);

    wc = *(pwstr + 1);
    printf("value of wc: %lc \n", wc);
}
```

Output

```
--- Wide Characters and Pointers ---
value of pwstr: 00000056FD2FC0C8 address of pwstr: 00000056FD2FC0F8
value of wc: H
value of pwstr: 00000056FD2FC0CA
value of wc: e
value of wc: l
```

Integers

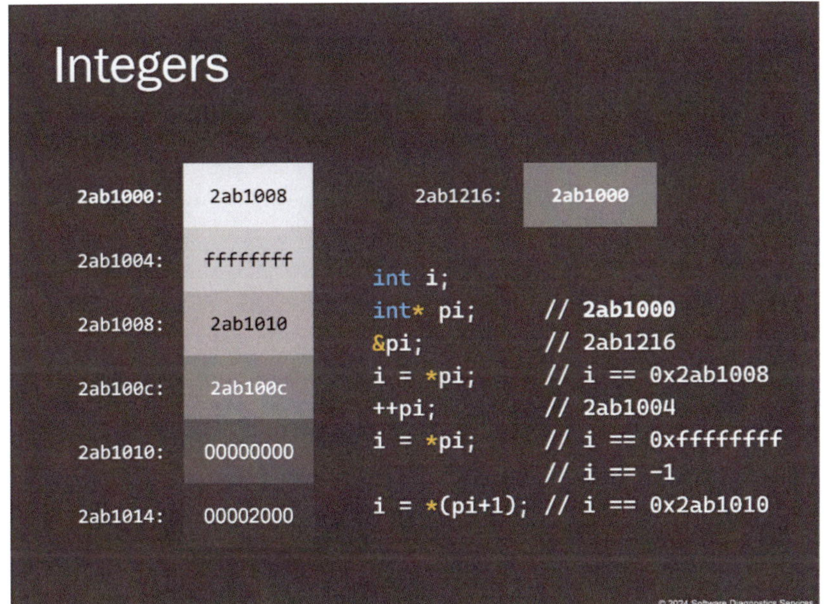

The next type we look at now is integers, which occupy 4 bytes.

C C++ as a better C

```
puts("--- Integers ---");
{
    int iarr[] = { 0x2ab1008, -1, 0x2ab1010, 0x2ab100c, 0, 0x2000 };

    int* pi = iarr;
    printf("value of pi: %p address of pi: %p \n", pi, &pi);

    int i = *pi;
    printf("value of i: %x \n", i);

    ++pi;
    printf("value of pi: %p \n", pi);

    i = *pi;
    printf("value of i: %x \n", i);

    i = *(pi + 1);
    printf("value of i: %x \n", i);
}
```

Output

```
--- Integers ---
value of pi: 00000056FD2FC138 address of pi: 00000056FD2FC168
value of i: 2ab1008
value of pi: 00000056FD2FC13C
value of i: ffffffff
value of i: 2ab1010
```

Long Integers

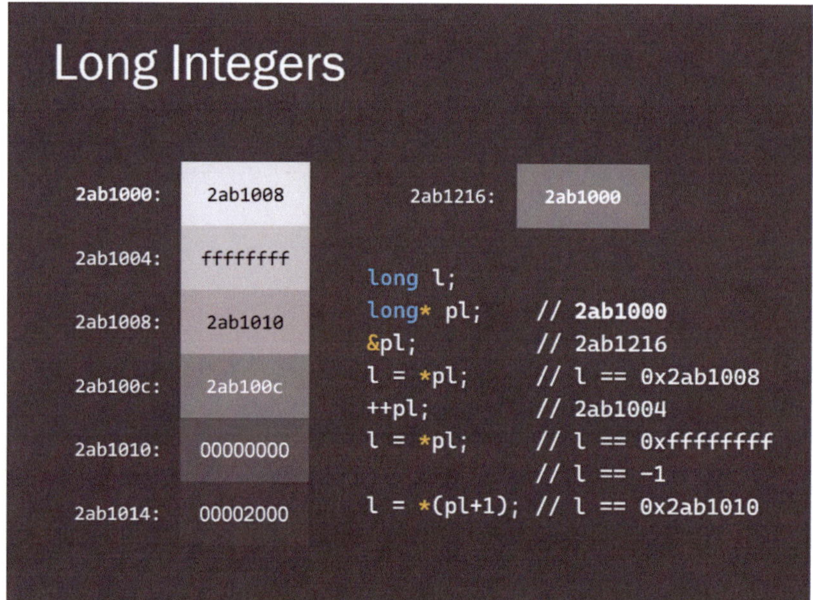

Long integers also occupy 4 bytes.

C C++ as a better C

```
puts("--- Long Integers ---");
{
    long larr[] = { 0x2ab1008, -1, 0x2ab1010, 0x2ab100c, 0, 0x2000 };

    long* pl = larr;
    printf("value of pl: %p address of pl: %p \n", pl , &pl);

    long l = *pl;
    printf("value of l: %x \n", l);

    ++pl;
    printf("value of pl: %p \n", pl);

    l = *pl;
    printf("value of l: %x \n", l);

    l = *(pl + 1);
    printf("value of l: %x \n", l);
}
```

Output

```
--- Long Integers ---
value of pl: 00000056FD2FC1A8 address of pl: 00000056FD2FC1D8
value of l: 2ab1008
value of pl: 00000056FD2FC1AC
value of l: ffffffff
value of l: 2ab1010
```

Little-Endian System

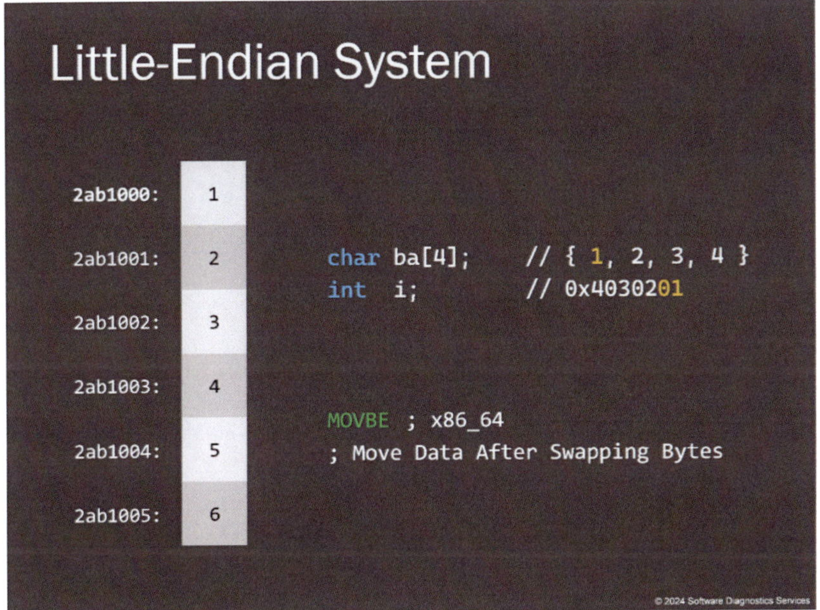

When converting between byte sequences and number values, we need to consider the little-endian system where the least significant digits reside at the lowest memory addresses.

C C++ as a better C

```
puts("--- Little-Endian System ---");
{
    char ba[4] = { 1, 2, 3, 4 };

    int i = *(int*)ba;

    printf("values of ba array: %x, %x, %x, %x value of i: %x \n",
        ba[0], ba[1], ba[2], ba[3], i);
}
```

Output

```
--- Little-Endian System ---
values of ba array: 1, 2, 3, 4 value of i: 4030201
```

Short Integers

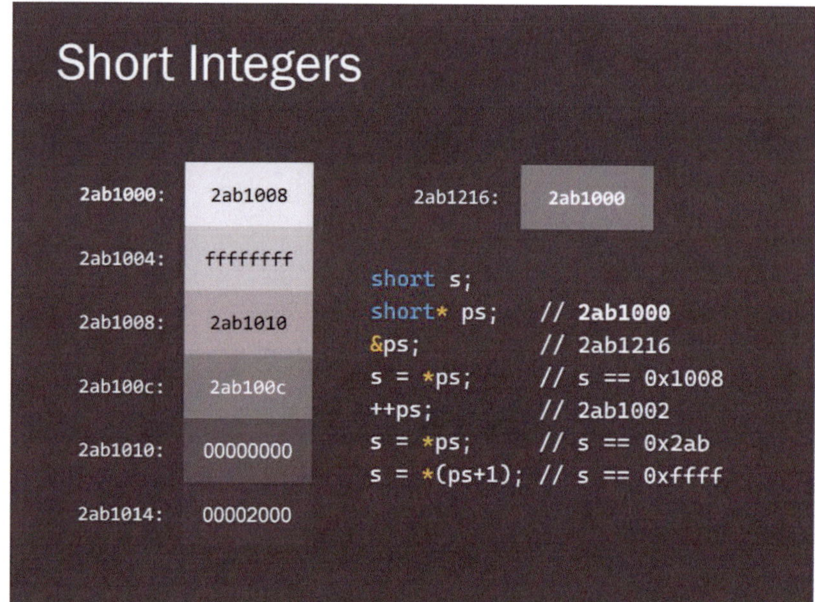

Short integers occupy 2 bytes.

C C++ as a better C

```
puts("--- Short Integers ---");
{
    int iarr[] = { 0x2ab1008, -1, 0x2ab1010, 0x2ab100c, 0, 0x2000 };

    short* ps = (short*)iarr;
    printf("value of ps: %p address of ps: %p \n", ps, &ps);

    short s = *ps;
    printf("value of s: %hx \n", s);

    ++ps;
    printf("value of ps: %p \n", ps);

    s = *ps;
    printf("value of s: %hx \n", s);

    s = *(ps + 1);
    printf("value of s: %hx \n", s);
}
```

Output

```
--- Short Integers ---
value of ps: 00000056FD2FC258 address of ps: 00000056FD2FC288
value of s: 1008
value of ps: 00000056FD2FC25A
value of s: 2ab
value of s: ffff
```

Long Long Integers

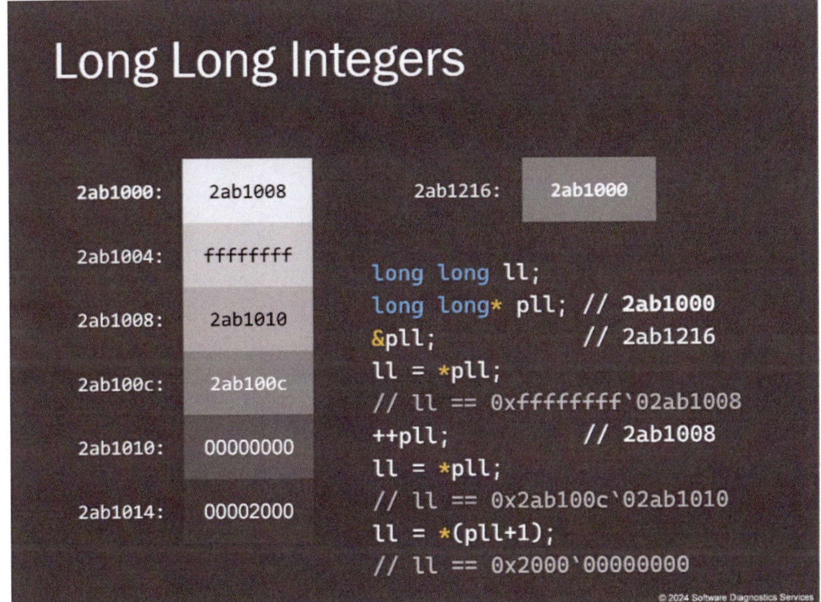

If we want 8-byte 64-bit integers, we need to use `long long`.

C C++ as a better C

```
puts("--- Long Long Integers ---");
{
    long larr[] = { 0x2ab1008, -1, 0x2ab1010, 0x2ab100c, 0, 0x2000 };

    long long* pll = (long long*)larr;
    printf("value of pll: %p address of pll: %p \n", pll, &pll);

    long long ll = *pll;
    printf("value of ll: %llx \n", ll);

    ++pll;
    printf("value of pll: %p \n", pll);

    ll = *pll;
    printf("value of ll: %llx \n", ll);

    ll = *(pll + 1);
    printf("value of ll: %llx \n", ll);
}
```

Output

```
--- Long Long Integers ---
value of pll: 00000056FD2FC2C8 address of pll: 00000056FD2FC2F8
value of ll: ffffffff02ab1008
value of pll: 00000056FD2FC2D0
value of ll: 2ab100c02ab1010
value of ll: 200000000000
```

Signed and Unsigned Integers

Signed and Unsigned Integers

- (signed) short / unsigned short
- signed / (signed) int / unsigned / unsigned int
- (signed) long (int) / unsigned long (int)
- (signed) long long (int) / unsigned long long (int)

```
for (unsigned i = 0xfff; i >= 0; --i)
{
        // ... Spiking Thread
}
```


We need to be careful to use unsigned index variables in classic loops. The following code example loops indefinitely since the loop variable is always positive:

C C++ as a better C

```
puts("--- Signed and Unsigned Integers ---");
{
    // for (unsigned i = 0xfff; i >= 0; --i) // hang
    for (signed i = 0xfff; i >= 0; --i)
    {
    }
}
```

Spiking Thread memory analysis pattern
https://www.dumpanalysis.org/blog/index.php/2007/05/11/crash-dump-analysis-patterns-part-14/

Fixed Size Integers

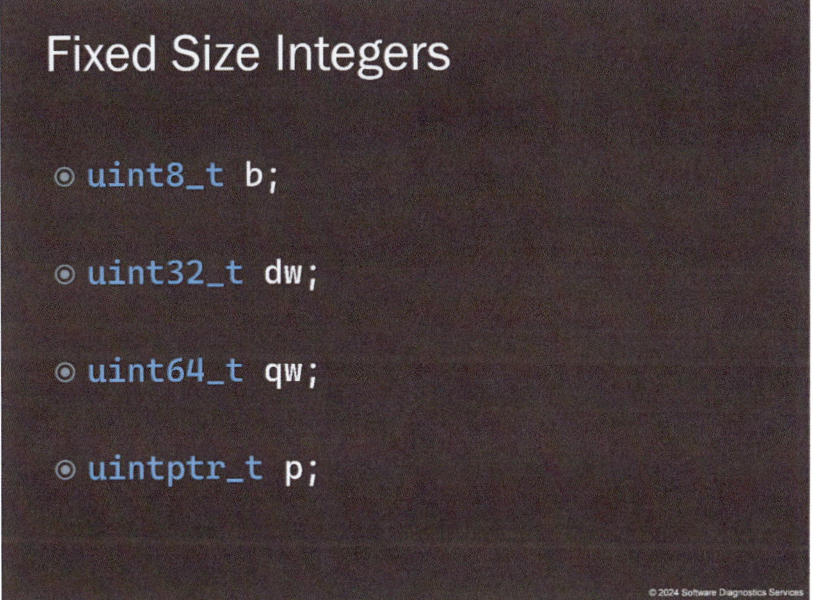

It is also possible to be precise and use portable fixed-size types.

C C++ as a better C

```
puts("--- Fixed Size Integers ---");
{
    uint8_t b = 0xfe;

    uint32_t dw = 0xfedcba98;

    uint64_t qw = 0x12345678ffffffff;

    uintptr_t p = (uintptr_t)&qw;
}
```

Booleans

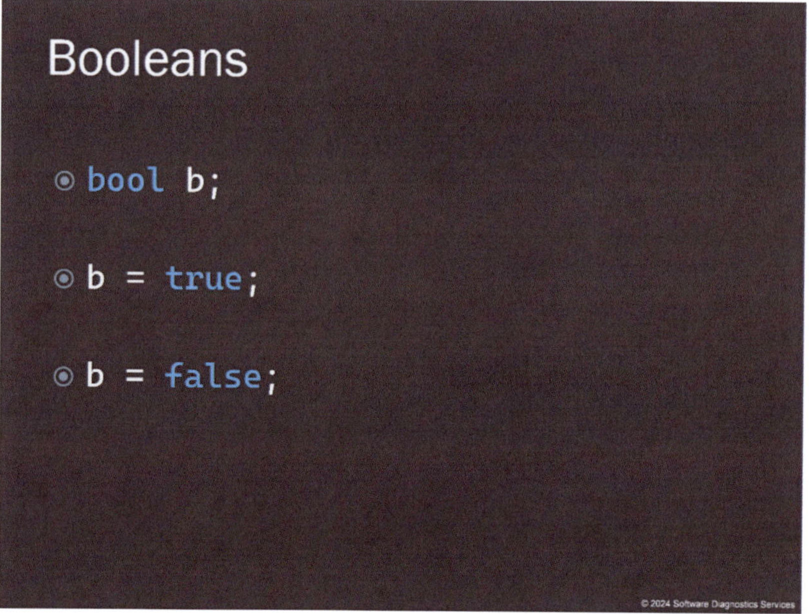

C++ also includes a native type for boolean variables. If you want to use it in pure C, you need to include the *stdbool.h* header.

C

```
puts("--- Booleans ---");
{
    bool b = true; // requires stdbool.h header in C

    b = false;
}
```

C++ as a better C

```
puts("--- Booleans ---");
{
    bool b = true;

    b = false;
}
```

Bytes

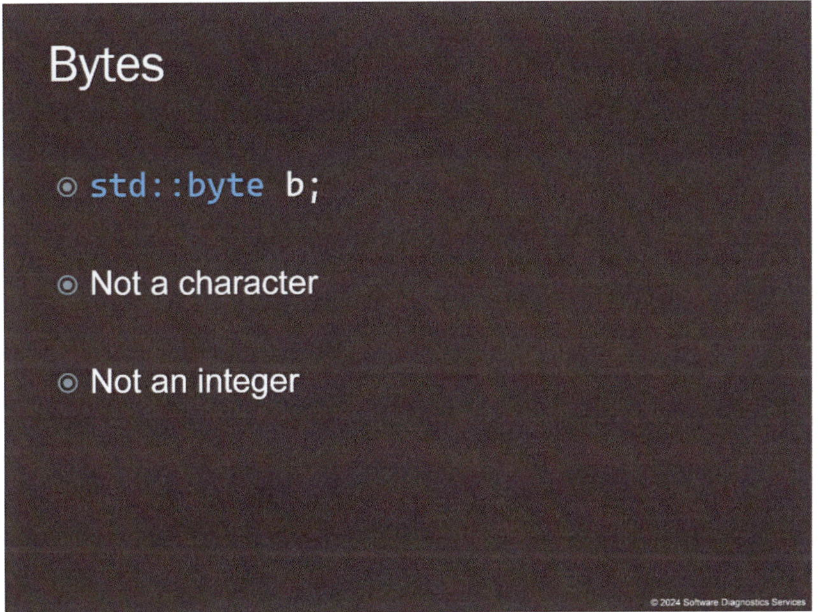

The latest C++ standards also include a distinct type for bytes.

Modern C++

```
std::println("--- Bytes ---");
{
    std::byte b{0xab};

    std::println("value of b: {}", b);
}
```

Output

```
--- Bytes ---
value of b: ab
```

Size

Size

- sizeof operator
- `size_t size = sizeof(int);`
- `int i; size = sizeof i;`
- `size = sizeof(1 + 1);`

The sizeof operator can evaluate the size of types, variables, and target result types of expressions (without expression evaluation).

C C++ as a better C

```
puts("--- Size ---");
{
    size_t size = sizeof(int);
    printf("value of size: %lld \n", size);

    int i = 0;
    size = sizeof i;
    printf("value of size: %lld \n", size);

    size = sizeof(1 + 1);
    printf("value of size: %lld \n", size);
}
```

Output

```
--- Size ---
value of size: 4
value of size: 4
value of size: 4
```

Alignment (C11)

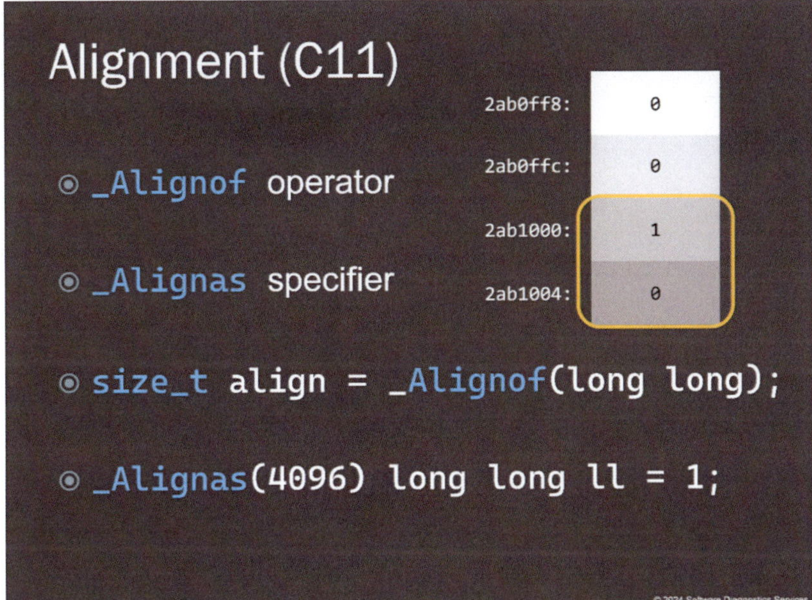

Variables are usually aligned in memory at offsets divisible by their type size value in bytes. In C11, you can get default alignment values using the _Alignof operator and change the default alignment using the _Alignas specifier.

C

```
puts("--- Alignment (C11) ---");
{
    size_t align = _Alignof(long long);

    printf("address of align: %p value of align: %lld \n", &align, align);

    _Alignas(4096) long long ll = 1;

    printf("address of ll: %p \n", &ll);
}
```

Output

```
--- Alignment (C11) ---
address of align: 00000056FD2FC438 value of align: 8
address of ll: 00000056FD2FD000
```

Alignment (C++11)

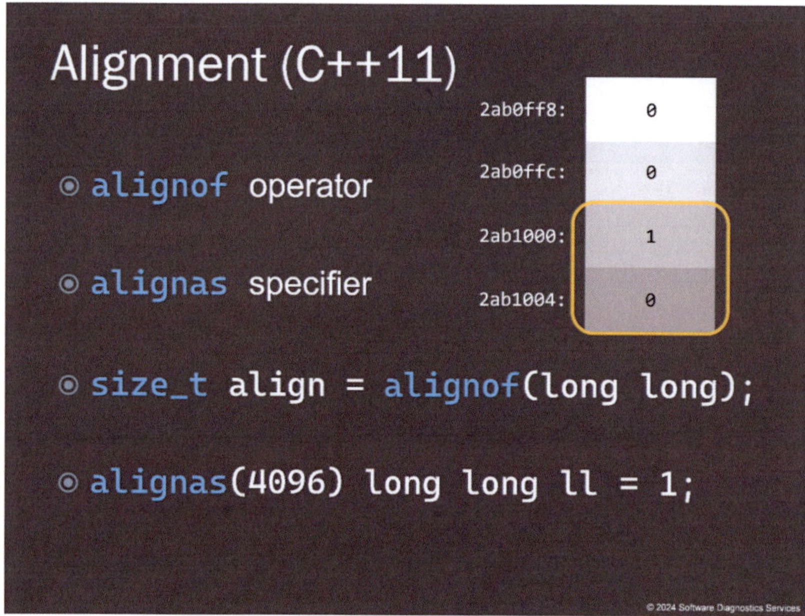

Variables are usually aligned in memory at offsets divisible by their type size value in bytes. In C++11, you can get default alignment values using the alignof operator and change the default alignment using the alignas specifier.

C++ as a better C

```
puts("--- Alignment (C++11) ---");
{
    size_t align = alignof(long long);

    printf("address of align: %p value of align: %lld \n", &align, align);

    alignas(4096) long long ll = 1;

    printf("address of ll: %p \n", &ll);
}
```

Output

```
--- Alignment (C++11) ---
address of align: 0000008107AFC438 value of align: 8
address of ll: 0000008107AFD000
```

LLP64

LLP64

- sizeof(int) == 4
- sizeof(int*) == 8
- sizeof(long) == 4
- sizeof(long long) == 8

Windows uses the so-called LLP64 data model where only `long long` integers and pointers are 64-bit.

C C++ as a better C

```
puts("--- LLP64 ---");
{
    printf("size of int: %lld \n"
        "size of int*: %lld \n"
        "size of long: %lld \n"
        "size of long long: %lld \n",
        sizeof(int), sizeof(int*), sizeof(long), sizeof(long long));
}
```

Output

```
--- LLP64 ---
size of int: 4
size of int*: 8
size of long: 4
size of long long: 8
```

Nothing and Anything

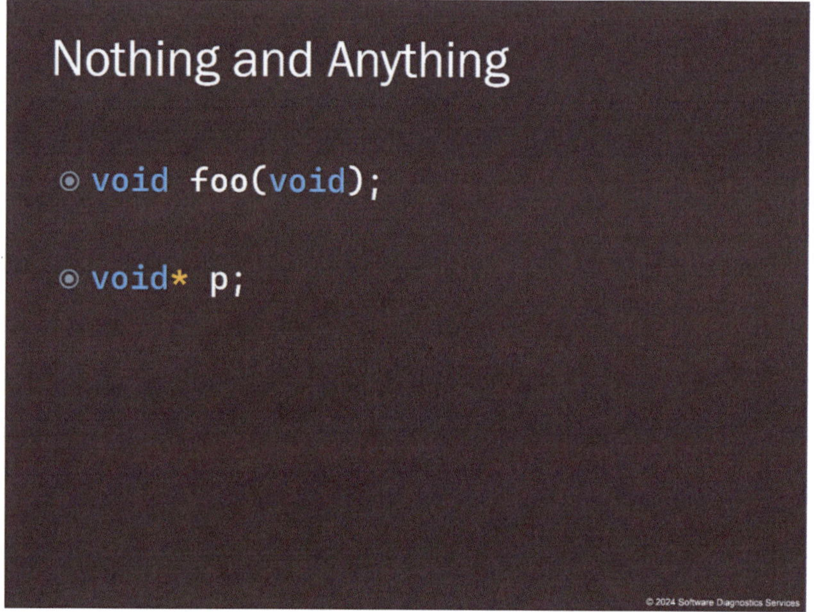

Two distinct types correspond to the concepts of *Nothing* and *Anything* you can find in other programming languages: `void` and `void *`. The latter is a pointer to any type.

C C++ as a better C

```
puts("--- Nothing and Anything ---");
{
    char c;
    char* pc = &c;

    long long ll;
    long long* pll = &ll;

    void* p = pc;
    p = pll;
}
```

Automatic Type Inference

Automatic Type Inference

```
auto a = "Hello";

auto func(decltype("Hello") cstr)
{
    return cstr;
}
```

© 2024 Software Diagnostics Services

C++11 added automatic type specification, so the type is deduced from the initializing expression.

Modern C++

```
auto func(decltype("Hello") cstr) {
    return cstr;
}

std::println("--- Automatic Type Inference ---");
{
    auto a = "Hello";

    std::println("type of a: {}", typeid(a).name());
    std::println("type of func: {}", typeid(func).name());
}
```

Output

```
--- Automatic Type Inference ---
type of a: char const * __ptr64
type of func: char const * __ptr64 __cdecl(char const (& __ptr64)[6])
```

Entity Conversion

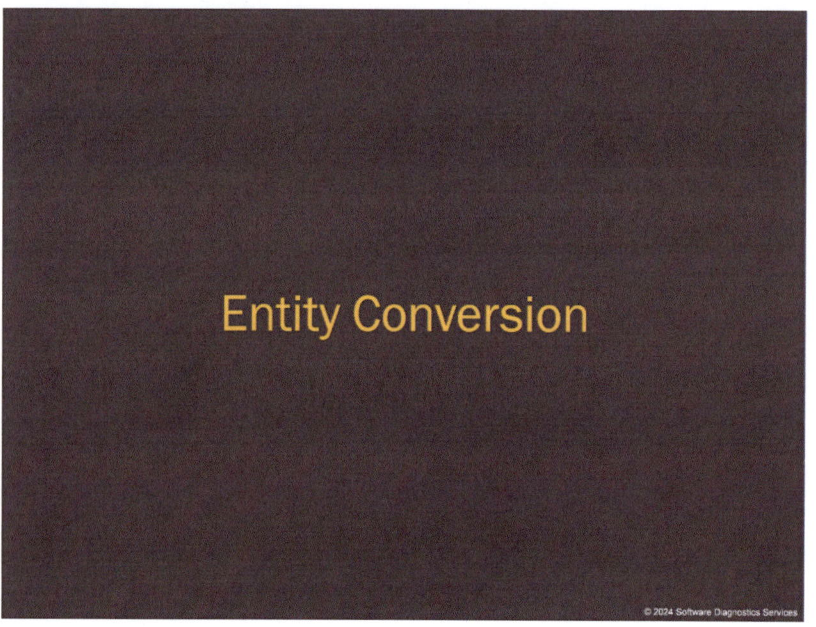

As you anticipate, the same memory cell addresses and their values are the basis of conversion between different entity types. So, let's look at some examples.

The **`entity_conversion`** projects:

- `entity_conversion_c` C
- `entity_conversion_c_cpp` C++ as a better C
- `entity_conversion_classic_cpp` Classic C++

can be found in the archive[4]. In the following slide descriptions, we only show relevant code snippets and their output.

[4] https://www.patterndiagnostics.com/Training/ACPPWD/ACPPWD.zip

Pointer Conversion (C-Style)

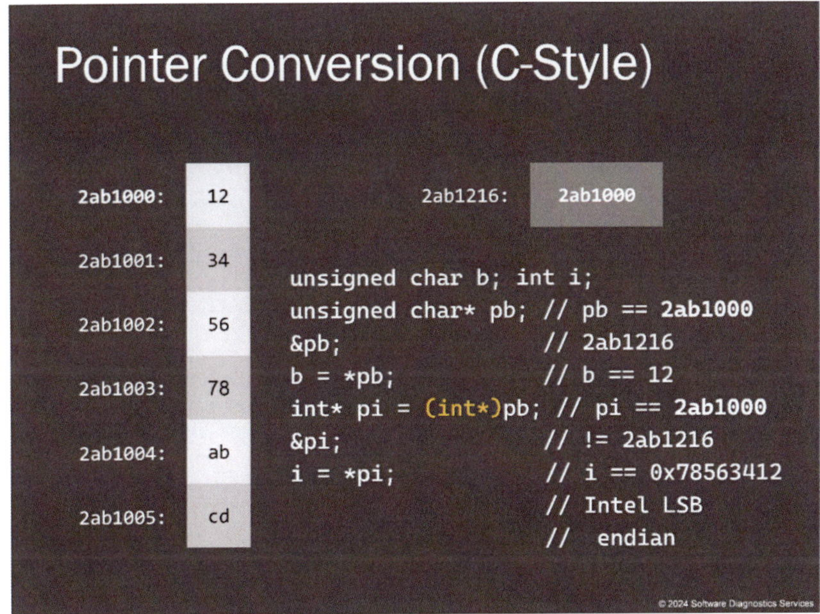

Pointers can be converted to each other freely because their value is just a memory address. However, when we dereference them, we get the value based on underlying memory contents, which don't change as illustrated here. Please also note that due to the least significant byte endian convention, the integer value we get differs from the memory layout byte order.

C C++ as a better C

```
puts("--- Pointer Conversion (C-Style) ---");
{
    unsigned char barr[] = { 0x12, 0x34, 0x56, 0x78, 0xab, 0xcd };

    unsigned char* pb = barr;
    printf("value of pb: %p address of pb: %p \n", pb, &pb);

    unsigned char b = *pb;
    printf("value of b: %x \n", b);

    int* pi = (int*)pb;

    printf("value of pi: %p address of pi: %p \n", pi, &pi);

    int i = *pi; // Intel LSB endian

    printf("value of i: %x \n", i);
}
```

Output

```
--- Pointer Conversion (C-Style) ---
value of pb: 00000033D759F714 address of pb: 00000033D759F738
value of b: 12
value of pi: 00000033D759F714 address of pi: 00000033D759F778
value of i: 78563412
```

Pointer Conversion (C++)

Classic C++

```
std::cout << "--- Pointer Conversion (C++) ---" << std::endl;
{
    unsigned char barr[] = { 0x12, 0x34, 0x56, 0x78, 0xab, 0xcd };

    unsigned char* pb = barr;
    std::cout << "value of pb: " << static_cast<void*>(pb) << // pb is interpreted as a C-string
        " address of pb: " << &pb << std::endl;

    unsigned char b = *pb;
    std::cout << "value of b: " << std::hex << static_cast<int>(b) << std::endl;

    int* pi = reinterpret_cast<int*>(pb);

    std::cout << "value of pi: " << pi << " address of pi: " << &pi << std::endl;

    int i = *pi; // Intel LSB endian

    std::cout << "value of i: " << std::hex << i << std::endl;
}
```

Output

```
--- Pointer Conversion (C++) ---
value of pb: 000000D4D60FF514 address of pb: 000000D4D60FF538
value of b: 12
value of pi: 000000D4D60FF514 address of pi: 000000D4D60FF578
value of i: 78563412
```

Numeric Promotion/Conversion

Numeric Promotion/Conversion

- `char c = 'a'; int n = c;`
- `short s = c;`
- `int n = 0x1234; char c = n;`

Values from the lesser range of values can be automatically promoted to types with a wider range of values. The opposite automatic conversion may lose some bits of information and should be carefully reviewed.

C C++ as a better C

```
puts("--- Numeric Promotion/Conversion ---");
{
    char c = 'a';
    int n = c;
    short s = c;

    printf("value of c: %x value of n: %x value of s: %x\n", c, n, s);

    n = 0x1234;
    c = n;

    printf("value of n: %x value of c: %x: \n", n, c);
}
```

Classic C++

```
std::cout << "--- Numeric Promotion/Conversion ---" << std::endl;
{
    char c = 'a';
    int n = c;
    short s = c;

    std::cout << "value of c: " << std::hex << static_cast<int>(c) << " value of n: " << n << "
value of s: " << s << std::endl;

    n = 0x1234;
    c = n;
```

```
    std::cout << "value of n: " << n << " value of c: " << static_cast<int>(c) << std::endl;
}
```

Output

```
--- Numeric Promotion/Conversion ---
value of c: 61 value of n: 61 value of s: 61
value of n: 1234 value of c: 34
```

Numeric Conversion

Numeric Conversion

- (type)(expr) // C-Style
- static_cast<type>(expr)

```
for (unsigned i = 0xfff; (int)i >= 0; --i)
{
}

for (unsigned i = 0xfff; static_cast<int>(i) >= 0; --i)
{
}
```


In the absence of automatic conversion for compatible types, we can use C-style casts or explicit, specific C++ casts.

C C++ as a better C

```
puts("--- Numeric Conversion ---");
{
    for (unsigned i = 0xfff; (int)i >= 0; --i)
    {
    }
}
```

Classic C++

```
std::cout << "--- Numeric Conversion ---" << std::endl;
{
    for (unsigned i = 0xfff; static_cast<int>(i) >= 0; --i)
    {
    }
}
```

Incompatible Types

When types are incompatible, for example, integers and pointers to them, we can use either C-style casts or the specific C++ type reinterpretation cast.

C C++ as a better C

```
puts("--- Incompatible Type ---");
{
    int* p = (int*)1;
}
```

Classic C++

```
std::cout << "--- Incompatible Type ---" << std::endl;
{
    int* p = reinterpret_cast<int*>(1);
}
```

Forcing

Forcing

```
struct A
{
      unsigned int u1;
      unsigned int u2;
};

struct B
{
      unsigned long long ull;
} b;

A a = reinterpret_cast<A>(b);

A a = *(A*)&b;
a = *reinterpret_cast<A *>(&b);
```


Different structures are even more incompatible with the failing direct C++ reinterpretation cast. However, we can force a reinterpretation of structures by reinterpreting a pointer to a source structure (an address of a source structure) as a pointer to a target structure (an address of a target structure) and then dereferencing it. In such a case, the underlying memory cells are reinterpreted as the target structure field values. You can review the code example after studying the next two sections on structures and memory:

C C++ as a better C

```
puts("--- Forcing ---");
{
    struct A
    {
        unsigned int u1;
        unsigned int u2;
    };

    struct B
    {
        unsigned long long ull;
    } b = {0xFFFFFFFF00000000};

    struct A a = *(struct A*)&b;

    printf("address of a: %p value of a: {%x, %x}: \n", &a, a.u1, a.u2);
    printf("address of b: %p value of b: %llx \n", &b, b.ull); // Intel LSB endian
}
```

Classic C++

```
std::cout << "--- Forcing ---" << std::endl;
{
    struct A
    {
        unsigned int u1;
        unsigned int u2;
    };

    struct B
```

```
    {
        unsigned long long ull;
    } b = { 0xFFFFFFFF00000000 };

    struct A a = *reinterpret_cast<A*>(&b);

    std::cout << "address of a: " << &a <<
        " value of a: {" << a.u1 << ", " << a.u2 << "}" << std::endl;
    std::cout << "address of b: " << &b <<
        " value of b: " << b.ull << std::endl; // Intel LSB endian
}
```

Output

```
--- Forcing ---
address of a: 000000D4D60FF678 value of a: {0, ffffffff}
address of b: 000000D4D60FF658 value of b: ffffffff00000000
```

Uniting

Uniting

```
struct A
{
      unsigned int u1;
      unsigned int u2;
};

struct B
{
      unsigned long long ull;
};

union AB
{
    struct A a;
    struct B b;
} ab;
```


We can superimpose different structures at the same location in memory. In this case the conversion is automatic when we choose between different discriminating union fields.

C C++ as a better C

```
puts("--- Uniting ---");
{
    struct A
    {
        unsigned int u1;
        unsigned int u2;
    };
```

```
    struct B
    {
        unsigned long long ull;
    };

    union AB
    {
        struct A a;
        struct B b;
    } ab = {0};

    ab.b.ull = 0xFFFFFFFF00000000;

    printf("address of ab: %p address of ab.a: %p address of ab.b: %p \n"
        "value of a : {% x, % x} value of b : % llx \n",
        &ab, &ab.a, &ab.b, ab.a.u1, ab.a.u2, ab.b.ull); // Intel LSB endian
}
```

Classic C++

```
std::cout << "--- Uniting ---" << std::endl;
{
    struct A
    {
        unsigned int u1;
        unsigned int u2;
    };

    struct B
    {
        unsigned long long ull;
    };

    union AB
    {
        struct A a;
        struct B b;
    } ab = { 0 };

    ab.b.ull = 0xFFFFFFFF00000000;

    std::cout << "address of ab: " << &ab <<
        " address of ab.a: " << &ab.a << " address of ab.b: " << &ab.b <<
        " value of a: {" << ab.a.u1 << ", " << ab.a.u2 << "}" <<
        " value of b: " << ab.b.ull << std::endl; // Intel LSB endian
}
```

Output

```
--- Uniting ---
address of ab: 0000009A370FFAD8 address of ab.a: 0000009A370FFAD8 address of ab.b: 0000009A370FFAD8
value of a : {0, ffffffff} value of b : ffffffff00000000
```

Structures, Classes, and Objects

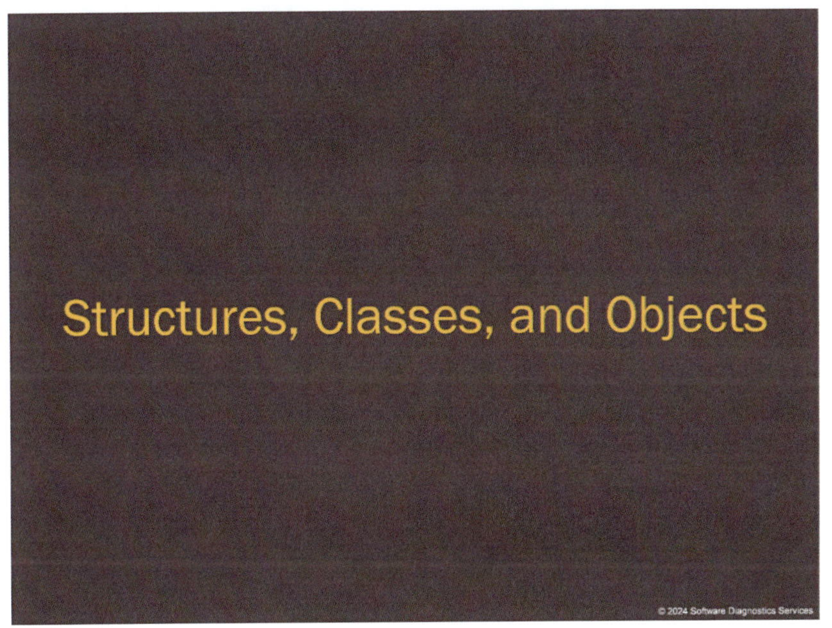

Now, we cover structures, classes, and their objects.

The `structures` projects:

- `structures_c` C
- `structures_c_cpp` C++ as a better C
- `structures_classic_cpp` Classic C++

can be found in the archive[5]. In the following slide descriptions, we only show relevant code snippets and their output.

[5] https://www.patterndiagnostics.com/Training/ACPPWD/ACPPWD.zip

Structures

Structures

```
struct MyStruct
{
    int field;
    // ...
};

struct MyStruct myStruct;
MyStruct myStruct2;

struct MyStruct* pMyStruct;
MyStruct* pMyStruct2;
```

```
struct
{
    int field;
    // ...
} myOtherStruct;

struct
{
    int field;
    // ...
}* pMyOtherStruct;
```


We can view structures as collections of fields laid out in memory. Structures may have names or can be anonymous, as on the right.

C

```
puts("--- Structures ---");
{
    struct MyStruct
    {
        int field;
        // ...
    };

    struct MyStruct myStruct;

    struct MyStruct* pMyStruct;

    struct
    {
        int field;
        // ...
    } myOtherStruct;

    struct
    {
        int field;
        // ...
    }* pMyOtherStruct;
}
```

C++ as a better C

```
puts("--- Structures ---");
{
    struct MyStruct
    {
        int field;
        // ...
    };

    MyStruct myStruct; // in C++ struct keyword can be omitted

    MyStruct* pMyStruct;

    struct
    {
        int field;
        // ...
    } myOtherStruct;

    struct
    {
        int field;
        // ...
    }* pMyOtherStruct;
}
```

Access Level

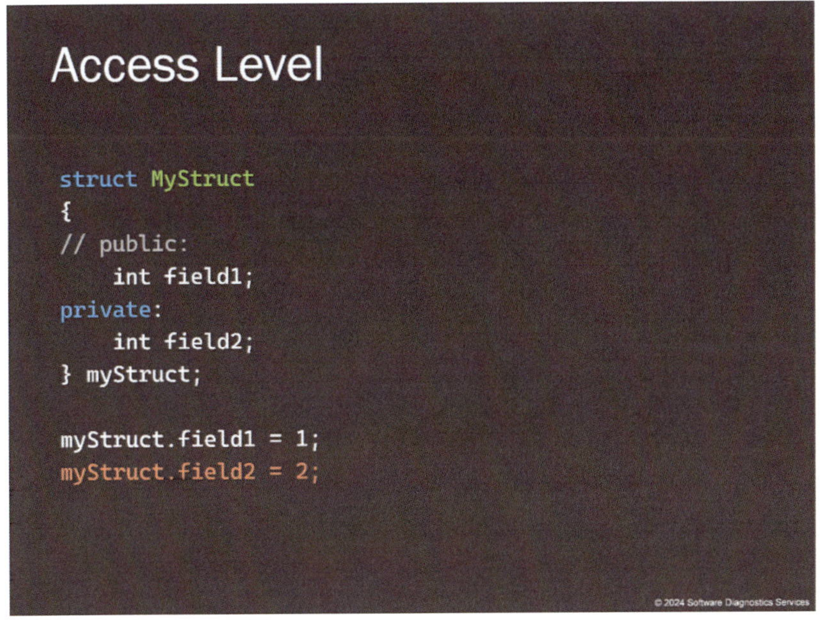

Fields with the `private` access specifier cannot be referenced from the outside.

Classic C++

```
std::cout << "--- Access Level ---" << std::endl;
{
    struct MyStruct
    {
        // public:
        int field1;
    private:
        int field2;
    } myStruct;

    myStruct.field1 = 1;
    // myStruct.field2 = 2; // error
}
```

Classes and Objects

Classes and Objects

```
class MyClass
{
    int field;
    // ...
};

class MyClass myClass;
MyClass myClass2;

class MyClass* pMyClass;
MyClass* pMyClass2;
```

```
class
{
    int field;
    // ...
} myOtherClass;

class
{
    int field;
    // ...
}* pMyOtherClass;
```


Classes have the same structure.

Classic C++

```
std::cout << "--- Classes and Objects ---" << std::endl;
{
    class MyClass {
        int field;
    };

    MyClass myStruct; // class keyword can be omitted

    MyClass* pMyStruct;
```

```
    class {
        int field;
    } myOtherClass;

    class
    {
        int field;
    }* pMyOtherClass;
}
```

Structures and Classes

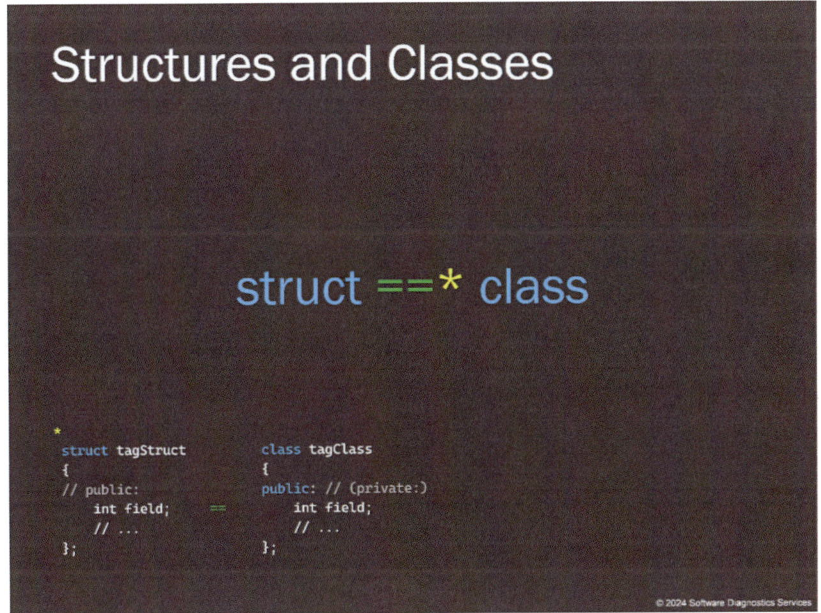

Both structures and classes are completely the same in C++ and can be used interchangeably. This is why you can always see `struct` in good modern C++ books. The only difference (if we ignore inheritance for now) is the field access, which is public by default in structures and private in classes.

Classic C++

```
std::cout << "--- Structures and Classes ---" << std::endl;
{
    struct tagStruct
    {
    // public:
        int field;
    };

    class tagClass
    {
    public: // (private:)
        int field;
    };
}
```

Pointer to Structure

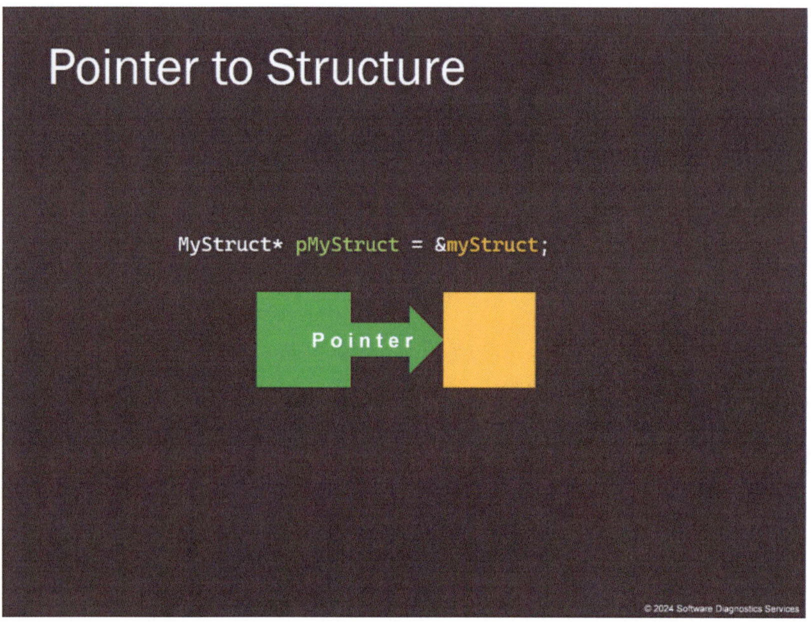

Here, we go again through our conceptual philosophy of pointers pictures and annotate them with C and C++ code.

C

```
puts("--- Pointer to Structure ---");
{
    struct MyStruct
    {
        int field;
        // ...
    } myStruct;

    struct MyStruct* pMyStruct = &myStruct;

    printf("address of myStruct: %p address of pMyStruct: %p value of pMyStruct: %p \n",
        &myStruct, &pMyStruct, pMyStruct);
}
```

C++ as a better C

```
puts("--- Pointer to Structure ---");
{
    struct MyStruct
    {
        int field;
        // ...
    } myStruct;

    MyStruct* pMyStruct = &myStruct;

    printf("address of myStruct: %p address of pMyStruct: %p value of pMyStruct: %p \n",
        &myStruct, &pMyStruct, pMyStruct);
}
```

Output

```
--- Pointer to Structure ---
address of myStruct: 0000008380F6F364 address of pMyStruct: 0000008380F6F388 value of pMyStruct:
0000008380F6F364
```

Pointer to Structure Dereference

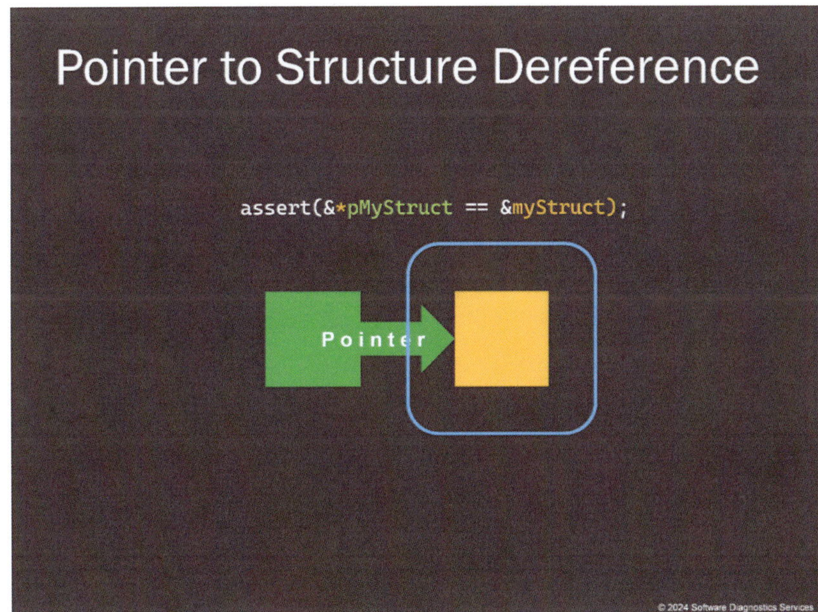

Here, we dereference a pointer to some structure. We get the structure value.

C

```
puts("--- Pointer to Structure Dereference ---");
{
    struct MyStruct
    {
        int field;
        // ...
    } myStruct;

    struct MyStruct* pMyStruct = &myStruct;

    printf("address of myStruct: %p address of pMyStruct: %p value of pMyStruct: %p \n",
        &myStruct, &pMyStruct, pMyStruct);

    assert(&*pMyStruct == &myStruct);

    printf("address of pMyStruct dereference: %p address of myStruct: %p \n",
        &*pMyStruct, &myStruct);
}
```

C++ as a better C

```
puts("--- Pointer to Structure Dereference ---");
{
    struct MyStruct
    {
        int field;
        // ...
    } myStruct;

    MyStruct* pMyStruct = &myStruct;

    printf("address of myStruct: %p address of pMyStruct: %p value of pMyStruct: %p \n",
        &myStruct, &pMyStruct, pMyStruct);

    assert(&*pMyStruct == &myStruct);

    printf("address of pMyStruct dereference: %p address of myStruct: %p \n",
        &*pMyStruct, &myStruct);
}
```

Output

```
--- Pointer to Structure Dereference ---
address of myStruct: 0000008380F6F3A4 address of pMyStruct: 0000008380F6F3C8 value of pMyStruct:
0000008380F6F3A4
address of pMyStruct dereference: 0000008380F6F3A4 address of myStruct: 0000008380F6F3A4
```

One to Many

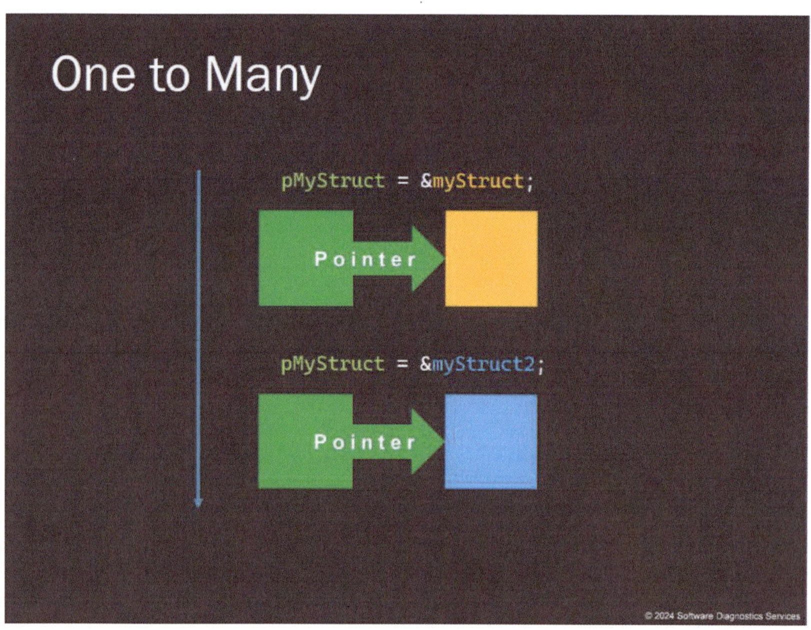

A pointer may contain memory addresses of different structure objects during its lifetime. If such objects are dynamically allocated (not in static or stack memory) then we may have a possibility of a memory leak.

C

```
puts("--- One to Many ---");
{
    struct MyStruct
    {
        int field;
        // ...
    } myStruct, myStruct2;

    struct MyStruct* pMyStruct = &myStruct;

    printf("address of myStruct: %p address of pMyStruct: %p value of pMyStruct: %p \n",
        &myStruct, &pMyStruct, pMyStruct);

    pMyStruct = &myStruct2; // no leak

    printf("address of myStruct2: %p address of pMyStruct: %p value of pMyStruct: %p \n",
        &myStruct2, &pMyStruct, pMyStruct);
}
```

C++ as a better C

```
puts("--- One to Many ---");
{
    struct MyStruct
    {
        int field;
        // ...
    } myStruct, myStruct2;

    MyStruct* pMyStruct = &myStruct;

    printf("address of myStruct: %p address of pMyStruct: %p value of pMyStruct: %p \n",
        &myStruct, &pMyStruct, pMyStruct);

    pMyStruct = &myStruct2; // no leak

    printf("address of myStruct2: %p address of pMyStruct: %p value of pMyStruct: %p \n",
        &myStruct2, &pMyStruct, pMyStruct);
}
```

Output

```
--- One to Many ---
address of myStruct: 0000008380F6F3E4 address of pMyStruct: 0000008380F6F428 value of pMyStruct:
0000008380F6F3E4
address of myStruct2: 0000008380F6F404 address of pMyStruct: 0000008380F6F428 value of pMyStruct:
0000008380F6F404
```

Memory Leak

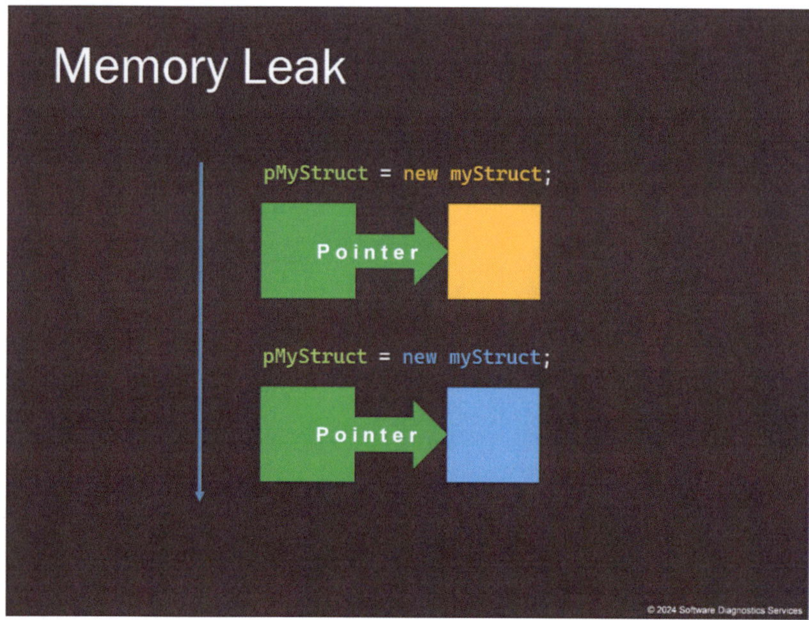

C

```
puts("--- Memory Leak ---");
{
    struct MyStruct
    {
        int field;
        // ...
    };

    struct MyStruct* pMyStruct = malloc(sizeof(struct MyStruct));

    printf("address of pMyStruct: %p value of pMyStruct: %p \n", &pMyStruct, pMyStruct);

    // free(pMyStruct);

    pMyStruct = malloc(sizeof(struct MyStruct)); // leak

    printf("address of pMyStruct: %p value of pMyStruct: %p \n", &pMyStruct, pMyStruct);

    free(pMyStruct);
}
```

C++ as a better C

```
puts("--- Memory Leak ---");
{
    struct MyStruct
    {
        int field;
        // ...
    };

    MyStruct* pMyStruct = (MyStruct*)malloc(sizeof(MyStruct)); // needs casting in C++

    printf("address of pMyStruct: %p value of pMyStruct: %p \n", &pMyStruct, pMyStruct);

    // free(pMyStruct);

    pMyStruct = (MyStruct*)malloc(sizeof(MyStruct)); // leak

    printf("address of pMyStruct: %p value of pMyStruct: %p \n", &pMyStruct, pMyStruct);

    free(pMyStruct);
}
```

Classic C++

```
std::cout << "--- Memory Leak ---" << std::endl;
{
    struct MyStruct
    {
        int field;
        // ...
    };

    MyStruct* pMyStruct = new MyStruct;

    std::cout << "address of pMyStruct: " << &pMyStruct <<
        " value of pMyStruct: " << pMyStruct << std::endl;

    // delete pMyStruct;

    pMyStruct = new MyStruct; // leak

    std::cout << "address of pMyStruct: " << &pMyStruct <<
        " value of pMyStruct: " << pMyStruct << std::endl;

    delete pMyStruct;
}
```

Output

```
--- Memory Leak ---
address of pMyStruct: 0000008380F6F448 value of pMyStruct: 000001D5E3417C50
address of pMyStruct: 0000008380F6F448 value of pMyStruct: 000001D5E34174D0
```

Many Pointers to One Structure

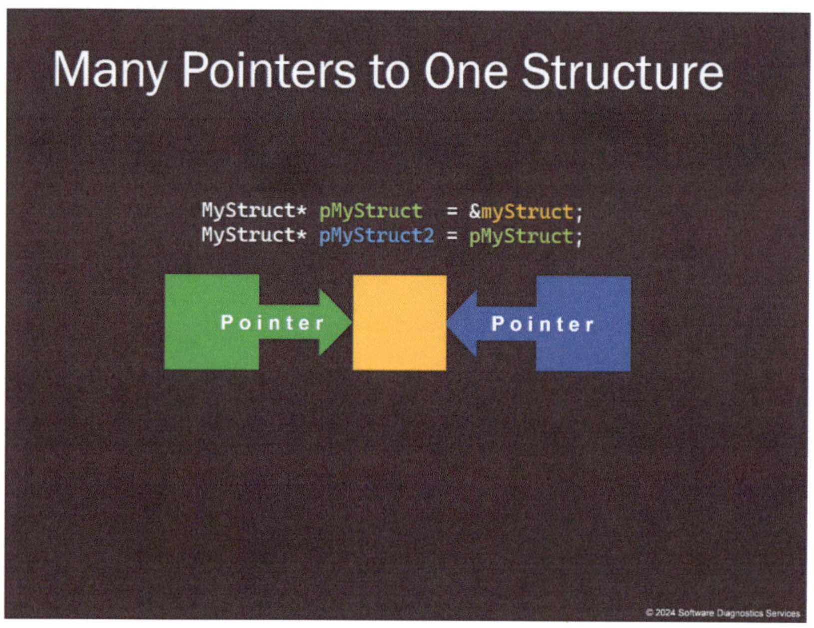

Here, we assign the value of one pointer to another, and both now point to the same structure.

C

```
puts("--- Many Pointers to One Structure ---");
{
    struct MyStruct
    {
        int field;
        // ...
    } myStruct;

    struct MyStruct* pMyStruct = &myStruct;

    printf("address of myStruct: %p address of pMyStruct: %p value of pMyStruct: %p \n",
        &myStruct, &pMyStruct, pMyStruct);

    struct MyStruct* pMyStruct2 = &myStruct;

    printf("address of myStruct: %p address of pMyStruct2: %p value of pMyStruct2: %p \n",
        &myStruct, &pMyStruct2, pMyStruct2);
}
```

C++ as a better C

```
puts("--- Many Pointers to One Structure ---");
{
    struct MyStruct
    {
        int field;
        // ...
    } myStruct;

    MyStruct* pMyStruct = &myStruct;
```

```
    printf("address of myStruct: %p address of pMyStruct: %p value of pMyStruct: %p \n",
        &myStruct, &pMyStruct, pMyStruct);

    MyStruct* pMyStruct2 = &myStruct;

    printf("address of myStruct: %p address of pMyStruct2: %p value of pMyStruct2: %p \n",
        &myStruct, &pMyStruct2, pMyStruct2);
}
```

Output

```
--- Many Pointers to One Structure ---
address of myStruct: 0000008380F6F464 address of pMyStruct: 0000008380F6F488 value of pMyStruct:
0000008380F6F464
address of myStruct: 0000008380F6F464 address of pMyStruct2: 0000008380F6F4A8 value of pMyStruct2:
0000008380F6F464
```

Many to One Dereference

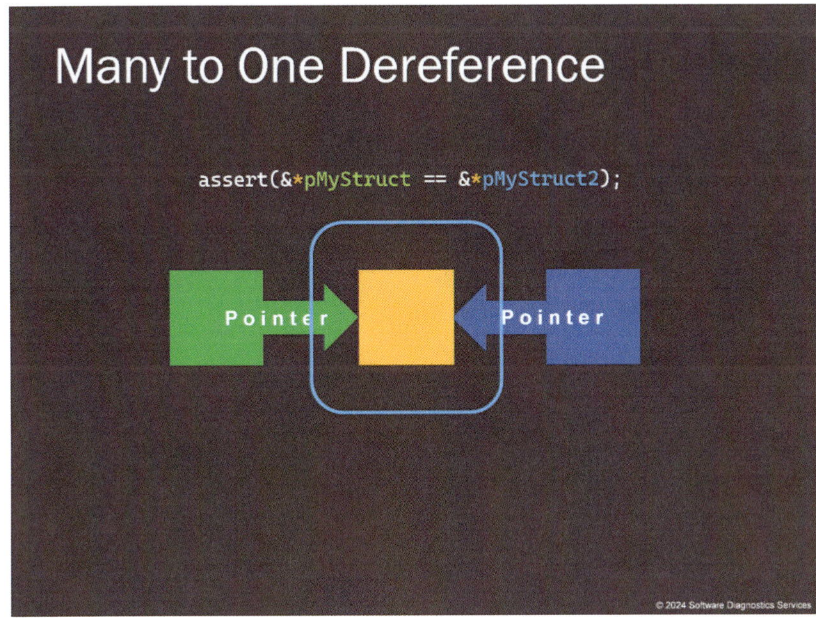

If we dereference both, we get the same value with the same address.

C

```
puts("--- Many to One Dereference ---");
{
    struct MyStruct
    {
        int field;
        // ...
    } myStruct;

    struct MyStruct* pMyStruct = &myStruct;
```

```
    struct MyStruct* pMyStruct2 = &myStruct;

    assert(&*pMyStruct == &*pMyStruct2);

    printf("address of myStruct: %p address of pMyStruct: %p value of pMyStruct: %p \n",
        &myStruct, &pMyStruct, pMyStruct);
    printf("address of myStruct: %p address of pMyStruct2: %p value of pMyStruct2: %p \n",
        &myStruct, &pMyStruct2, pMyStruct2);
    printf("address of pMyStruct dereference: %p address of pMyStruct2 dereference: %p \n",
        &*pMyStruct, &*pMyStruct2);
}
```

C++ as a better C

```
puts("--- Many to One Dereference ---");
{
    struct MyStruct
    {
        int field;
        // ...
    } myStruct;

    MyStruct* pMyStruct = &myStruct;
    MyStruct* pMyStruct2 = &myStruct;

    assert(&*pMyStruct == &*pMyStruct2);

    printf("address of myStruct: %p address of pMyStruct: %p value of pMyStruct: %p \n",
        &myStruct, &pMyStruct, pMyStruct);
    printf("address of myStruct: %p address of pMyStruct2: %p value of pMyStruct2: %p \n",
        &myStruct, &pMyStruct2, pMyStruct2);
    printf("address of pMyStruct dereference: %p address of pMyStruct2 dereference: %p \n",
        &*pMyStruct, &*pMyStruct2);
}
```

Output

```
--- Many to One Dereference ---
address of myStruct: 0000008380F6F4C4 address of pMyStruct: 0000008380F6F4E8 value of pMyStruct:
0000008380F6F4C4
address of myStruct: 0000008380F6F4C4 address of pMyStruct2: 0000008380F6F508 value of pMyStruct2:
0000008380F6F4C4
address of pMyStruct dereference: 0000008380F6F4C4 address of pMyStruct2 dereference: 0000008380F6F4C4
```

Invalid Pointer to Structure

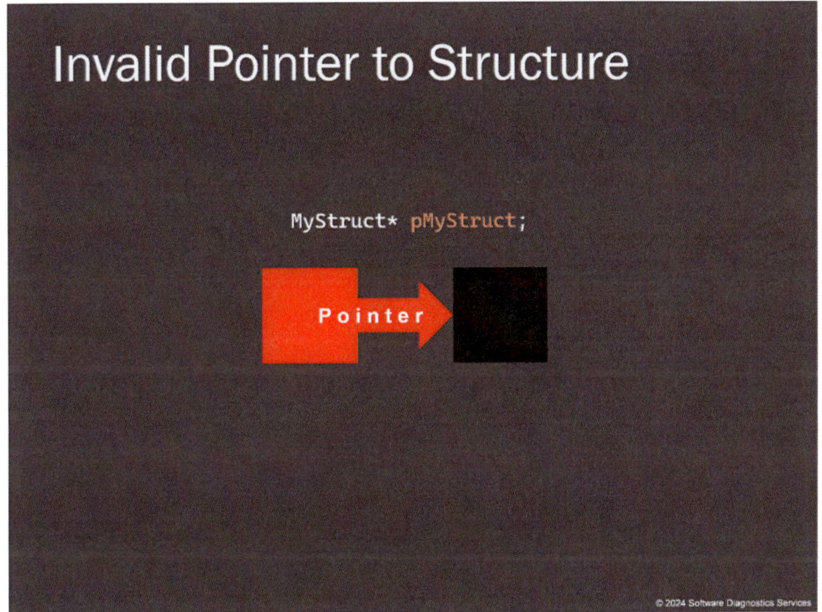

Here, we depict an uninitialized pointer that, depending on the memory storage type, can be a NULL pointer or some random value.

C

```
puts("--- Invalid Pointer to Structure ---");
{
    struct MyStruct
    {
        int field;
        // ...
    } myStruct;

    struct MyStruct* pMyStruct = (struct MyStruct*)0xffffffff00000000;

    printf("address of pMyStruct: %p value of pMyStruct: %p \n", &pMyStruct, pMyStruct);

    struct MyStruct* pUninitialized;

    // Basic Runtime Checks: Default and SDL Checks: No (/sdl-)

    printf("address of pUninitialized: %p value of pUninitialized: %p \n", &pUninitialized,
pUninitialized);
}
```

C++ as a better C

```
puts("--- Invalid Pointer to Structure ---");
{
    struct MyStruct
    {
        int field;
        // ...
    } myStruct;

    MyStruct* pMyStruct = (MyStruct*)0xffffffff00000000;

    printf("address of pMyStruct: %p value of pMyStruct: %p \n", &pMyStruct, pMyStruct);

    MyStruct* pUninitialized;

    // Basic Runtime Checks: Default and SDL Checks: No (/sdl-)
    printf("address of pUninitialized: %p value of pUninitialized: %p \n", &pUninitialized,
pUninitialized);
}
```

Output

```
--- Invalid Pointer to Structure ---
address of pMyStruct: 000000D7095FFA70 value of pMyStruct: FFFFFFFF00000000
address of pUninitialized: 000000D7095FFA78 value of pUninitialized: 00007FF88F0411FE
```

Classic C++

```
puts("--- Invalid Pointer to Structure ---");
{
    struct MyStruct
    {
        int field;
        // ...
    } myStruct;

    MyStruct* pMyStruct = reinterpret_cast<MyStruct*>(0xffffffff00000000);

    std::cout << "address of pMyStruct: " << &pMyStruct <<
        " value of pMyStruct: " << pMyStruct << std::endl;

    MyStruct* pUninitialized;

    std::cout << "address of pUninitialized: " << &pUninitialized << " value of pUninitialized: "
<< pUninitialized << std::endl;
}
```

Output

```
--- Invalid Pointer to Structure ---
address of pMyStruct: 000000D7468FF6A8 value of pMyStruct: FFFFFFFF00000000
address of pUninitialized: 000000D7468FF6C8 value of pUninitialized: CCCCCCCCCCCCCCCC
```

Invalid Pointer Dereference

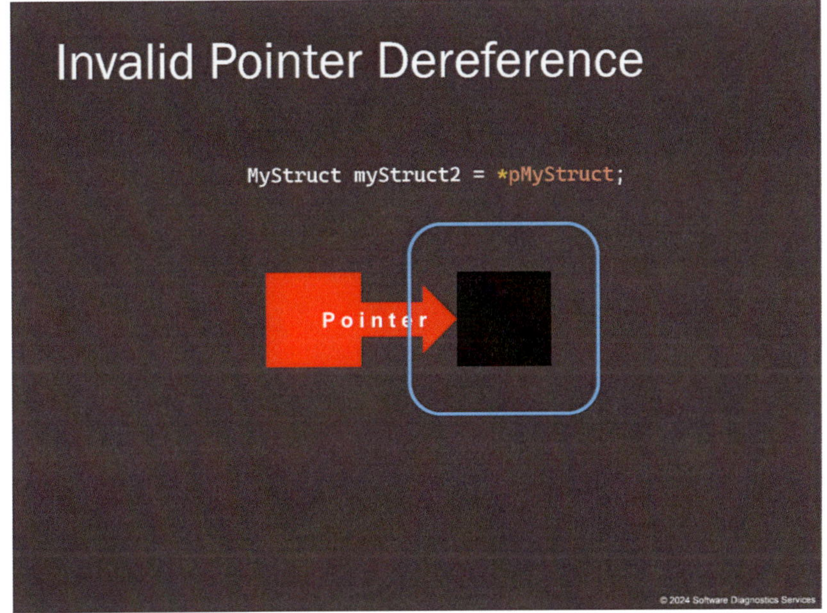

Dereferencing an uninitialized pointer can have undefined behavior, most likely an access violation leading to a crash.

C

```
puts("--- Invalid Pointer Dereference ---");
{
    struct MyStruct
    {
        int field;
        // ...
    } myStruct;

    struct MyStruct* pMyStruct = (struct MyStruct*)4;

    printf("address of pMyStruct: %p value of pMyStruct: %p \n", &pMyStruct, pMyStruct);

    // struct MyStruct myStruct2 = *pMyStruct; // crash
}
```

C++ as a better C

```
puts("--- Invalid Pointer Dereference ---");
{
    struct MyStruct
    {
        int field;
        // ...
    } myStruct;

    MyStruct* pMyStruct = (MyStruct*)4;

    printf("address of pMyStruct: %p value of pMyStruct: %p \n", &pMyStruct, pMyStruct);

    // MyStruct myStruct2 = *pMyStruct; // crash
}
```

Classic C++

```
puts("--- Invalid Pointer Dereference ---");
{
    struct MyStruct
    {
        int field;
        // ...
    } myStruct;

    MyStruct* pMyStruct = reinterpret_cast<MyStruct*>(4);

    std::cout << "address of pMyStruct: " << &pMyStruct <<
        " value of pMyStruct: " << pMyStruct << std::endl;

    // MyStruct myStruct2 = *pMyStruct; // crash
}
```

Output

```
--- Invalid Pointer Dereference ---
address of pMyStruct: 0000008380F6F588 value of pMyStruct: 0000000000000004
```

Wild (Dangling) Pointer

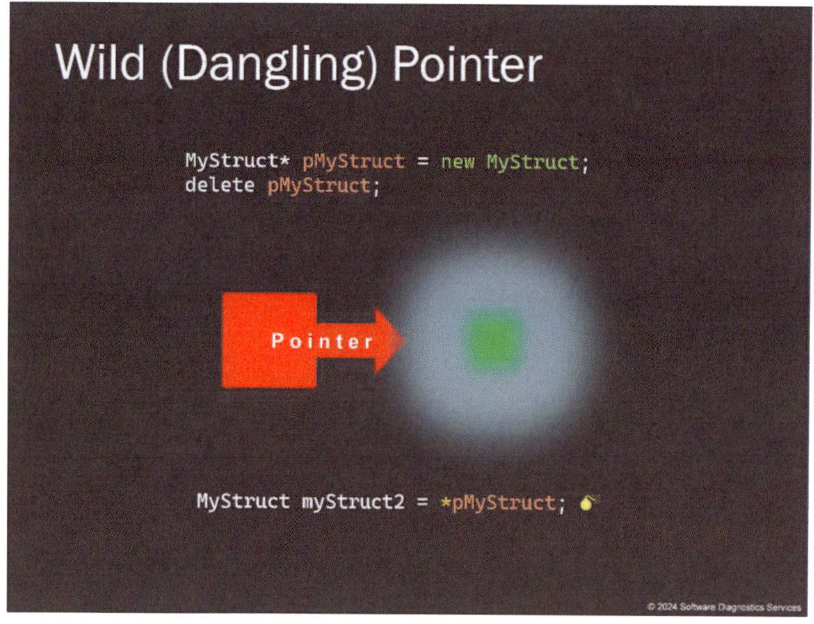

Memory for a structure can be dynamically allocated and then deallocated, but if a pointer is not reset to some value easy to check, such as 0, then we have a dangling pointer with its dereferencing resulting in undefined behavior that could lead to further corruption.

C

```
puts("--- Wild (Dangling) Pointer ---");
{
    struct MyStruct
    {
        int field;
        // ...
    };

    struct MyStruct* pMyStruct = malloc(sizeof(struct MyStruct));
    if (pMyStruct == NULL) return -1;

    *(int*)pMyStruct = 0x12345678;

    printf("address of pMyStruct: %p value of pMyStruct: %p dereference of pMyStruct: %x \n",
        &pMyStruct, pMyStruct, *(int*)pMyStruct);

    free(pMyStruct); // dangling pointer

    printf("address of pMyStruct: %p value of pMyStruct: %p \n",
        &pMyStruct, pMyStruct);

    // printf("dereference of pMyStruct: %x \n", *(int*)pMyStruct); // may crash

    // assert(*(int*)pMyStruct == 0x12345678); // may fail or crash

    pMyStruct = NULL; // Not dangling
}
```

C++ as a better C

```
puts("--- Wild (Dangling) Pointer ---");
{
    struct MyStruct
    {
        int field;
        // ...
    };

    MyStruct* pMyStruct = (MyStruct*)malloc(sizeof(MyStruct));
    if (pMyStruct == NULL) return -1;

    *(int*)pMyStruct = 0x12345678;

    printf("address of pMyStruct: %p value of pMyStruct: %p dereference of pMyStruct: %x \n",
        &pMyStruct, pMyStruct, *(int*)pMyStruct);

    free(pMyStruct); // dangling pointer

    printf("address of pMyStruct: %p value of pMyStruct: %p \n",
        &pMyStruct, pMyStruct);

    // printf("dereference of pMyStruct: %x \n", *(int*)pMyStruct); // may crash

    // assert(*(int*)pMyStruct == 0x12345678); // may fail or crash

    pMyStruct = NULL; // Not dangling
}
```

Output

```
--- Wild (Dangling) Pointer ---
address of pMyStruct: 0000008380F6F5A8 value of pMyStruct: 000001D5E34170D0 dereference of pMyStruct:
12345678
address of pMyStruct: 0000008380F6F5A8 value of pMyStruct: 000001D5E34170D0
```

Classic C++

```
puts("--- Wild (Dangling) Pointer ---");
{
    struct MyStruct
    {
        int field;
        // ...
    };

    MyStruct* pMyStruct = new MyStruct;

    *reinterpret_cast<int*>(pMyStruct) = 0x12345678;

    std::cout << "address of pMyStruct: " << &pMyStruct << " value of pMyStruct: " <<
        pMyStruct << " dereference of pMyStruct: " << *reinterpret_cast<int*>(pMyStruct) <<
std::endl;

    delete pMyStruct; // dangling pointer

    std::cout << "address of pMyStruct: " << &pMyStruct <<
        " value of pMyStruct: " << pMyStruct << std::endl;

    // std::cout << " dereference of pMyStruct: "
    //     << *reinterpret_cast<int*>(pMyStruct) << std::endl; // may crash

    // assert(*reinterpret_cast<int*>(pMyStruct) == 0x12345678); // may fail or crash

    pMyStruct = NULL; // Not dangling
    // pMyStruct = nullptr;  // C++11
}
```

Output

```
--- Wild (Dangling) Pointer ---
address of pMyStruct: 00000001F31EF888 value of pMyStruct: 000001215C8D7A90 dereference of pMyStruct:
305419896
address of pMyStruct: 00000001F31EF888 value of pMyStruct: 0000000000008123
```

Pointer to Pointer to Structure

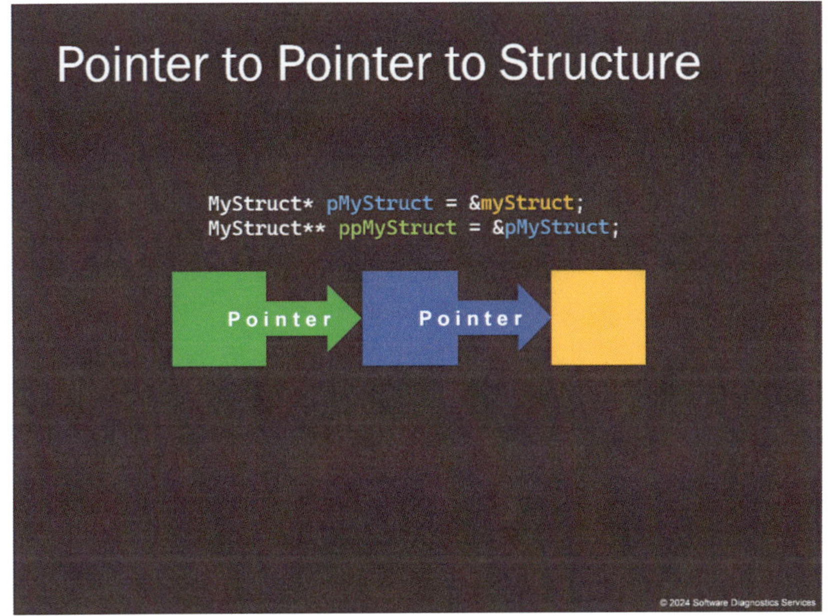

We can also have pointers to pointers to structures and so on, with double and more dereferences needed to get the value. We'll see why we need double-pointers later when we discuss passing parameters to functions.

C

```
puts("--- Pointer to Pointer to Structure ---");
{
    struct MyStruct
    {
        int field;
        // ...
    } myStruct;

    struct MyStruct* pMyStruct = &myStruct;

    printf("address of myStruct: %p address of pMyStruct: %p value of pMyStruct: %p \n",
        &myStruct, &pMyStruct, pMyStruct);

    struct MyStruct** ppMyStruct = &pMyStruct;

    printf("address of ppMyStruct: %p value of ppMyStruct: %p \n",
        &ppMyStruct, ppMyStruct);
}
```

C++ as a better C

```
puts("--- Pointer to Pointer to Structure ---");
{
    struct MyStruct
    {
        int field;
        // ...
    } myStruct;

    MyStruct* pMyStruct = &myStruct;
```

```
    printf("address of myStruct: %p address of pMyStruct: %p value of pMyStruct: %p \n",
        &myStruct, &pMyStruct, pMyStruct);

    MyStruct** ppMyStruct = &pMyStruct;

    printf("address of ppMyStruct: %p value of ppMyStruct: %p \n",
        &ppMyStruct, ppMyStruct);
}
```

Output

```
--- Pointer to Pointer to Structure ---
address of myStruct: 0000002D7AEFFC88 address of pMyStruct: 0000002D7AEFFC90 value of pMyStruct:
0000002D7AEFFC88
address of ppMyStruct: 0000002D7AEFFC98 value of ppMyStruct: 0000002D7AEFFC90
```

Pointer to Pointer Dereference

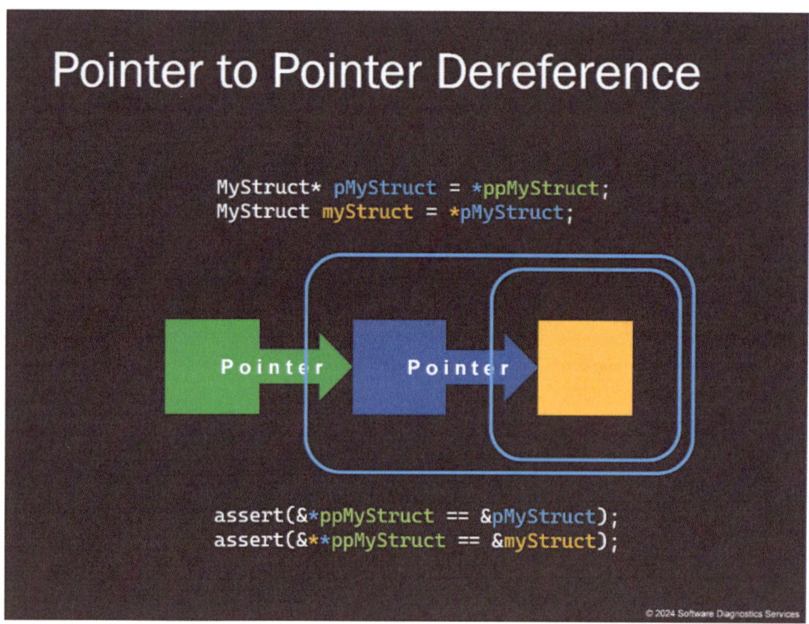

Here, we have double dereference illustrated. Please notice an example of Hungarian notation.

C

```
puts("--- Pointer to Pointer to Dereference ---");
{
    struct MyStruct
    {
        int field;
        // ...
    } myStruct;

    struct MyStruct* pMyStruct = &myStruct;
```

```
    printf("address of myStruct: %p address of pMyStruct: %p value of pMyStruct: %p \n",
        &myStruct, &pMyStruct, pMyStruct);

    struct MyStruct** ppMyStruct = &pMyStruct;

    printf("address of ppMyStruct: %p value of ppMyStruct: %p value of ppMyStruct dereference: %p
\n",
        &ppMyStruct, ppMyStruct, *ppMyStruct);

    assert(&*ppMyStruct == &pMyStruct);

    printf("address of ppMyStruct dereference: %p address of pMyStruct: %p \n",
        &*ppMyStruct, &pMyStruct);

    assert(&**ppMyStruct == &myStruct);

    printf("address of ppMyStruct double dereference: %p address of myStruct: %p \n",
        &**ppMyStruct, &myStruct);
}
```

C++ as a better C

```
puts("--- Pointer to Pointer to Dereference ---");
{
    struct MyStruct
    {
        int field;
        // ...
    } myStruct;

    MyStruct* pMyStruct = &myStruct;

    printf("address of myStruct: %p address of pMyStruct: %p value of pMyStruct: %p \n",
        &myStruct, &pMyStruct, pMyStruct);

    MyStruct** ppMyStruct = &pMyStruct;

    printf("address of ppMyStruct: %p value of ppMyStruct: %p value of ppMyStruct dereference: %p
\n",
        &ppMyStruct, ppMyStruct, *ppMyStruct);

    assert(&*ppMyStruct == &pMyStruct);

    printf("address of ppMyStruct dereference: %p address of pMyStruct: %p \n",
        &*ppMyStruct, &pMyStruct);

    assert(&**ppMyStruct == &myStruct);

    printf("address of ppMyStruct double dereference: %p address of myStruct: %p \n",
        &**ppMyStruct, &myStruct);
}
```

Output

```
--- Pointer to Pointer to Dereference ---
address of myStruct: 0000008380F6F624 address of pMyStruct: 0000008380F6F648 value of pMyStruct:
0000008380F6F624
address of ppMyStruct: 0000008380F6F668 value of ppMyStruct: 0000008380F6F648 value of ppMyStruct
dereference: 0000008380F6F624
address of ppMyStruct dereference: 0000008380F6F648 address of pMyStruct: 0000008380F6F648
address of ppMyStruct double dereference: 0000008380F6F624 address of myStruct: 0000008380F6F624
```

Memory and Structures

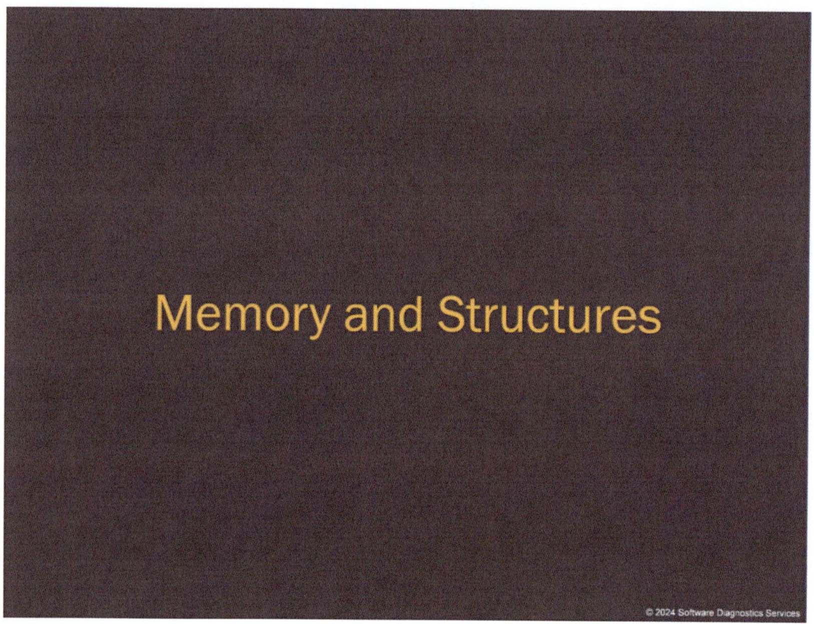

Now, we look at the memory representation of structures.

The `memory_and_structures` projects:

- `memory_and_structures_c` C
- `memory_and_structures_c_cpp` C++ as a better C
- `memory_and_structures_classic_cpp` Classic C++

can be found in the archive[6]. In the following slide descriptions, we only show relevant code snippets and their output.

[6] https://www.patterndiagnostics.com/Training/ACPPWD/ACPPWD.zip

Addresses and Structures

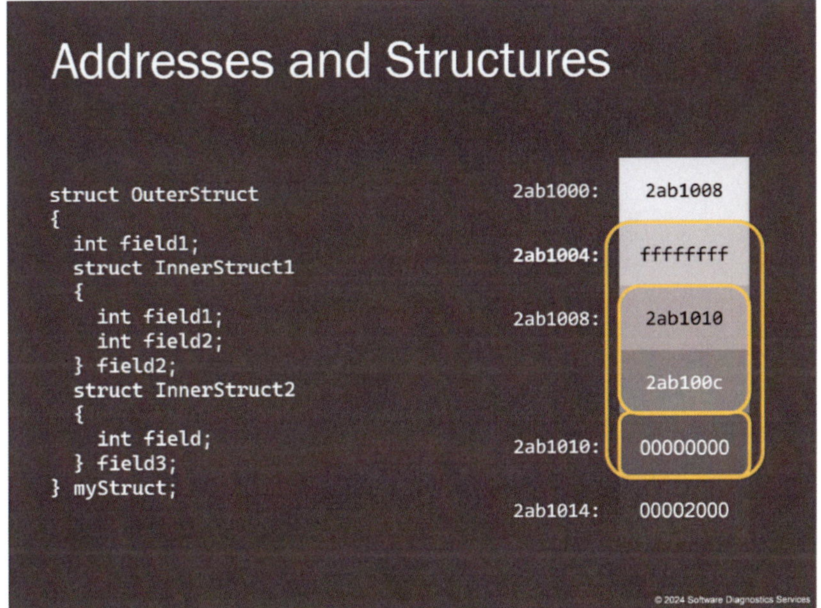

A structure in memory is a sequential collection of memory cells; some may be multicell and themselves sub-structures. Each part of a structure, its member, or structure field has its own address as well, in addition to the overall address of the structure.

C C++ as a better C

```
puts("--- Addresses and Structures ---");
{
    struct OuterStruct
    {
        int field1;
        struct InnerStruct1
        {
            int field1;
            int field2;
        } field2;
        struct InnerStruct2
        {
            int field;
        } field3;
    } myStruct;

    printf("address of myStruct: %p address of field2: %p address of field3: %p \n",
        &myStruct, &myStruct.field2, &myStruct.field3);
}
```

Output

```
--- Addresses and Structures ---
address of myStruct: 000000D79E79FBD8 address of field2: 000000D79E79FBDC address of field3:
000000D79E79FBE4
```

Structure Field Access

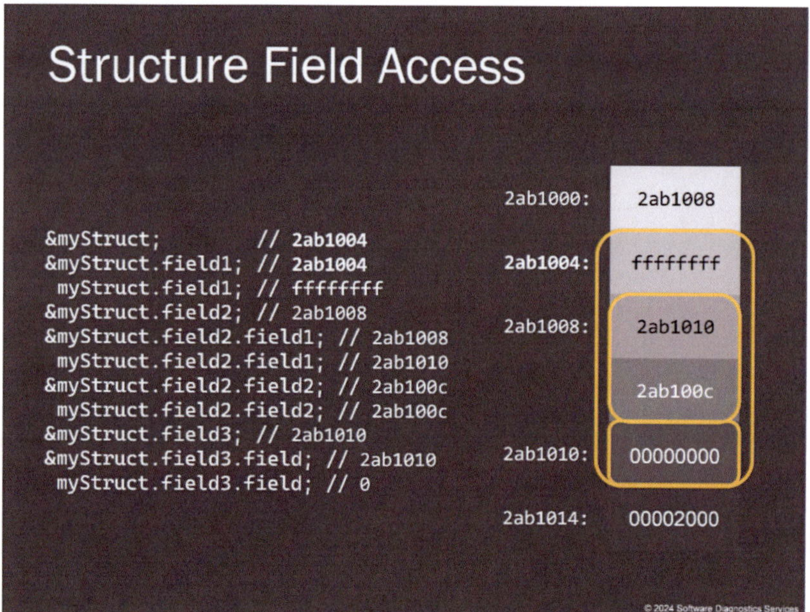

This example shows field addresses and access when we have a structure value.

C

```
puts("--- Structure Field Access  ---");
{
    struct OuterStruct
    {
        int field1;
        struct InnerStruct1
        {
            int field1;
            int field2;
        } field2;
        struct InnerStruct2
        {
            int field;
        } field3;
    } myStruct = { 0xffffffff, { 0x2ab1010, 0x2ab100c }, { 0 } };

    printf("&myStruct: %p \n"
        "&myStruct.field1: %p \n"
        "myStruct.field1: %x \n"
        "&myStruct.field2: %p \n"
        "&myStruct.field2.field1: %p \n"
        "myStruct.field2.field1: %x \n"
        "&myStruct.field2.field2: %p \n"
        "myStruct.field2.field2: %x \n"
        "&myStruct.field3: %p \n"
        "&myStruct.field3.field: %p \n"
        "myStruct.field3.field: %x \n",
        &myStruct,
        &myStruct.field1,
        myStruct.field1,
```

```
        &myStruct.field2,
        &myStruct.field2.field1,
        myStruct.field2.field1,
        &myStruct.field2.field2,
        myStruct.field2.field2,
        &myStruct.field3,
        &myStruct.field3.field,
        myStruct.field3.field);
}
```

C++ as a better C

```
puts("--- Structure Field Access  ---");
{
    struct OuterStruct
    {
        int field1;
        struct InnerStruct1
        {
            int field1;
            int field2;
        } field2;
        struct InnerStruct2
        {
            int field;
        } field3;
    } myStruct = { -1, { 0x2ab1010, 0x2ab100c }, { 0 } }; // warning about unsigned int -> int
conversion in C++

    printf("&myStruct: %p \n"
        "&myStruct.field1: %p \n"
        "myStruct.field1: %x \n"
        "&myStruct.field2: %p \n"
        "&myStruct.field2.field1: %p \n"
        "myStruct.field2.field1: %x \n"
        "&myStruct.field2.field2: %p \n"
        "myStruct.field2.field2: %x \n"
        "&myStruct.field3: %p \n"
        "&myStruct.field3.field: %p \n"
        "myStruct.field3.field: %x \n",
        &myStruct,
        &myStruct.field1,
        myStruct.field1,
        &myStruct.field2,
        &myStruct.field2.field1,
        myStruct.field2.field1,
        &myStruct.field2.field2,
        myStruct.field2.field2,
        &myStruct.field3,
        &myStruct.field3.field,
        myStruct.field3.field);
}
```

Output

```
--- Structure Field Access  ---
&myStruct: 000000D79E79FC08
&myStruct.field1: 000000D79E79FC08
myStruct.field1: ffffffff
&myStruct.field2: 000000D79E79FC0C
&myStruct.field2.field1: 000000D79E79FC0C
myStruct.field2.field1: 2ab1010
&myStruct.field2.field2: 000000D79E79FC10
```

```
myStruct.field2.field2: 2ab100c
&myStruct.field3: 000000D79E79FC14
&myStruct.field3.field: 000000D79E79FC14
myStruct.field3.field: 0
```

Pointers to Structures

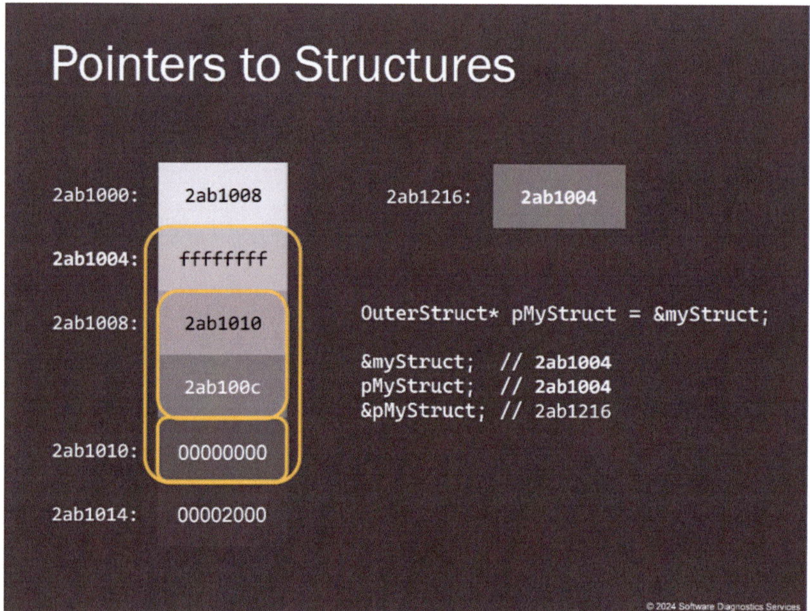

A structure has its address. A pointer to a structure is a memory cell that contains that address. It has its own address.

C

```
puts("--- Pointers to Structures ---");
{
    struct OuterStruct
    {
        int field1;
        struct InnerStruct1
        {
            int field1;
            int field2;
        } field2;
        struct InnerStruct2
        {
            int field;
        } field3;
    } myStruct;

    struct OuterStruct* pMyStruct = &myStruct;

    printf("address of myStruct: %p address of pMyStruct: %p value of pMyStruct: %p \n",
        &myStruct, &pMyStruct, pMyStruct);
}
```

C++ as a better C

```
puts("--- Pointers to Structures ---");
{
    struct OuterStruct
    {
        int field1;
        struct InnerStruct1
        {
            int field1;
            int field2;
        } field2;
        struct InnerStruct2
        {
            int field;
        } field3;
    } myStruct;

    OuterStruct* pMyStruct = &myStruct; // struct keyword can be omitted in C++

    printf("address of myStruct: %p address of pMyStruct: %p value of pMyStruct: %p \n",
        &myStruct, &pMyStruct, pMyStruct);
}
```

Output

```
--- Pointers to Structures ---
address of myStruct: 000000D79E79FC38 address of pMyStruct: 000000D79E79FC68 value of pMyStruct:
000000D79E79FC38
```

Pointers to Structure Fields

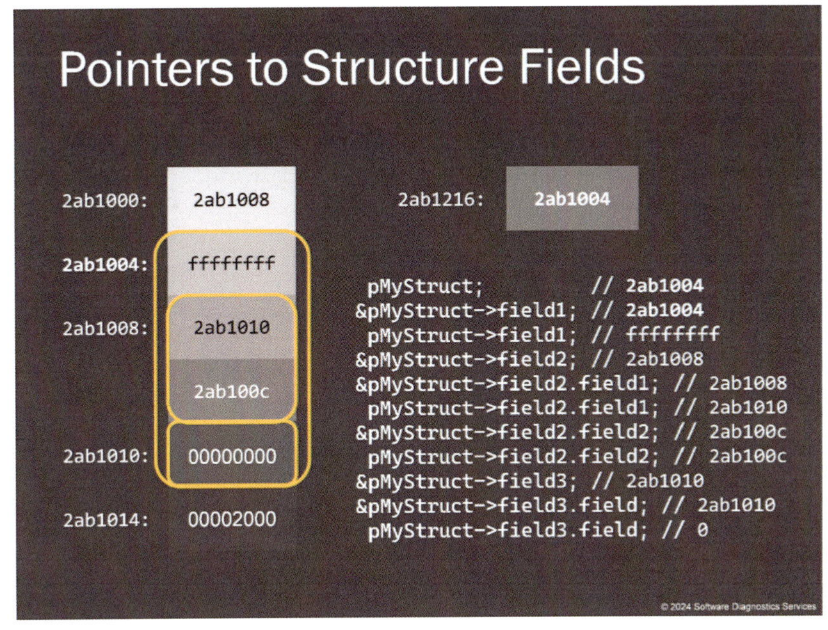

This example shows field addresses and access when we have a pointer to a structure value.

C

```
puts("--- Pointers to Structure Fields ---");
{
    struct OuterStruct
    {
        int field1;
        struct InnerStruct1
        {
            int field1;
            int field2;
        } field2;
        struct InnerStruct2
        {
            int field;
        } field3;
    } myStruct = { 0xffffffff, { 0x2ab1010, 0x2ab100c }, { 0 } };

    struct OuterStruct* pMyStruct = &myStruct;

    printf("pMyStruct: %p \n"
        "&pMyStruct->field1: %p \n"
        "pMyStruct->field1: %x \n"
        "&pMyStruct->field2: %p \n"
        "&pMyStruct->field2.field1: %p \n"
        "pMyStruct->field2.field1: %x \n"
        "&pMyStruct->field2.field2: %p \n"
        "pMyStruct->field2.field2: %x \n"
        "&pMyStruct->field3: %p \n"
        "&pMyStruct->field3.field: %p \n"
        "pMyStruct->field3.field: %x \n",
        pMyStruct,
        &pMyStruct->field1,
        pMyStruct->field1,
        &pMyStruct->field2,
        &pMyStruct->field2.field1,
        pMyStruct->field2.field1,
        &pMyStruct->field2.field2,
        pMyStruct->field2.field2,
        &pMyStruct->field3,
        &pMyStruct->field3.field,
        pMyStruct->field3.field);
}
```

C++ as a better C

```
puts("--- Pointers to Structure Fields ---");
{
    struct OuterStruct
    {
        int field1;
        struct InnerStruct1
        {
            int field1;
            int field2;
        } field2;
        struct InnerStruct2
        {
            int field;
        } field3;
    } myStruct = { -1, { 0x2ab1010, 0x2ab100c }, { 0 } };

    OuterStruct* pMyStruct = &myStruct;
```

```
    printf("pMyStruct: %p \n"
        "&pMyStruct->field1: %p \n"
        "pMyStruct->field1: %x \n"
        "&pMyStruct->field2: %p \n"
        "&pMyStruct->field2.field1: %p \n"
        "pMyStruct->field2.field1: %x \n"
        "&pMyStruct->field2.field2: %p \n"
        "pMyStruct->field2.field2: %x \n"
        "&pMyStruct->field3: %p \n"
        "&pMyStruct->field3.field: %p \n"
        "pMyStruct->field3.field: %x \n",
        pMyStruct,
        &pMyStruct->field1,
        pMyStruct->field1,
        &pMyStruct->field2,
        &pMyStruct->field2.field1,
        pMyStruct->field2.field1,
        &pMyStruct->field2.field2,
        pMyStruct->field2.field2,
        &pMyStruct->field3,
        &pMyStruct->field3.field,
        pMyStruct->field3.field);
}
```

Output

```
--- Pointers to Structure Fields ---
pMyStruct: 000000D79E79FC88
&pMyStruct->field1: 000000D79E79FC88
pMyStruct->field1: ffffffff
&pMyStruct->field2: 000000D79E79FC8C
&pMyStruct->field2.field1: 000000D79E79FC8C
pMyStruct->field2.field1: 2ab1010
&pMyStruct->field2.field2: 000000D79E79FC90
pMyStruct->field2.field2: 2ab100c
&pMyStruct->field3: 000000D79E79FC94
&pMyStruct->field3.field: 000000D79E79FC94
pMyStruct->field3.field: 0
```

Structure Inheritance

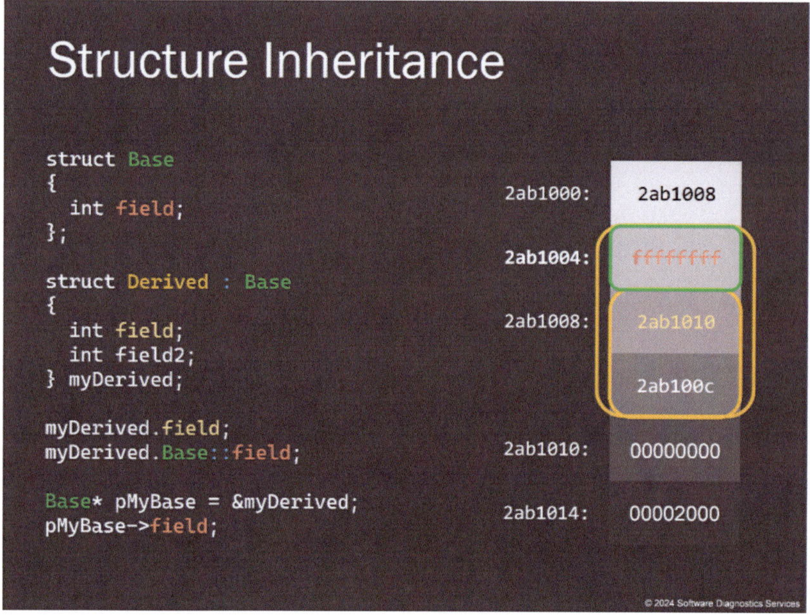

Structures can inherit fields from other structures. In the case of the same field names, the derived structure hides the base structure fields, but they can be accessed by explicit base structure name qualification.

Classic C++

```
std::cout << "--- Structure Inheritance ---" << std::endl;
{
    struct Base
    {
        int field;
    };

    struct Derived : Base
    {
        int field;
        int field2;
    } myDerived = { -1, 0x2ab1010, 0x2ab100c };

    std::cout << std::hex << "address of myDerived: " << &myDerived << std::endl <<
        "address of myDerived.field: " << &myDerived.field <<
        " value of myDerived.field: " << myDerived.field << std::endl <<
        "address of myDerived.Base::field: " << &myDerived.Base::field <<
        " value of myDerived.Base::field: " << myDerived.Base::field << std::endl;

    Base* pMyBase = &myDerived;

    std::cout << std::hex << "address of myDerived: " << &myDerived <<
        " address of pMyBase: " << &pMyBase << " value of pMyBase: " << pMyBase << std::endl <<
        "address of pMyBase->field: " << &pMyBase->field <<
        " value of pMyBase->field: " << pMyBase->field << std::endl;
}
```

Output

```
--- Structure Inheritance ---
address of myDerived: 00000008094FF7D8
address of myDerived.field: 00000008094FF7DC value of myDerived.field: 2ab1010
address of myDerived.Base::field: 00000008094FF7D8 value of myDerived.Base::field: ffffffff
address of myDerived: 00000008094FF7D8 address of pMyBase: 00000008094FF808 value of pMyBase:
00000008094FF7D8
address of pMyBase->field: 00000008094FF7D8 value of pMyBase->field: ffffffff
```

Structure Slicing

Structure Slicing

```
struct Base
{
  int field;
};

struct Derived : Base
{
  int field2;
} myDerived { 0, 1 };

Base myBase = myDerived;
myDerived = myBase;
Derived myDerived2 = static_cast<Derived>(myBase);

Base* pMyBase = &myDerived;
Derived* pMyDerived = pMyBase;

Derived* pMyDerived = static_cast<Derived*>(pMyBase);
```


It is possible to copy a derived structure to a base structure variable, but in this case, the former contents are sliced since the base structure occupies less memory. The other way around, from the base structure to the derived, is forbidden by default because the compiler doesn't know how to fill the new derived-only fields. However, this can be forced with a static cast where the derived fields may be either default initialized with zeroes or filled with the existing adjacent memory content, which can be completely random. The same downcast can be done between pointers, but when we try to dereference a target pointer to the derived structure later, we may get random data.

Classic C++

```
std::cout << "--- Structure Slicing ---" << std::endl;
{
    struct Base
    {
        int field;
    };

    struct Derived : Base
    {
        int field2;
    } myDerived = { 0, 1 };

    Base myBase = myDerived;
    // myDerived = myBase; // error
    Derived myDerived2 = static_cast<Derived>(myBase);
```

```
    std::cout << "address of myDerived: " << &myDerived <<
        " value of myDerived: { " << myDerived.field << ", " << myDerived.field2 << " }" <<
std::endl <<
        "address of myBase: " << &myBase <<
        " value of myBase: " << myBase.field << std::endl <<
        "address of myDerived2: " << &myDerived2 <<
        " value of myDerived2: { " << myDerived2.field << ", " << myDerived2.field2 << " }" <<
std::endl;

    Base* pMyBase = &myDerived;
    // Derived* pMyDerived = pMyBase; // error

    Derived* pMyDerived = static_cast<Derived*>(pMyBase);

    std::cout << "address of pMyBase: " << &pMyBase << " value of pMyBase: " << pMyBase <<
std::endl <<
        "address of pMyDerived: " << &pMyDerived << " value of pMyDerived: " << pMyDerived <<
std::endl;
}
```

Output

```
--- Structure Slicing ---
address of myDerived: 00000008094FF828 value of myDerived: { 0, 1 }
address of myBase: 00000008094FF844 value of myBase: 0
address of myDerived2: 00000008094FF868 value of myDerived2: { 0, 0 }
address of pMyBase: 00000008094FF888 value of pMyBase: 00000008094FF828
address of pMyDerived: 00000008094FF8A8 value of pMyDerived: 00000008094FF828
```

Inheritance Access Level

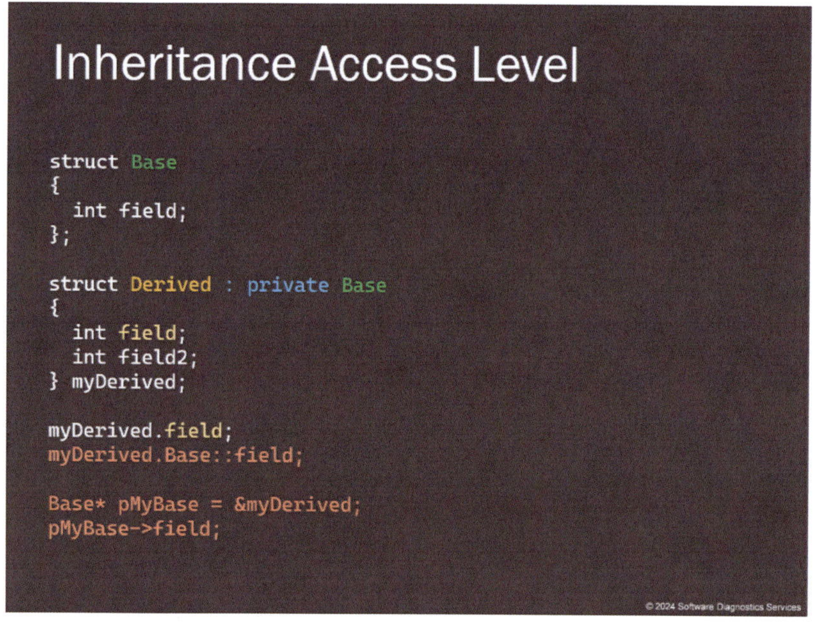

It is possible to inherit privately. In such a case, the base structure fields are inaccessible from the outside, even with the explicit qualification.

Classic C++

```
std::cout << "--- Inheritance Access Level ---" << std::endl;
{
    struct Base {
        int field;
    };

    struct Derived : private Base
    {
        int field;
        int field2;
    } myDerived;

    myDerived.field;
    // myDerived.Base::field; // error

    // Base* pMyBase = &myDerived; // error
    // pMyBase->field;
}
```

Structures and Classes II

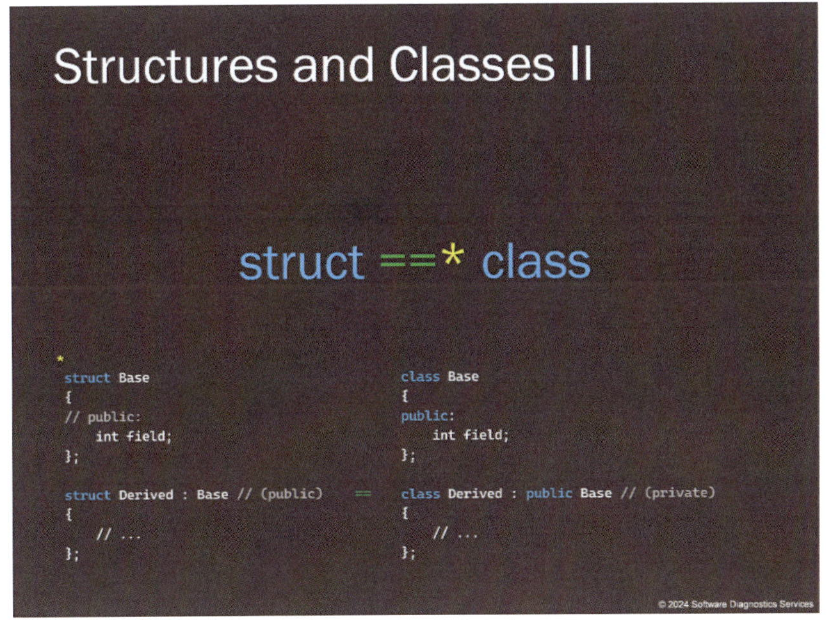

Again, structures and classes are almost equivalent except for the default inheritance access (and field access), which is, by default, public for structures and private for classes. Public access needs to be specified explicitly for classes. We do not discuss protected access in this training, which is not really relevant for memory thinking when we look at built code.

Classic C++

```
std::cout << "--- Structures and Classes II ---" << std::endl;
{
    class Base
    {
    public:
        int field;
    };

    class Derived : public Base // (private by default)
    {
        // ...
    };
}
```

Internal Structure Alignment

Internal Structure Alignment

```
struct Struct
{
  bool field1;
  short field2;
  long long field8;
} myStruct;

#pragma pack(1)
struct StructPacked
{
  bool field1;
  short field2;
  long long field8;
} myStructPacked;
```

```
0:000> dt Struct
Struct
   +0x000 field1           : Bool
   +0x002 field2           : Int2B
   +0x008 field8           : Int8B

0:000> dt StructPacked
StructPacked
   +0x000 field1           : Bool
   +0x001 field2           : Int2B
   +0x003 field8           : Int8B
```


Fields may be aligned according to their default type alignment, which may introduce gaps, increasing the overall structure size.

Classic C++

```
std::cout << "--- Internal Structure Alignment ---" << std::endl;
{
    struct Struct
    {
        bool field1;
        short field2;
        long long field8;
    } myStruct;

    #pragma pack(1)
```

```
    struct StructPacked
    {
        bool field1;
        short field2;
        long long field8;
    } myStructPacked;

    std::cout << "address of myStruct: " << &myStruct <<
        " size of myStruct: " << sizeof(myStruct) << std::endl <<
        "address of myStruct.field2: " << &myStruct.field2 <<
        " address of myStruct.field8: " << &myStruct.field8 << std::endl <<
        "address of myStructPacked: " << &myStructPacked <<
        " size of myStructPacked: " << sizeof(myStructPacked) << std::endl <<
        "address of myStructPacked.field2: " << &myStructPacked.field2 <<
        " address of myStructPacked.field8: " << &myStructPacked.field8 << std::endl;
}
```

Output

```
--- Internal Structure Alignment ---
address of myStruct: 00000008094FF8F8 size of myStruct: 10
address of myStruct.field2: 00000008094FF8FA address of myStruct.field8: 00000008094FF900
address of myStructPacked: 00000008094FF928 size of myStructPacked: b
address of myStructPacked.field2: 00000008094FF929 address of myStructPacked.field8: 00000008094FF92B
```

Static Structure Fields

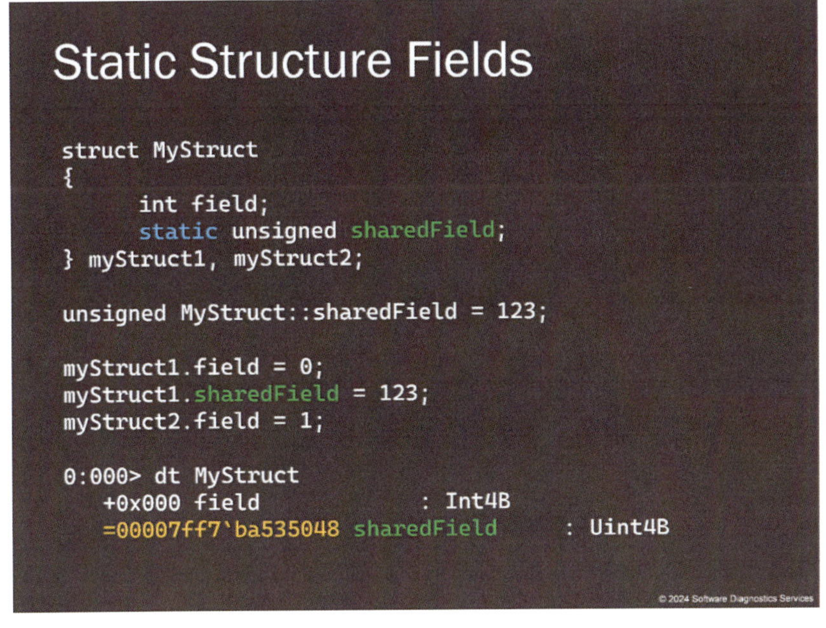

Static structure field values are shared between the different objects of the same structure type. They occupy uniquely separate memory cells from the objects' memory.

Classic C++

```
struct MyStructS
{
    int field;
    static unsigned sharedField;
};

unsigned MyStructS::sharedField = 123;

// ...

std::cout << "--- Static Structure Fields ---" << std::endl;
{
    MyStructS myStruct1, myStruct2;

    myStruct1.field = 0;
    myStruct1.sharedField = 0x123;
    myStruct2.field = 1;

    std::cout << "address of myStruct1: " << &myStruct1 <<
        " address of myStruct2: " << &myStruct2 << std::endl <<
        "address of myStruct1.sharedField: " << &myStruct1.sharedField <<
        " value of myStruct1.sharedField: " << myStruct1.sharedField << std::endl <<
        "address of myStruct2.sharedField: " << &myStruct2.sharedField <<
        " value of myStruct2.sharedField: " << myStruct2.sharedField << std::endl;
}
```

Output

```
--- Static Structure Fields ---
address of myStruct1: 00000008094FF954 address of myStruct2: 00000008094FF974
address of myStruct1.sharedField: 00007FF664BBF000 value of myStruct1.sharedField: 123
address of myStruct2.sharedField: 00007FF664BBF000 value of myStruct2.sharedField: 123
```

Uniform Initialization

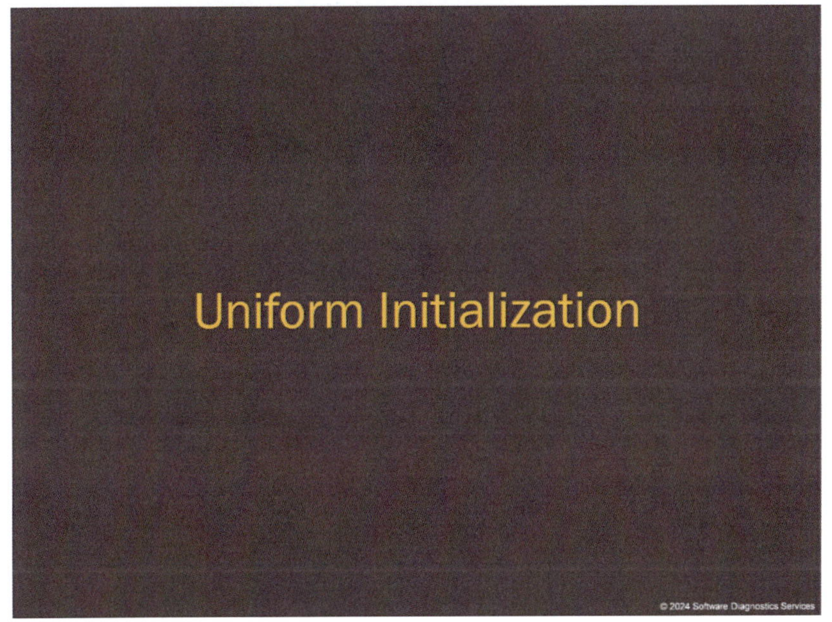

Throughout C++ history, there were several ways to initialize variables. Finally, there is some uniform way to do it consistently.

The `uniform_initialization` project:

- `uniform_initialization_modern_cpp` Modern C++

can be found in the archive[7]. In the following slide descriptions, we only show relevant code snippets and their output.

[7] https://www.patterndiagnostics.com/Training/ACPPWD/ACPPWD.zip

Old Initialization Ways

When we omit an initialization value, a variable is considered uninitialized if its memory belongs to certain memory classes, such as stack. For static memory, it may be default-initialized with zero memory values.

Modern C++

```
std::println("--- Old Initialization Ways ---");
{
    struct OuterStruct
    {
        int field1;
        struct InnerStruct1
        {
            int field1;
            int field2;
        } field2;
        struct InnerStruct2
        {
            int field;
        } field3;
    };

    OuterStruct* pMyStruct1; // uninitialized
    OuterStruct* pMyStruct2 = NULL;
    OuterStruct* pMyStruct3(NULL);
    OuterStruct* pMyStruct4 = nullptr;
}
```

New Way {}

New Way {}

- OuterStruct* pMyStruct{};
- OuterStruct* pMyStruct{NULL};
- OuterStruct* pMyStruct{nullptr};
- OuterStruct* pMyStruct{&myStruct};

When we use the new way of initialization in modern C++, we can use empty {} to signal default initialization even for stack memory.

Modern C++

```
std::println("--- New Way {{}} ---"); // prints --- New Way {} ---
{
    struct OuterStruct
    {
        int field1;
        struct InnerStruct1
        {
            int field1;
            int field2;
        } field2;
        struct InnerStruct2
        {
            int field;
        } field3;
    } myStruct;

    OuterStruct* pMyStruct1{};
    OuterStruct* pMyStruct2{NULL};
    OuterStruct* pMyStruct3{nullptr};
    OuterStruct* pMyStruct4{&myStruct};
}
```

Uniform Structure Initialization

Uniform Structure Initialization

```
struct OuterStructA
{
  int field1;
  struct InnerStruct1
  {
    int field1;
    int field2;
  } field2;
  struct InnerStruct2
  {
    int field;
  } field3;
} myStructA {1, {2, 3}, {4}};
```

```
struct OuterStructB
{
  int field1{1};
  struct InnerStruct1
  {
    int field1{2};
    int field2{3};
  } field2;
  struct InnerStruct2
  {
    int field{4};
  } field3;
} myStructB;
```


It is possible to uniformly initialize the structure outside or provide default field initializers in the structure definition.

Modern C++

```
std::println("--- Uniform Structure Initialization ---");
{
    struct OuterStructA
    {
        int field1;
        struct InnerStruct1
        {
            int field1;
            int field2;
        } field2;
        struct InnerStruct2
        {
            int field;
        } field3;
    } myStructA{ 1, {2, 3}, {4} };

    std::println("value of myStructA: {{ {}, {{{}, {}}}, {{{}}} }}",
        myStructA.field1, myStructA.field2.field1, myStructA.field2.field2,
myStructA.field3.field);

    struct OuterStructB
    {
        int field1{1};
        struct InnerStruct1
        {
            int field1{2};
            int field2{3};
        } field2;
        struct InnerStruct2
        {
```

```
            int field{4};
        } field3;
    } myStructB;

    std::println("value of myStructB: {{ {}, {{{}, {}}}, {{{}}} }}",
        myStructB.field1, myStructB.field2.field1, myStructB.field2.field2,
myStructB.field3.field);

    OuterStructB myStructC;

    std::println("value of myStructC: {{ {}, {{{}, {}}}, {{{}}} }}",
        myStructC.field1, myStructC.field2.field1, myStructC.field2.field2,
myStructC.field3.field);
}
```

Output

```
--- Uniform Structure Initialization ---
value of myStructA: { 1, {2, 3}, {4} }
value of myStructB: { 1, {2, 3}, {4} }
value of myStructC: { 1, {2, 3}, {4} }
```

Static Field Initialization

Static Field Initialization

```
struct MyStruct
{
      int field;
      inline static unsigned sharedField{123};
} myStruct1, myStruct2;

// unsigned MyStruct::sharedField = 123;

myStruct1.field = 0;
assert(myStruct1.sharedField == 123);
myStruct2.field = 1;
```


The latest C++ standards allow static field initialization inside the structure definition instead of the classic C++ ways of outside initialization (shown in comments).

Modern C++

```
struct MyStructS
{
    int field;
    inline static unsigned sharedField{123};
};

// ...

std::println("--- Static Field Initialization ---");
{
    MyStructS myStruct1, myStruct2;

    myStruct1.field = 0;
    assert(myStruct1.sharedField == 123);
    myStruct2.field = 1;

    std::println("value of myStruct1: {{ {}, {} }} value of myStruct2: {{ {}, {} }}",
        myStruct1.field, myStruct1.sharedField, myStruct2.field, myStruct2.sharedField);
}
```

Output

```
--- Static Field Initialization ---
value of myStruct1: { 0, 123 } value of myStruct2: { 1, 123 }
```

Macros, Types, and Synonyms

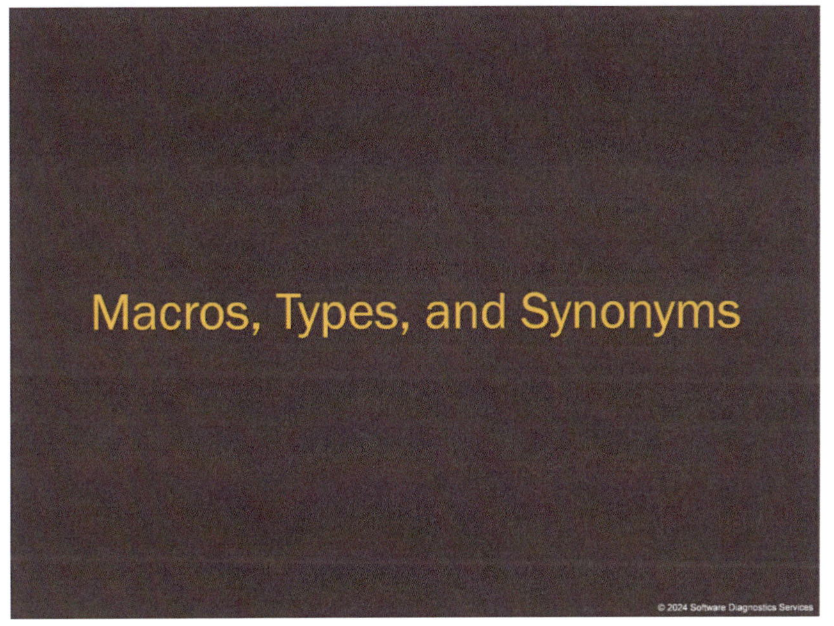

Type names may be long or inconvenient. There are some ways to construct easier type names.

The `macros_types_synonyms` projects:

- `macros_types_synonyms_c` C
- `macros_types_synonyms_c_cpp` C++ as a better C
- `macros_types_synonyms_modern_cpp` Modern C++

can be found in the archive[8]. In the following slide descriptions, we only show relevant code snippets and their output.

[8] https://www.patterndiagnostics.com/Training/ACPPWD/ACPPWD.zip

Macros

Macros

- #define TRUE 1
- #define BYTE unsigned char
- #define PBYTE unsigned char*
- #define PMyStruct struct MyStruct*

C

```
puts("--- Macros ---");
{
#define TRUE 1
#define BYTE unsigned char
#define PBYTE unsigned char*

    struct MyStruct { BYTE _dummy; } myStruct = {TRUE};

#define PMyStruct struct MyStruct*

    PMyStruct pMyStruct = NULL;
}
```

C++ as a better C

```
puts("--- Macros ---");
{
#define TRUE 1
#define BYTE unsigned char
#define PBYTE unsigned char*

    struct MyStruct {} myStruct; // In C++ structs can be without members

    printf("size of myStruct: %lld \n", sizeof(myStruct));

#define PMyStruct struct MyStruct*

    PMyStruct pMyStruct = NULL;
}
```

Output

```
--- Macros ---
size of myStruct: 1
```

Old Way

C

```
puts("--- Old Way ---");
{
#undef BYTE
#undef PBYTE
#undef PMyStruct

    typedef unsigned char BYTE;
    typedef unsigned char* PBYTE;
    typedef unsigned char BYTE, * PBYTE;
    typedef struct { BYTE _dummy; } MyStruct, * PMyStruct;

    MyStruct myStruct = {TRUE};
    PMyStruct pMyStruct = &myStruct;
}
```

C++ as a better C

```
puts("--- Old Way ---");
{
#undef BYTE
#undef PBYTE
#undef PMyStruct

    typedef unsigned char BYTE;
    typedef unsigned char* PBYTE;
    typedef unsigned char BYTE, * PBYTE;
    typedef struct {} MyStruct, * PMyStruct;

    MyStruct myStruct;
    PMyStruct pMyStruct = &myStruct;
}
```

New Way

New Way

- `using BYTE = unsigned char;`
- `using PBYTE = unsigned char*;`
- `using MyStruct = struct {};`

Modern C++

```
std::println("--- New Way ---");
{
    using BYTE = unsigned char;
    using PBYTE = unsigned char*;
    using MyStruct = struct { BYTE field; };

    MyStruct myStruct{1};
}
```

Enumerations

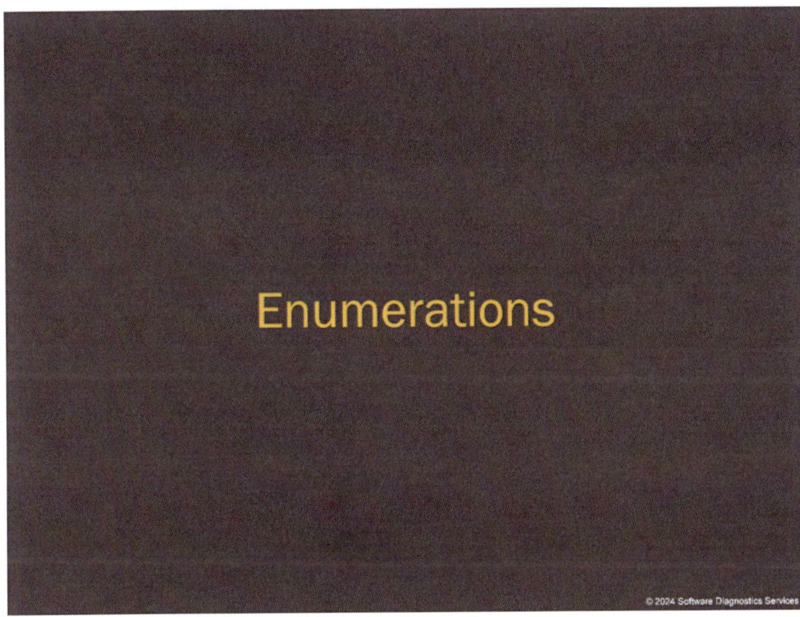

The `enumerations` projects:

- `enumerations_c` C
- `enumerations_c_cpp` C++ as a better C
- `enumerations_modern_cpp` Modern C++

can be found in the archive[9]. In the following slide descriptions, we only show relevant code snippets and their output.

[9] https://www.patterndiagnostics.com/Training/ACPPWD/ACPPWD.zip

Old Way

Old Way

- enum MEMORY_DUMP_TYPE
  { PROCESS = 1, KERNEL, COMPLETE = 10 };
- assert(sizeof(MEMORY_DUMP_TYPE) == 4);
- MEMORY_DUMP_TYPE dumpType = KERNEL;
- int d = dumpType;
- dumpType = (MEMORY_DUMP_TYPE)3;
- enum MEMORY_DUMP_TYPE2
  { PROCESS = 1, KERNEL, COMPLETE = 10, ACTIVE };

When using the old C-style enums, you cannot reuse the same enum value names for other enums, for example, when extending them. Also, all such enums have the same type.

C

```
puts("--- Old Way ---");
{
    enum MEMORY_DUMP_TYPE { PROCESS = 1, KERNEL, COMPLETE = 10 };

    enum MEMORY_DUMP_TYPE dumpType = KERNEL;

    printf("address of dumpType: %p size of dumpType: %llx value of dumpType: %x \n",
        &dumpType, sizeof(dumpType), dumpType);

    assert(sizeof(enum MEMORY_DUMP_TYPE) == 4);

    int d = dumpType;

    dumpType = 3;

    printf("value of dumpType: %x \n", dumpType);

    // enum MEMORY_DUMP_TYPE_EX { PROCESS, KERNEL, COMPLETE, ACTIVE }; // error
}
```

C++ as a better C

```
puts("--- Old Way ---");
{
    enum MEMORY_DUMP_TYPE { PROCESS = 1, KERNEL, COMPLETE = 10 };

    MEMORY_DUMP_TYPE dumpType = KERNEL; // enum can omitted in C++

    printf("address of dumpType: %p size of dumpType: %llx value of dumpType: %x \n",
        &dumpType, sizeof(dumpType), dumpType);
```

```
    assert(sizeof(MEMORY_DUMP_TYPE) == 4);

    int d = dumpType;

    dumpType = (MEMORY_DUMP_TYPE)3; // requires a cast

    printf("value of dumpType: %x \n", dumpType);

    // enum MEMORY_DUMP_TYPE_EX { PROCESS = 1, KERNEL, COMPLETE = 10, ACTIVE }; // error
}
```

Output

```
--- Old Way ---
address of dumpType: 0000009F89D2FC54 size of dumpType: 4 value of dumpType: 2
value of dumpType: 3
```

New Way

New Way

- enum class MEMORY_DUMP_TYPE
  { PROCESS = 1, KERNEL, COMPLETE = 10 };
- assert(sizeof(MEMORY_DUMP_TYPE) == 4);
- MEMORY_DUMP_TYPE dumpType = MEMORY_DUMP_TYPE::KERNEL;
- int d = static_cast<int>(dumpType);
- dumpType = static_cast<MEMORY_DUMP_TYPE>(3);
- enum class MEMORY_DUMP_TYPE_EX
  { PROCESS, KERNEL, COMPLETE, ACTIVE };

The modern C++ way allows reusing enum value names since the type of each enum is distinct; we have to qualify the value names.

Modern C++

```
std::println("--- New Way ---");
{
    enum class MEMORY_DUMP_TYPE
    {
        PROCESS = 1, KERNEL, COMPLETE = 10
    };

    MEMORY_DUMP_TYPE dumpType = MEMORY_DUMP_TYPE::KERNEL;

    std::println("address of dumpType: {} size of dumpType: {} value of dumpType: {}",
```

```
        reinterpret_cast<uintptr_t>(&dumpType), sizeof(dumpType), static_cast<int>(dumpType));

    assert(sizeof(MEMORY_DUMP_TYPE) == 4);

    int d = static_cast<int>(dumpType);

    dumpType = static_cast<MEMORY_DUMP_TYPE>(3);

    std::println("value of dumpType: {}", static_cast<int>(dumpType));

    enum class MEMORY_DUMP_TYPE_EX {
        PROCESS = MEMORY_DUMP_TYPE::PROCESS,
        KERNEL = MEMORY_DUMP_TYPE::KERNEL, COMPLETE = MEMORY_DUMP_TYPE::COMPLETE,
        ACTIVE
    };
}
```

Output

```
--- New Way ---
address of dumpType: 00000068CABCF934 size of dumpType: 4 value of dumpType: 2
value of dumpType: 3
```

Memory Storage

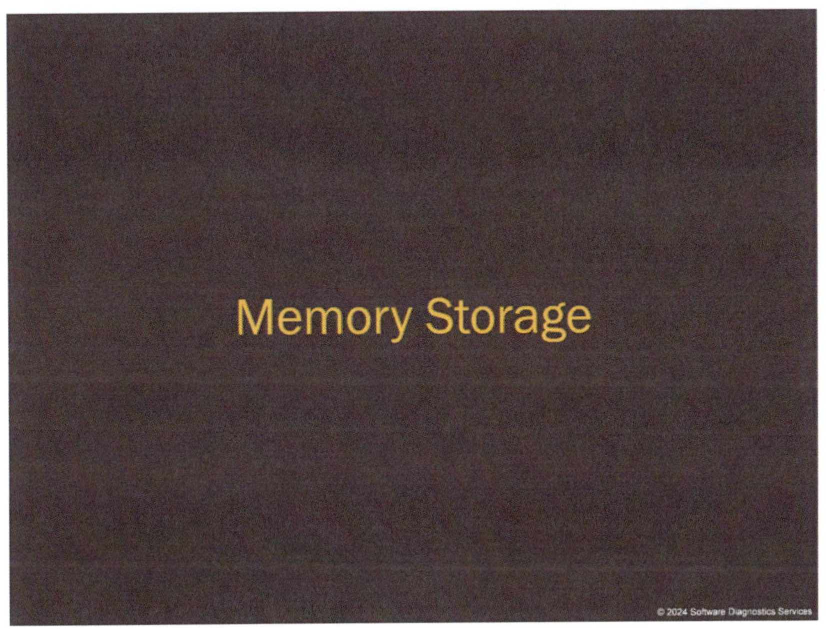

What memory storage is used to store values ultimately influences program behavior and possible defects.

The `memory_storage` projects:

- `memory_storage_c` C
- `memory_storage_c_cpp` C++ as a better C
- `memory_storage_classic_cpp` Classic C++

can be found in the archive[10]. In the following slide descriptions, we only show relevant code snippets and their output.

[10] https://www.patterndiagnostics.com/Training/ACPPWD/ACPPWD.zip

Overview

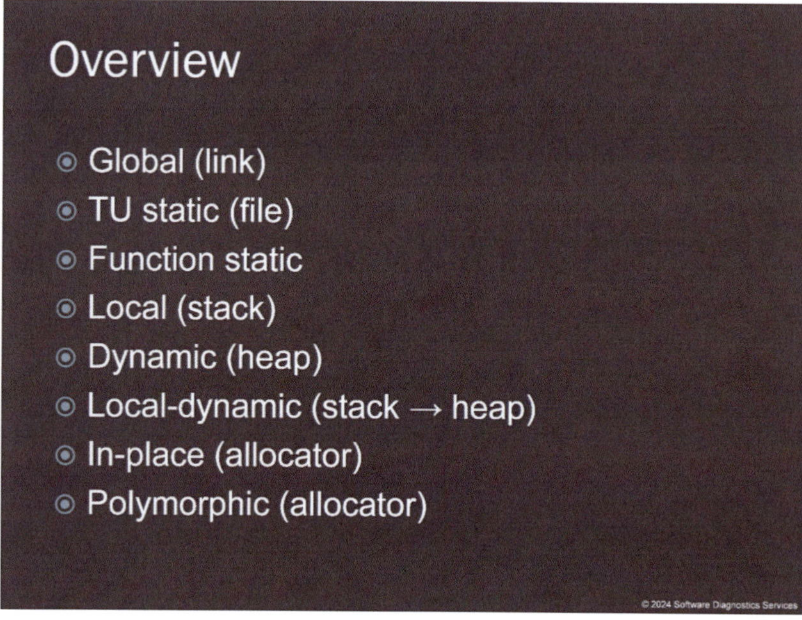

Here, we show the list of different storage types and talk about them in detail later. We cover the polymorphic allocators in the next edition.

Memory Regions

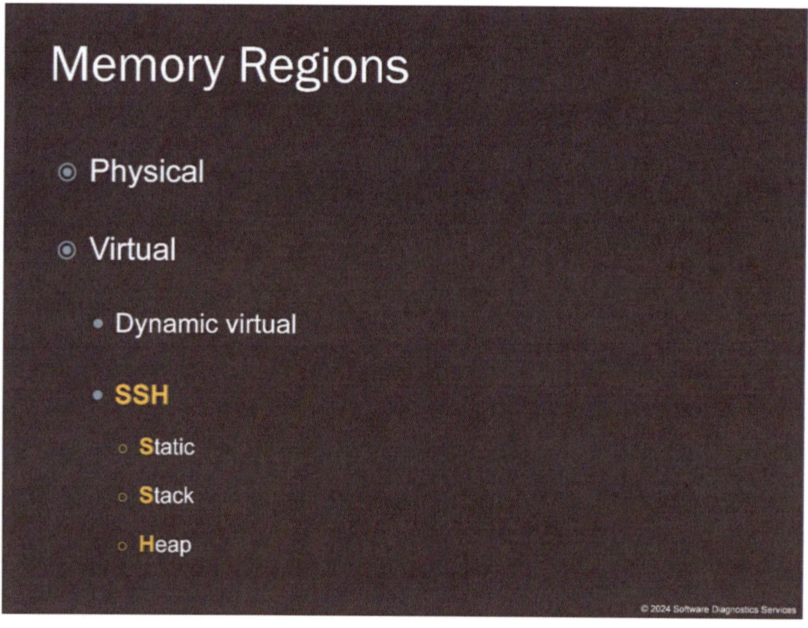

All computer memory is physical memory. However, unless you write specific hardware-related kernel-mode drivers or modules, you don't really work with physical memory in your applications and services. You work with the so-called virtual memory, an abstraction that allows you to think that your process works with linearly ordered computer memory cells, each with its own memory address. Processes allocate memory in pages of virtual memory. But they can dedicate some of the virtual memory regions for specialized purposes. SSH abbreviation is a good mnemonic for static, stack, and heap types of memory regions. We now look at these three region types separately.

Dynamic Virtual Memory

Dynamic Virtual Memory

- OS managed
- Base for static, stack, and heap
- `VirtualAlloc`

© 2024 Software Diagnostics Services

Virtual memory is dynamic – we have terabytes of virtual memory for an x64 process. But it is not really a memory you can write or read to. It needs to be committed – physical memory pages associated with virtual memory regions. All these committed virtual memory regions are used as underlying memory pages for static data, stack, and heap regions. Even large heap blocks are allocated using this mechanism. You can use Windows API to allocate large chunks of virtual memory for your own usage.

Static Memory

Static Memory

- Per process
- Program data
- Can be read-only
- Shared between all threads
- "Always there"
- Persists across function calls

© 2024 Software Diagnostics Services

Static memory is per process and usually contains program data, such as string literals. It can be read-only memory pages. Static memory is shared between all process threads, so caution is needed for multithreaded access. It is "always there", having a static lifetime, so any pointers or references to it are valid for the duration of the process.

Stack Memory

Stack Memory

- Per thread (sort of memory isolation)
- Function frame data
- Temporary
- Undefined frame values (garbage) before and after a call
- Values may be pointers to static, stack, and heap memory

Stack memory regions are separate for each process thread and provide some degree of isolation. The purpose of stack memory is to have some space for function frame data such as parameters and local values. Such frames are temporary: once a function returns to its caller frame, frame memory can be reused by subsequent function calls so we should treat memory values before and after each call as undefined, containing garbage. However, for the duration of a function call, frame memory values can point to (contain addresses of) static, stack, and heap memory.

Thread Stack Frames

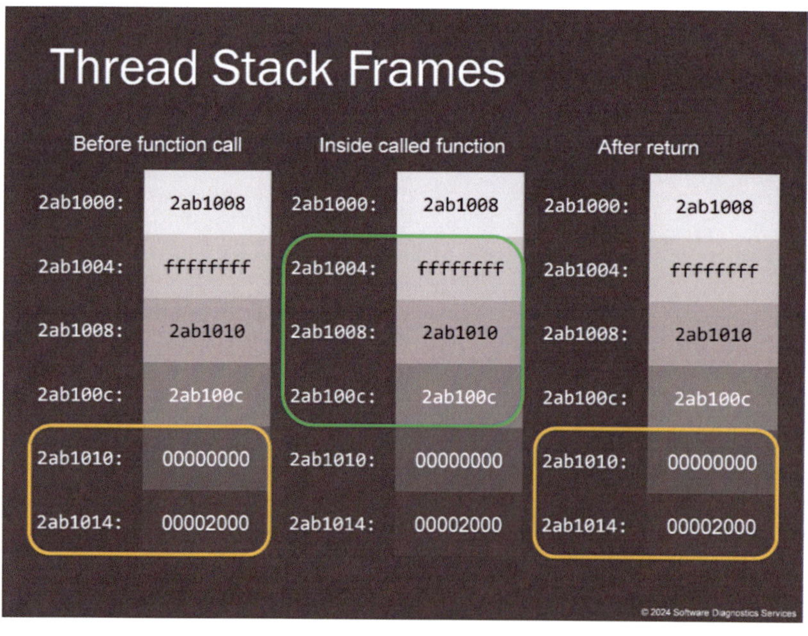

When a function is called, a stack frame is allocated in the thread stack memory region to hold local variables' values.

Local Variable Value Lifecycle

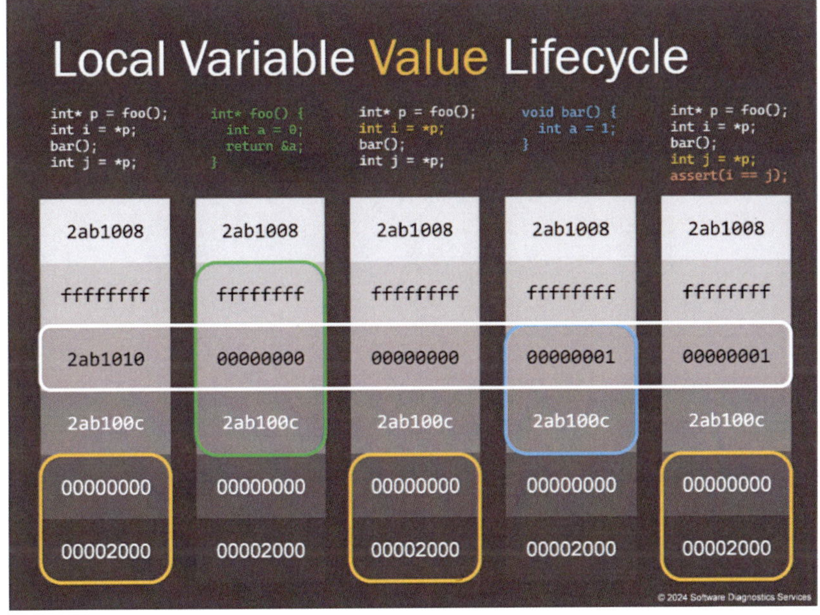

Since the stack frame memory values can be overwritten after the return from the function by subsequent function calls, local variable values have definite values only during the function call where they were initialized.

The code examples corresponding to the memory diagrams.

Before calling the `foo` function, the memory values below the current stack frame are undefined:

```
int *p = foo();
int i = *p;
bar();
int j = *p;
```

When we enter the `foo` function, the corresponding stack frame is created. The function code also initializes the local variable a with 0 value. The function also returns the stack address of that local variable:

```
int *foo()
{
  int a = 0;
  return &a;
}
```

In the caller, we save that value at that address in the i variable. Then we call the `bar` function:

```
int *p = foo();
int i = *p;
bar();
int j = *p;
```

When we enter the `bar` function, the corresponding stack frame is created. The function code also initializes the local variable a with 1. Coincidentally, the variable a occupies the same stack memory location as the local variable a in the previous `foo` function call:

```
void bar()
{
  int a = 1;
}
```

Upon the return from the `bar` function, we dereference the same p address but get a different value:

```
int *p = foo();
int i = *p;
bar();
```

```
int j = *p;
assert(i == j);
```

C C++ as a better C

```
puts("--- Local Variable Value Lifecycle ---");
{
    int* p = foo();
    int i = *p;
    bar();
    int j = *p;

    printf("value of i: %d value of j: %d \n", i, j);

    // assert(i == j); // fails
}
```

Output

```
--- Local Variable Value Lifecycle ---
value of i: 0 value of j: 1
```

Scope

Scope

```
{
    int a;
    {
        int a;
        {
            int a;
        }
    }
}
```


Scopes of variables can be nested with variable names in the nested scope, hiding variables with the same name in the enclosing scope.

C C++ as a better C

```
puts("--- Scope ---");
{
    int a = 0;
    int b = 0xb;
    {
        int a = 1;
        {
            int a = 2;
            printf("value of a: %d value of b: %x \n", a, b);
        }
        printf("value of a: %d value of b: %x \n", a, b);
    }
    printf("value of a: %d value of b: %x \n", a, b);
}
```

Output

```
--- Scope ---
value of a: 2 value of b: b
value of a: 1 value of b: b
value of a: 0 value of b: b
```

Stack Allocation Pitfalls

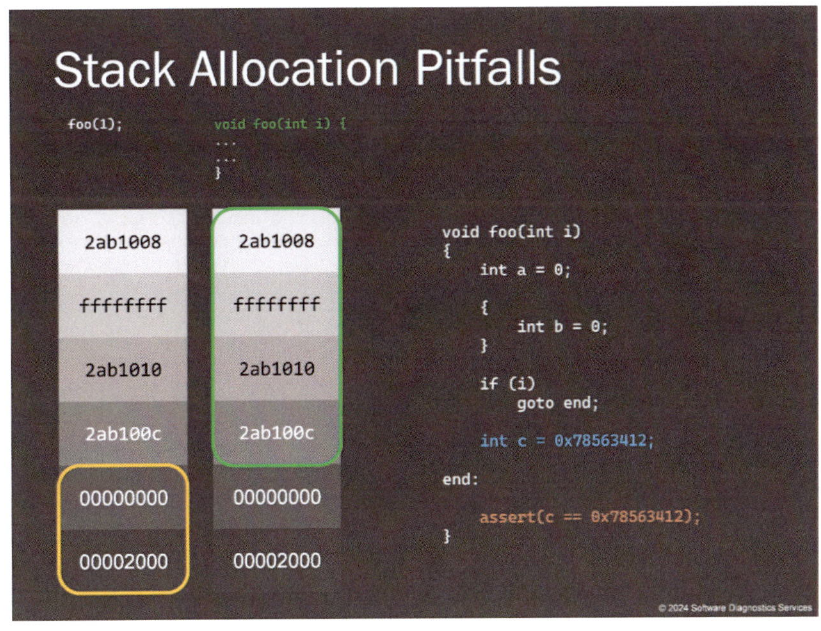

Please don't forget that stack frame memory for all function local variables is allocated at the entrance of the function, but individual variables may be initialized at a later time.

The code example corresponding to the memory diagram:

```
foo(1);
```

When we enter the `foo` function, the allocated stack frame includes the local variable `c`, which is initially uninitialized:

```
void foo(int i) {
...
}
```

If the value of the `i` function parameter is positive, the initialization of the local variable `c` is skipped, and the assertion is failed.

C

```
puts("--- Stack Allocation Pitfalls ---");
{
    int a = 0;

    {
        int b = 0;
    }

    if (/*some condition*/ 1)
        goto end;

    int c = 0x78563412;

end:;

    printf("value of c: %x \n", c);
    // Basic Runtime Checks: Default and SDL Checks: No (/sdl-)
    // assert(c == 0x78563412); // fail
}
```

C++ as a better C

```
puts("--- Stack Allocation Pitfalls ---");
{
    int a = 0;

    {
        int b = 0;
    }

    if (/*some condition*/ 1)
        goto end; // requires /Zc:gotoScope-

    int c = 0x78563412;

end:;

    printf("value of c: %x \n", c);
    // Basic Runtime Checks: Default and SDL Checks: No (/sdl-)
    // assert(c == 0x78563412); // fail
}
```

Output

```
--- Stack Allocation Pitfalls ---
value of c: ee960dab
```

Explicit Local Allocation

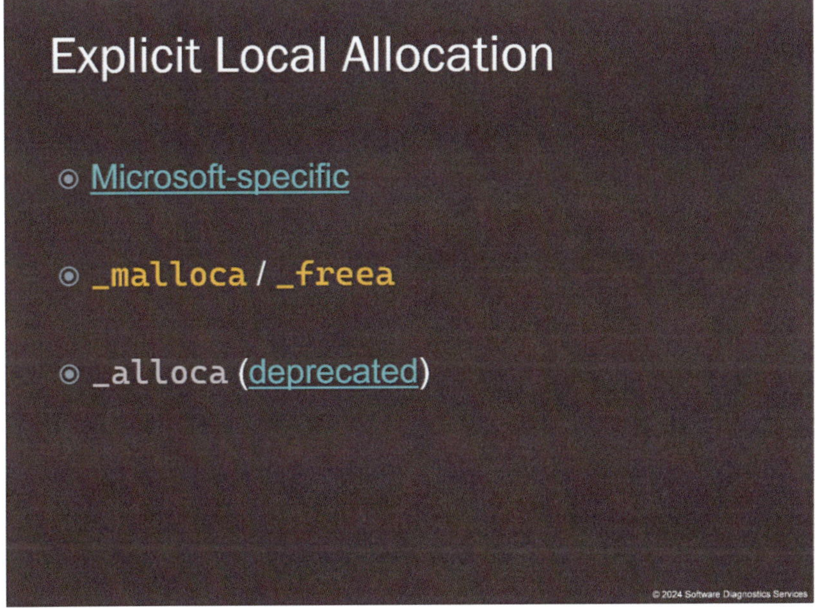

It is possible to explicitly allocate memory on the thread stack, for example, for some variable-length array storage. However, be aware of the possible stack overflow.

Microsoft-specific _malloca / _freea
https://learn.microsoft.com/en-us/cpp/c-runtime-library/reference/malloca

deprecated _alloca
https://learn.microsoft.com/en-us/cpp/c-runtime-library/reference/alloca

C C++ as a better C

```
puts("--- Explicit Local Allocation ---");
{
    int i;

    void* pBlock = _malloca(0x200); // In Debug does heap allocation

    int j;

    printf("address of i: %p address of j: %p address of pBlock: %p value of pBlock: %p \n",
        &i, &j, &pBlock, pBlock);

    _freea(pBlock);

    int k;

    printf("address of i: %p address of j: %p address of k: %p \n"
        "address of pBlock: %p value of pBlock: %p \n",
        &i, &j, &k, &pBlock, pBlock);
}
```

Debug Output

```
--- Explicit Local Allocation ---
address of i: 000000579F4FFC9C address of j: 000000579F4FFCA8 address of pBlock: 000000579F4FFCA0 value of
pBlock: 000001D82FD154F0
address of i: 000000579F4FFC9C address of j: 000000579F4FFCA8 address of k: 000000579F4FFCAC
address of pBlock: 000000579F4FFCA0 value of pBlock: 000001D82FD154F0
```

Release Output

```
--- Explicit Local Allocation ---
address of i: 000000A5646FF860 address of j: 000000A5646FF870 address of pBlock: 000000A5646FF868 value of
pBlock: 000000A5646FF660
address of i: 000000A5646FF860 address of j: 000000A5646FF870 address of k: 000000A5646FF874
address of pBlock: 000000A5646FF868 value of pBlock: 000000A5646FF660
```

Heap Memory

Heap Memory

- Per process
- Can be shared between threads
- Dynamic memory
- Undefined (garbage) after the end of the lifetime
- Values may be pointers to static and heap memory

Like static memory, heap memory is also accessible to and shared between all process threads. It is also dynamic, with the total amount of allocated memory changing over time. After heap-allocated memory is freed or released, its contents become undefined due to subsequent allocations or heap compactification. Values allocated from the heap may contain pointers to static and other heap memory. Generally, if heap memory contains pointers to stack memory, it may be a red flag since stack memory is defined only for the duration of the function call unless heap memory is also released before the return of the function call.

Dynamic Allocation (C-style)

Dynamic Allocation (C-style)

- Persistent across function calls
- `(m|c|re)alloc`
- `free`
- Can be replaced

There are some advantages to a dynamic memory allocation compared to a local stack allocation. The allocated memory and its values persist across function calls. Since allocations are implemented by library calls, they can be replaced with other libraries and custom code that provides debugging capabilities for tracking memory allocations and deallocations, as well as other checks.

Dynamic Allocation (C++)

Dynamic Allocation (C++)

- Persistent across function calls
- Global operators
- Structure-specific operators
- Can be replaced

C++ has its own implementation of dynamic memory that is often internally implemented by underlying C-style calls and Windows API. However, these high-level allocation facilities are more flexible and customizable to the needs of structure designers. It provides replaceable operators for global allocations for chunks of memory and structure-specific allocations.

Memory Expressions

Memory Expressions

- Use memory operators
- `new`
- `delete` / `delete[]`
- `new` throws `std::bad_alloc` exception (do not check for `nullptr`) unless told not to via `std::nothrow` value

Memory allocation expressions are used for allocating memory for values, structures, and their arrays. Internally, they may use memory operators. The same advice for non-array/array deallocation and checking return addresses is applicable here.

Memory Operators

Memory Operators

- `operator new` / `operator delete`
- `operator new[]` / `operator delete[]`
- `operator new` throws `std::bad_alloc` exception (do not check for `nullptr`) unless told not to via `std::nothrow` value

When freeing globally allocated memory, always pay attention to whether it was allocated in the array form to avoid memory leaks, crashes, and other undefined behavior. Also, never check the allocated memory address for `nullptr` as done in the C-style allocations: C++ allocation operators throw an exception in-stead.

Classic C++

```
// allocate from the stack instead of heap

void* operator new(std::size_t size)
{
    std::cout << "operator new(std::size_t size) called" << std::endl;

    void* p = _malloca(size); // In Debug does heap allocation
    if (p) return p;

    throw std::bad_alloc{};
}

void* operator new(std::size_t size, const std::nothrow_t&) noexcept
{
    std::cout << "operator new(std::size_t size, const std::nothrow_t&) called" << std::endl;

    return _malloca(size); // In Debug does heap allocation
}

void* operator new[](std::size_t size)
{
    std::cout << "operator new[](std::size_t size) called" << std::endl;

    void* p = _malloca(size); // In Debug does heap allocation
    if (p) return p;

    throw std::bad_alloc{};
}

void* operator new[](std::size_t size, const std::nothrow_t&) noexcept
{
    std::cout << "operator new[](std::size_t size, const std::nothrow_t&) called" << std::endl;

    return _malloca(size); // In Debug does heap allocation
}

void operator delete(void* p, std::size_t size) noexcept
{
    std::cout << "operator delete(void* p, std::size_t size) called" << std::endl;

    _freea(p);
}

void operator delete[](void* p) noexcept
{
    std::cout << "operator delete(void* p) called" << std::endl;

    _freea(p);
}

// ...

std::cout << "--- Memory Expressions ---" << std::endl;
{
    int* pi = new int;
    int* iarr = new int[10];

    std::cout << "address of pi: " << &pi << " value of pi: " << pi << std::endl;
    std::cout << "address of iarr: " << &iarr << " value of iarr: " << iarr << std::endl;

    delete[] iarr;
    delete pi;
```

```
    pi = new(std::nothrow) int;
    iarr = new(std::nothrow) int[10];

    std::cout << "address of pi: " << &pi << " value of pi: " << pi << std::endl;
    std::cout << "address of iarr: " << &iarr << " value of iarr: " << iarr << std::endl;

    delete[] iarr;
    delete pi;
}

std::cout << "--- Memory Operators ---" << std::endl;
{
    // see above
}
```

<u>Debug Output</u>

```
--- Memory Expressions ---
operator new(std::size_t size) called
operator new[](std::size_t size) called
address of pi: 00000032BF73F718 value of pi: 000001F9CDE66DB0
address of iarr: 00000032BF73F738 value of iarr: 000001F9CDE5B9D0
operator delete(void* p) called
operator delete(void* p, std::size_t size) called
operator new(std::size_t size, const std::nothrow_t&) called
operator new[](std::size_t size, const std::nothrow_t&) called
address of pi: 00000032BF73F718 value of pi: 000001F9CDE667C0
address of iarr: 00000032BF73F738 value of iarr: 000001F9CDE5B9D0
operator delete(void* p) called
operator delete(void* p, std::size_t size) called
```

<u>Release Output</u>

```
--- Memory Expressions ---
operator new(std::size_t size) called
operator new[](std::size_t size) called
address of pi: 000000B2AF8FFC48 value of pi: 000000B2AF8FFBE0
address of iarr: 000000B2AF8FFC40 value of iarr: 000000B2AF8FFBC0
operator delete(void* p) called
operator delete(void* p, std::size_t size) called
operator new(std::size_t size, const std::nothrow_t&) called
operator new[](std::size_t size, const std::nothrow_t&) called
address of pi: 000000B2AF8FFC48 value of pi: 000000B2AF8FFBF0
address of iarr: 000000B2AF8FFC40 value of iarr: 000000B2AF8FFBD0
operator delete(void* p) called
operator delete(void* p, std::size_t size) called
```

Local Pointers (Manual)

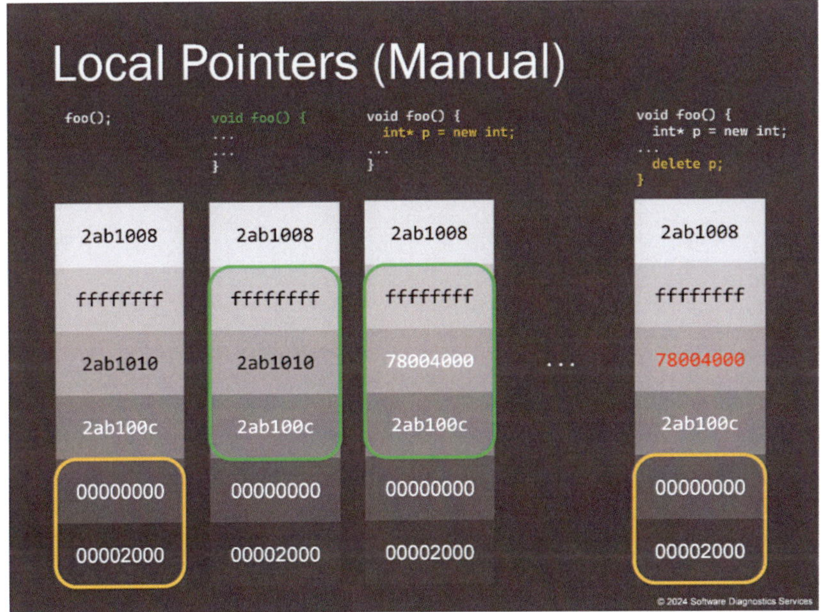

When allocating memory dynamically and assigning the memory address to a local variable, we must not forget to free/delete memory before returning from the function to avoid a memory leak.

The code example corresponding to the memory diagram:

```
foo();
```

When we enter the `foo` function, the allocated stack frame includes the local variables:

```
void foo()
{
...
...
}
```

The local variable `p` contains the address of the allocated memory for an integer value:

```
void foo()
{
  int *p = new int;
...
}
```

However, before exiting the function, we must free the memory; otherwise, there is a memory leak. Please note that neither `delete` nor `free` change the value of the variable `p`. It becomes a dangling pointer but it is ok because it goes out of scope here and is not reused for dereferencing unless saved somewhere else.

```
void foo()
{
  int *p = new int;
...
  delete p;
}
```

In-place Allocation

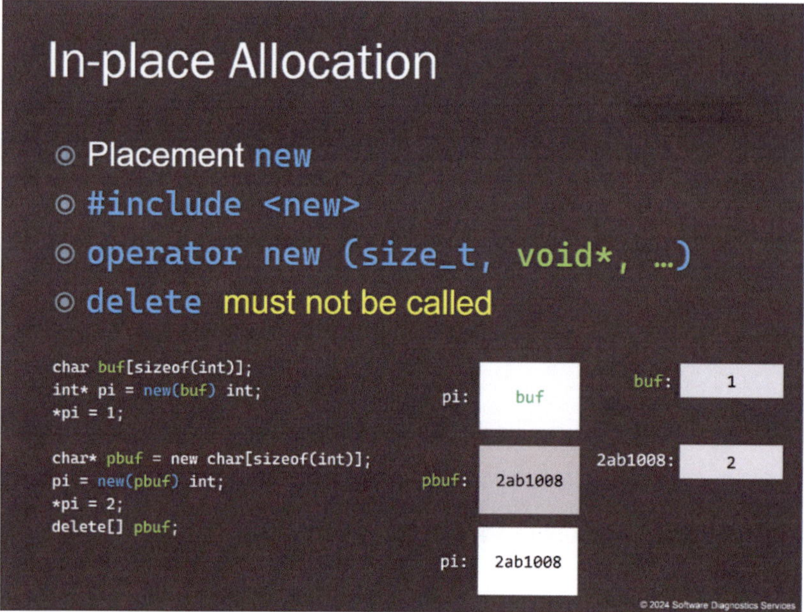

If we want to reuse existing memory buffers, we can use placement new.

Classic C++

```
std::cout << "--- In-place Allocation ---" << std::endl;
{
    char buf[sizeof(int)];
    int* pi = new(buf) int;
    *pi = 1;

    std::cout << "address of buf: " << &buf << " value of pi: " << pi << std::endl;

    char* pbuf = new char[sizeof(int)];
    pi = new(pbuf) int;
    *pi = 2;

    std::cout << "value of pbuf: " << static_cast<void*>(pbuf) << " value of pi: " << pi <<
std::endl;

    delete[] pbuf;
}
```

Debug Output

```
--- In-place Allocation ---
address of buf: 00000032BF73F754 value of pi: 00000032BF73F754
operator new[](std::size_t size) called
value of pbuf: 000001F9CDE66C70 value of pi: 000001F9CDE66C70
operator delete(void* p) called
```

Release Output

```
--- In-place Allocation ---
address of buf: 000000B2AF8FFC40 value of pi: 000000B2AF8FFC40
operator new[](std::size_t size) called
value of pbuf: 000000B2AF8FFBE0 value of pi: 000000B2AF8FFBE0
operator delete(void* p) called
```

Useful WinDbg Commands

Useful WinDbg Commands

- !address [<address>]
- lm
- bp module!main
- uf module!main
- dt module!main::<type>
- dps <address> [<address>]
- ~<thread>s
- !teb
- dv /i /V

Source Code Organisation

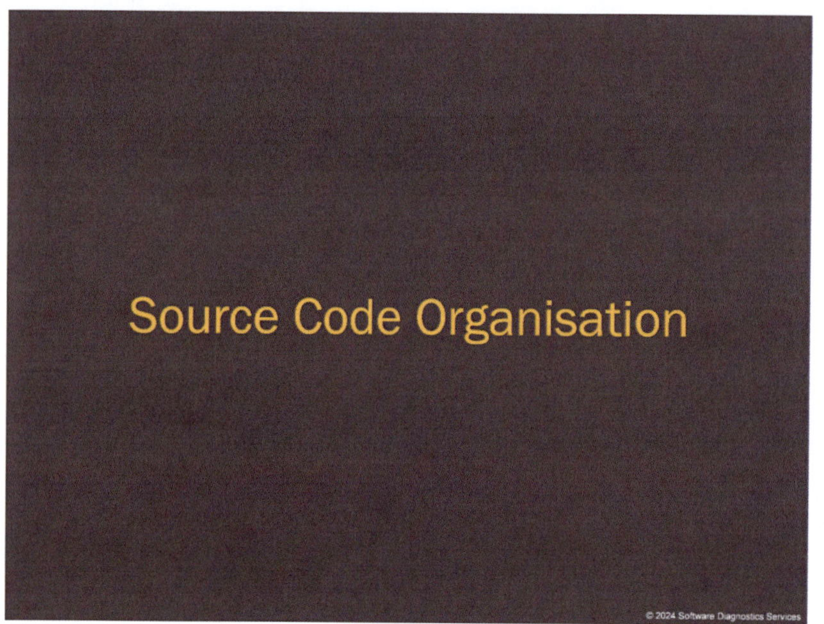

We now discuss C and C++ source code organization.

The `source_code_organization` project:

- `source_code_organization_classic_cpp` Classic C++

can be found in the archive[11]. In the following slide descriptions, we only show relevant code snippets and their output.

[11] https://www.patterndiagnostics.com/Training/ACPPWD/ACPPWD.zip

Logical Layer (Translation Units)

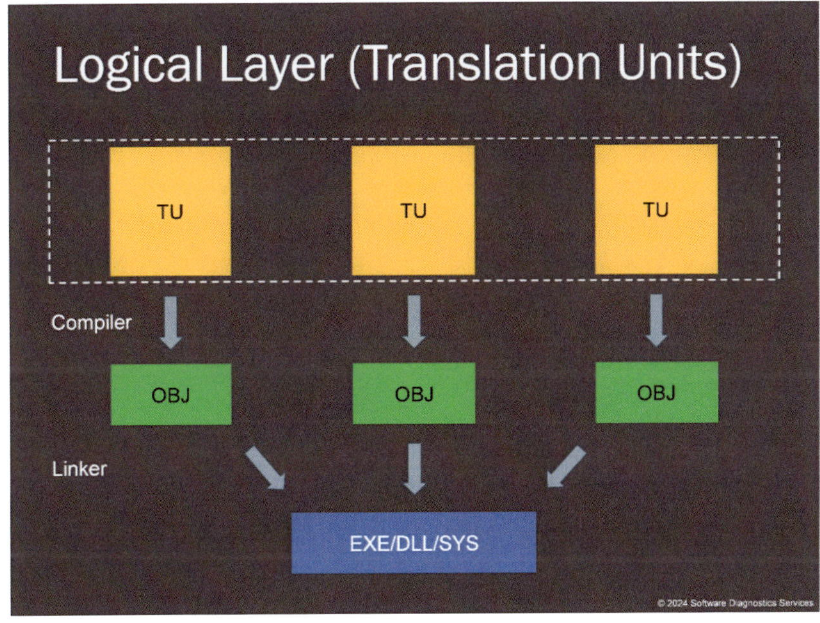

From a compiler perspective, it works with a translation unit as a whole and converts the source code of a translation unit to an object file. Several object files are combined by a linker into an executable file.

Physical Layer (Source Files)

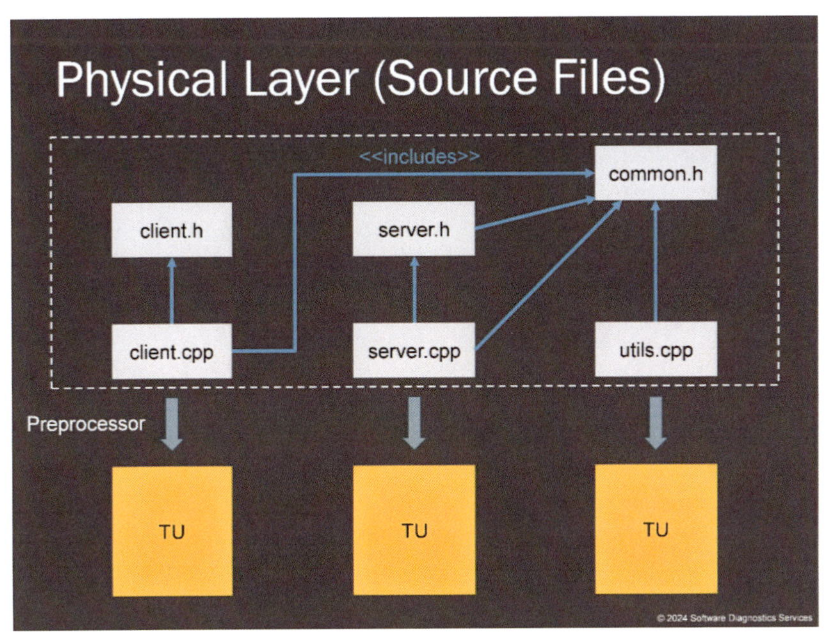

Although one physical source code file corresponds to one translation unit, it is passed through a preprocessor, which, among other things, looks for special directives to include other files, and those files may also contain directives to include other files. You can also see, as in the case of the *common.h* file, by transitivity of inclusion, that the same file may be included many times.

Inter-TU Sharing

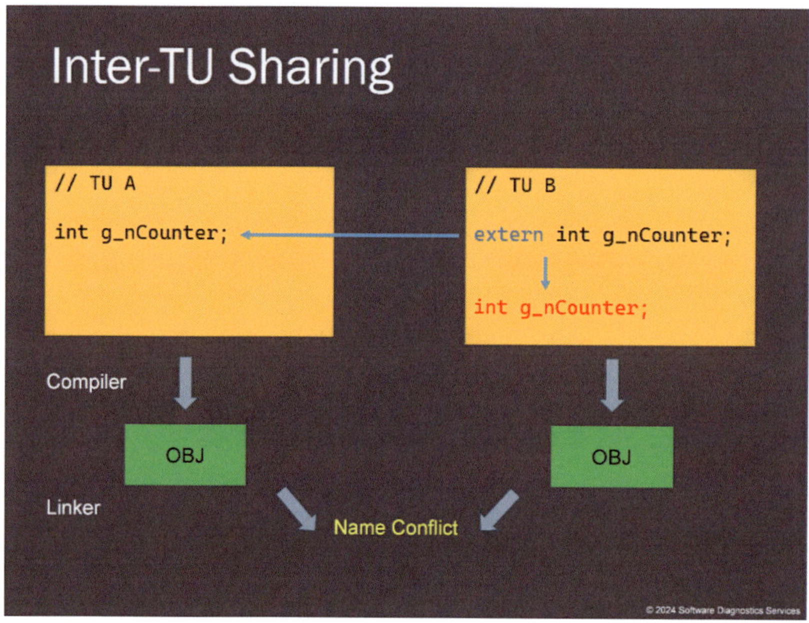

Variables in different translation units having the same name may conflict during the linkage phase.

Classic Static TU Isolation

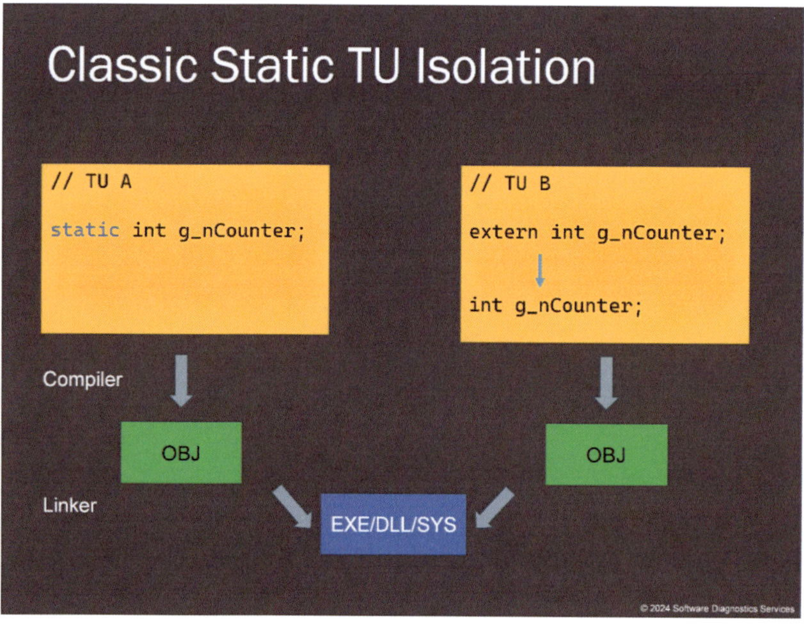

To avoid name conflicts during linkage, C and classic C++ suggest using the `static` specifier.

Namespace TU Isolation

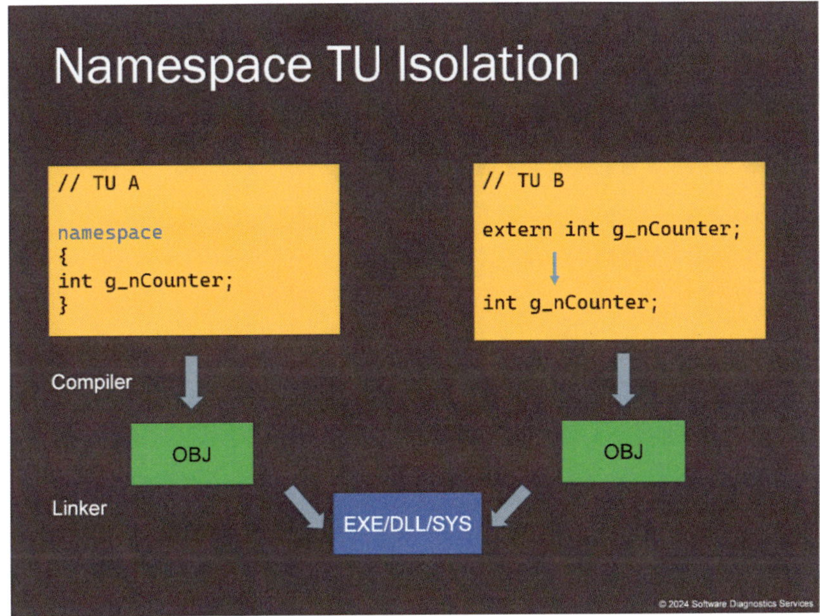

Modern C++ suggests using namespaces instead.

Declaration and Definition

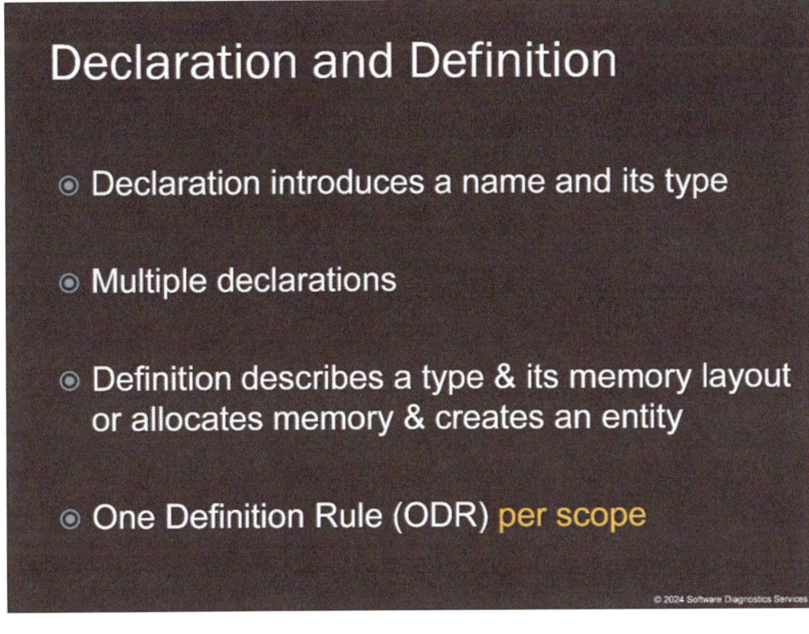

In C and C++, when reasoning about compilation, it is useful to consider the distinction between declaration and definition. The rule of thumb is that the latter usually describes the memory layout. Please also note that a definition is also a declaration.

TU Definition Conflicts

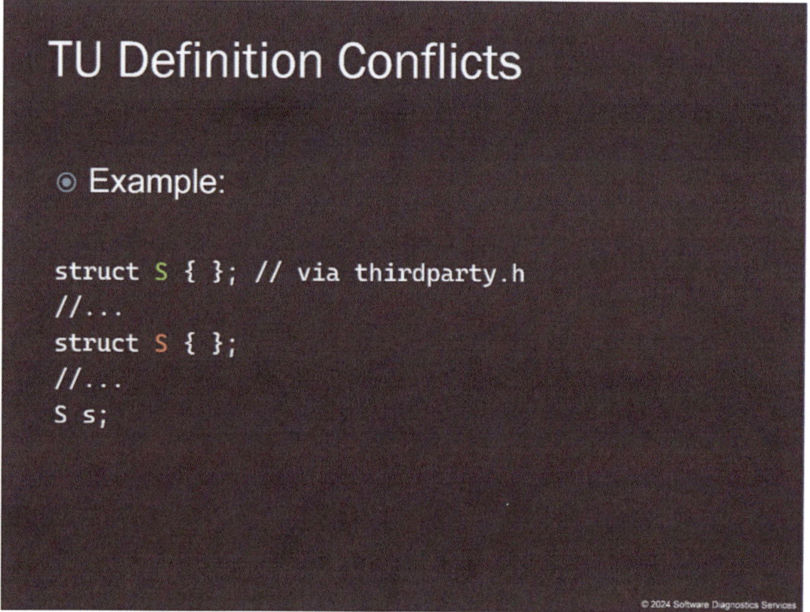

Multiple declarations of the same entity are allowed, but only one definition is allowed, the essence of ODR, One Definition Rule.

Classic C++

```
#include "thirdparty.h"

// struct S {}; // error

std::cout << "--- TU Definition Conflicts ---" << std::endl;
{
    struct S {}; // OK, different scope

    S s;

    std::cout << "size of s: " << sizeof(s) << std::endl;

    {
        struct S { int _dummy;  }; // OK, different scope

        S s;

        std::cout << "size of s: " << sizeof(s) << std::endl;
    }
}
```

Output

```
--- TU Definition Conflicts ---
size of s: 1
size of s: 4
```

Fine-grained TU Scope Isolation

Fine-grained TU Scope Isolation

- Named namespaces
- Example:

```
struct S { }; // via thirdparty.h
namespace mycode { struct S { }; }
//...
mycode::S s;
using namespace mycode;
S s2; // ambiguous
```


Named namespaces allow the fine-grained scope isolation.

Classic C++

```
#include "thirdparty.h"

namespace mycode { struct S {}; }

std::cout << "--- Fine-grained TU Scope Isolation ---" << std::endl;
{
    mycode::S s;

    using namespace mycode;
    // S s2; // ambiguous
}
```

Conceptual Layer (Design)

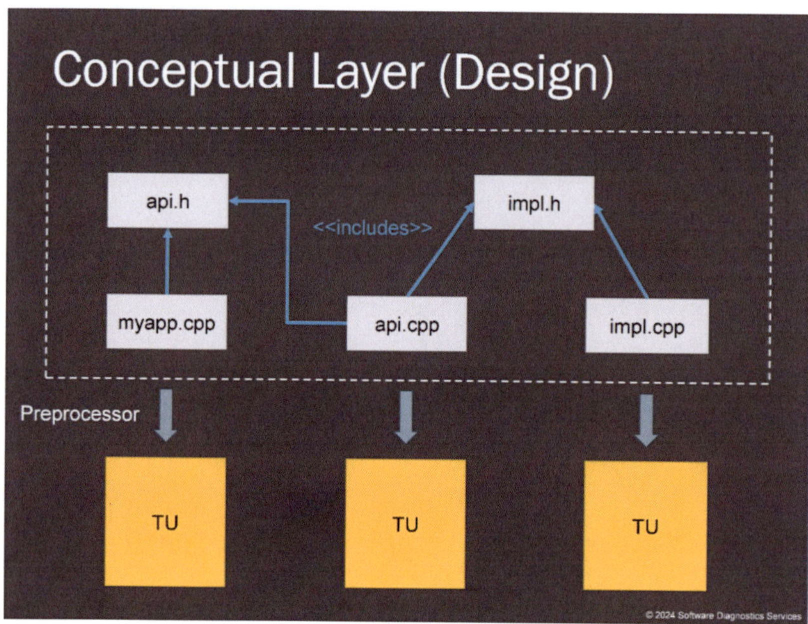

In the design layer, we may want to separate implementation details.

Incomplete Types

Incomplete Types

```
struct MyStruct; // declaration

MyStruct* pMyStruct; // (declaration and) definition

// PImpl (Pointer to Implementation) idiom

struct InstrumentImpl; // declaration

struct Instrument // (declaration and) definition
{
        int getMeasurement(); // declaration
private:
        InstrumentImpl* pImpl; // definition
};
```


Such separation is achieved via incomplete types and the so-called **PImpl** (**P**ointer to **Impl**ementation) idiom.

Classic C++

```
// source_code_organization_modern_cpp.cpp

#include "instrument.h"

std::cout << "--- Incomplete Types ---" << std::endl;
{
    struct MyStruct; // declaration

    MyStruct* pMyStruct; // (declaration and) definition

    Instrument instrument;

    instrument.getMeasurement();
}
```

```
// instrument.h

#pragma once

// PImpl (Pointer to Implementation) idiom

struct InstrumentImpl; // declaration

struct Instrument // (declaration and) definition
{
    Instrument();
    ~Instrument();

    int getMeasurement(); // declaration
private:
    InstrumentImpl* pImpl; // definition
};
```

```
// instrument.cpp

#include <iostream>
#include "instrument.h"
#include "instrumentImpl.h"

Instrument::Instrument() : pImpl(new InstrumentImpl) {}

Instrument::~Instrument()
{
        delete pImpl;
}

int Instrument::getMeasurement()
{
        std::cout << "Instrument::getMeasurement() called" << std::endl;
        return pImpl->getMeasurement();
}
```

```
// instrumentImpl.h

#pragma once

struct InstrumentImpl
{
	InstrumentImpl();
	int getMeasurement();

private:
	int value;
};


// instrumentImpl.cpp

#include <iostream>
#include "instrumentImpl.h"

InstrumentImpl::InstrumentImpl() : value(0) {}

int InstrumentImpl::getMeasurement()
{
	std::cout << "InstrumentImpl::getMeasurement() called" << std::endl;
	return value;
}
```

Output

```
--- Incomplete Types ---
Instrument::getMeasurement() called
InstrumentImpl::getMeasurement() called
```

References

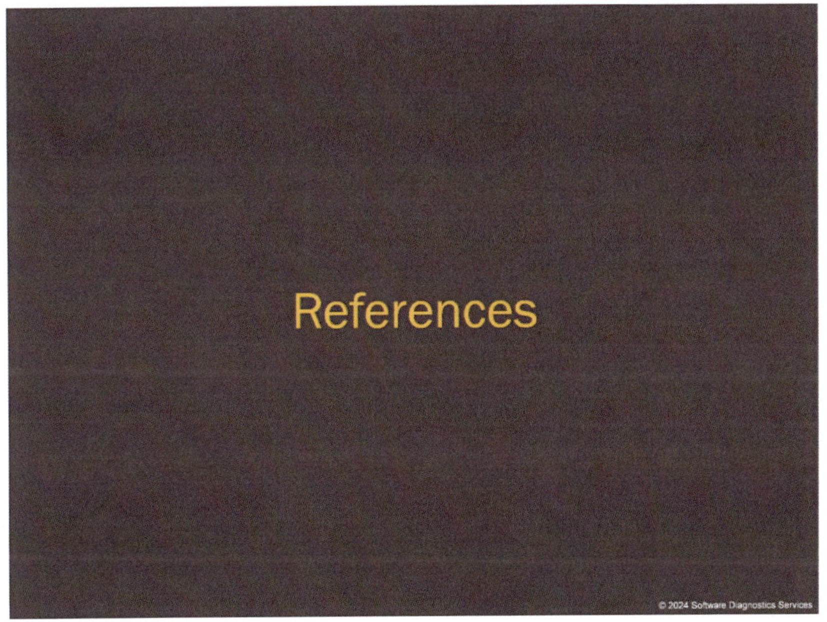

Now, a slide for C++ references. We plan to extend this section in the second edition.

The `references` project:

- `references_modern_cpp` Modern C++

can be found in the archive[12]. In the following slide descriptions, we only show relevant code snippets and their output.

[12] https://www.patterndiagnostics.com/Training/ACPPWD/ACPPWD.zip

Type& vs. Type*

Type& vs. Type*

- The same from a memory perspective (internally)
- Another name, not a separate entity (from C++ perspective)
- Definition: `int& ref{val}; int* ptr{&val};`
- Double references and pointers to references are not allowed
- Dereference: `ref; * ptr;`
- Field access: `rStruct.field;`
  `pStruct->field; (*pStruct).field;`

From the memory perspective, references and pointers are the same thing. The only difference is that you cannot have a dangling reference; it must be initialized.

Modern C++

```
std::println("--- Type& vs. Type* ---");
{
    int val{0};
    int& ref{val};
    int* ptr{&val};

    // int& & refref; // error
    // int&* pref; // error

    int i = ref;
    i = *ptr;

    std::println("value of ref as address: {} address of val: {}", &ref, &val);

    struct Struct
    {
        int field{0};
    } myStruct, * pStruct{&myStruct}, & rStruct{myStruct};

    rStruct.field;
    pStruct->field;
    (*pStruct).field;
}
```

Output

```
--- Type& vs. Type* ---
value of ref as address: 000000322231F804 address of val: 000000322231F804
```

Values

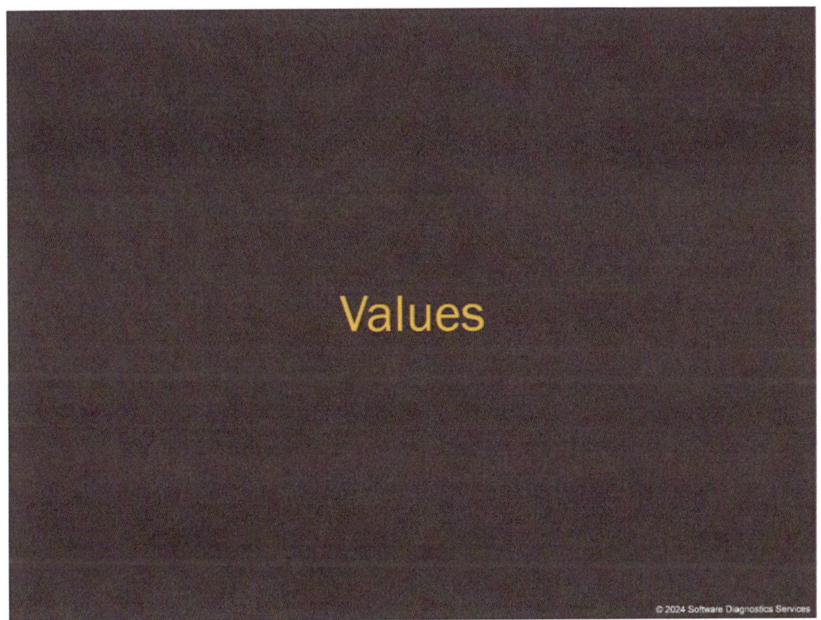

Let's now briefly discuss various categories of values. These are what is stored in memory. A pointer value is also a value that is interpreted as a memory address pointing to some other value elsewhere.

The `values` projects:

- `values_c` C
- `values_c_cpp` C++ as a better C
- `values_modern_cpp` Modern C++

can be found in the archive[13]. In the following slide descriptions, we only show relevant code snippets and their output.

[13] https://www.patterndiagnostics.com/Training/ACPPWD/ACPPWD.zip

Value Categories

Value Categories

- lvalues vs. rvalues classification
- Expression: left vs. right
- Memory: lvalue is backed up by memory cell(s)
- Temporaries and literals: rvalue

```
int lvalue = rvalue(); lvalue = 1;
```


When reading serious C++ documentation, you frequently see the so-called **lvalues** and **rvalues** mentioned. Crudely, you can think about them as **l**eft and **r**ight values in expressions, where the **r**ight value can be temporary, and the **l**eft value has to be backed up by some memory.

Classification
https://learn.microsoft.com/en-us/cpp/cpp/lvalues-and-rvalues-visual-cpp

C C++ as a better C

```
int rvalue()
{
    return 0;
}

puts("--- Value Categories ---");
{
    int lvalue = rvalue(); lvalue = 1;
}
```

Constant Values

The values can also be constant, facilitating functional programming and code safety. Please note that there can be pointers and references to constant values, constant pointers to mutable variables, and both. The way to read such declarations is from right to left.

C C++ as a better C

```
puts("--- Constant Values ---");
{
    const int cv = 1;
    int v = 0;

    printf("address of cv: %p address of v: %p \n", &cv, &v);

    const int* pc = NULL;
    pc = NULL;
    // *pc = 0; // error

    int* const cp = &v;
    // cp = NULL; // error
    *cp = 1;

    const int* const cpc = cp;
    // cpc = NULL; // error
    // *cpc = 0; // error
}
```

Output

```
--- Constant Values ---
address of cv: 000000CAAA50FA54 address of v: 000000CAAA50FA74
```

Modern C++

```
std::println("--- Constant Values ---");
{
    int v{0};

    const int& rc{v};
    // rc = 1; // error

    int& r{v};
    r = 1;
}
```

Constant Expressions

Constant Expressions

- #define myConstExpr 1 + 1
- const int myConstExpr = 1 + 1;
- constexpr int myConstExpr = 1 + 1;

There are different ways to define constants for later symbolic use. The C and classic C++ way is to use preprocessor (legacy) and `const`. The modern way is to use `constexpr`, which is more flexible.

Modern C++

```
std::println("--- Constant Expressions ---");
{
    const int myConst = 1 + 1;

    constexpr int myConstExpr = 1 + 1;

    std::println("address of myConst: {} address of myConstExpr: {}", &myConst, &myConstExpr);
}
```

Output

```
--- Constant Expressions ---
address of myConst: 00000059BAF1F9A4 address of myConstExpr: 00000059BAF1F9C4
```

Functions

This section is the largest. We may split it up in the third edition once it grows more.

The `functions` projects:

- `functions_c` C
- `functions_c_cpp` C++ as a better C
- `functions_classic_cpp` Classic C++
- `functions_modern_cpp` Modern C++

can be found in the archive[14]. In the following slide descriptions, we only show relevant code snippets and their output.

[14] https://www.patterndiagnostics.com/Training/ACPPWD/ACPPWD.zip

Macro Functions

Macro Functions

```
#define SQUARE(x) x * x

assert(9 == SQUARE(2+1));

#define SQUARE(x) (x) * (x)

assert(9 == SQUARE(2+1));
```


Implementing the compilation phase functions during source code preprocessing to avoid runtime calculations is the oldest method starting from C. However, if not done carefully, these functions may produce incorrect results.

C C++ as a better C

```
puts("--- Macro Functions ---");
{
#define SQUARE(x) x * x

    printf("value of SQUARE(2): %x value of SQUARE(2 + 1): %x \n",
        SQUARE(2), SQUARE(2 + 1));

    // assert(9 == SQUARE(2 + 1)); // fails

#undef SQUARE
#define SQUARE(x) (x) * (x)

    printf("value of SQUARE(2): %x value of SQUARE(2 + 1): %x \n",
        SQUARE(2), SQUARE(2 + 1));

    assert(9 == SQUARE(2 + 1));
}
```

Output

```
--- Macro Functions ---
value of SQUARE(2): 4 value of SQUARE(2 + 1): 5
value of SQUARE(2): 4 value of SQUARE(2 + 1): 9
```

constexpr Functions

constexpr Functions

- `constexpr int SQUARE(int x)`
  ```
  {
    return x * x;
  }
  ```
- `constexpr int i = SQUARE(2+1);`
- Function is generated for non-constexpr use

`constexpr` functions are calculated during compilation if they are used in the `constexpr` context. In other contexts, the compiler generates function bodies for runtime execution.

Modern C++

```
std::println("--- constexpr Functions ---");
{
    // No function calls
    constexpr int result = SQUARE(2);
    constexpr int result2 = SQUARE(2 + 1);

    std::println("value of SQUARE(2): {} value of SQUARE(2+1): {}",
        result, result2);

    assert(9 == result2);

    // A function is generated because we use it in a non-constexpr expression
    int result3 = SQUARE(3);
}
```

Output

```
--- constexpr Functions ---
value of SQUARE(2): 4 value of SQUARE(2+1): 9
```

Pointers to Functions

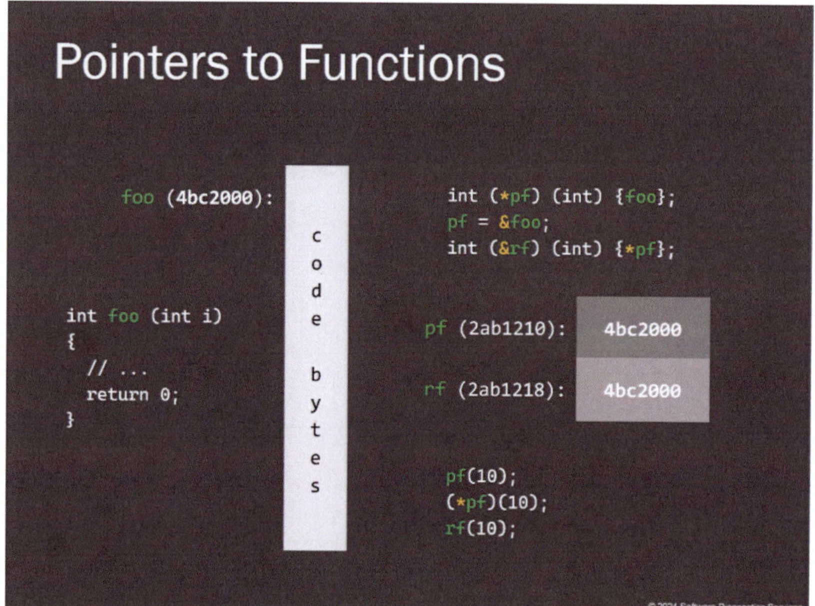

Functions are code bytes and, therefore, occupy some memory locations with their start addresses. It is possible to have pointers and references to functions:

```
int (*pf) (int) {foo};
pf = &foo;
int (&rf) (int) {*pf};
```

When having a pointer or reference to a function, it is possible to call the function with or without using the dereferencing syntax (*):

```
pf(10);
(*pf)(10);
rf(10)
```

C C++ as a better C

```
int foo(int i)
{
    // ...
    return 0;
}

puts("--- Pointers to Functions ---");
{
    int (*pf) (int) = foo;
    pf = &foo;

    printf("address of foo: %p address of pf: %p value of pf: %p \n",
        foo, &pf, pf);

    pf(10);
    (*pf)(10);
}
```

Output

```
--- Pointers to Functions ---
address of foo: 00007FF70E961113 address of pf: 0000009260CFF6B8 value of pf: 00007FF70E961113
```

Classic C++

```
int foo(int i)
{
    // ...
    return 0;
}

std::cout << "--- Pointers to Functions ---" << std::endl;
{
    int (*pf) (int) = foo;
    pf = &foo;
    int(&rf) (int) = *pf;

    std::cout << "address of foo: " << foo << " address of pf: " << &pf <<
        " value of pf: " << pf << " value of rf: " << rf << std::endl;

    pf(10);
    (*pf)(10);
    rf(10);
}
```

Output

```
--- Pointers to Functions ---
address of foo: 00007FF795CF11F4 address of pf: 0000002BC331ECE8 value of pf: 00007FF795CF11F4 value of
rf: 00007FF795CF11F4
```

Function Pointer Types

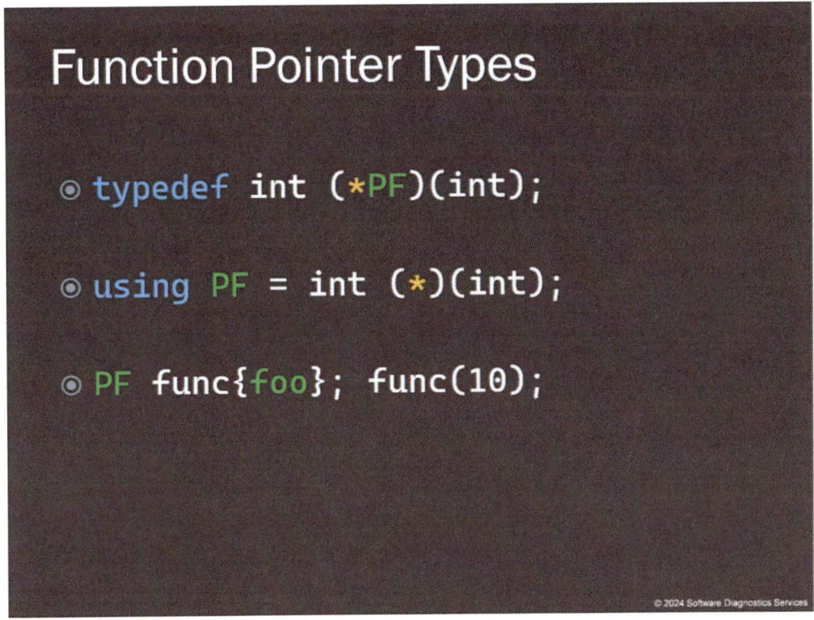

Function pointer type declarations can be done using the classic `typedef` syntax or via the more modern `using` type alias.

C C++ as a better C

```
puts("--- Function Pointer Types ---");
{
    typedef int (*PF)(int);

    PF func = foo;
    func(10);

}
```

Modern C++

```
std::println("--- Function Pointer Types ---");
{
    using PF = int (*)(int);

    PF func{foo};
    func(10);
}
```

Reading Declarations

It is worth knowing the rules of reading declarations since function pointer types can be quite complicated. The first example reads as an array of 10 elements, with each element a pointer to a pointer of constant pointers to constant integers. The next example is a pointer to a function that accepts a pointer to a function that accepts an integer and returns an integer, and accepts another integer, and returns a pointer to a function that accepts an integer and returns an integer. It can be simplified by using the common subtype PF. We can verify the compatibility of the two descriptions by initialization. GPT-4 is very good at deciphering such types.

Modern C++

```
std::println("--- Reading Declarations ---");
{
    const int* const** arr[10]{};

    int (*(*difficult)(int (*)(int), int))(int){};

    using PF = int (*)(int);
    using DF = PF(*)(PF, int);
    DF difficult2{ difficult };
}
```

Structure Function Fields

Structure Function Fields

```
struct
{
      int field;
      PF  pFunc;
} myStruct {0, foo};

myStruct.pFunc(0);
```


Structures may contain fields that are pointers to functions: the obvious way to implement OOP in C.

C C++ as a better C

```
puts("--- Structure Function Fields ---");
{
    typedef int (*PF)(int);

    struct
    {
        int field;
        PF  pFunc;
    } myStruct = { 0, foo };

    myStruct.pFunc(0);

    printf("address of foo: %p address of myStruct: %p \n"
        "address of myStruct.pFunc: %p value of myStruct.pFunc: %p \n",
        foo, &myStruct, &myStruct.pFunc, myStruct.pFunc);
```

```
}
```

Output

```
--- Structure Function Fields ---
address of foo: 00007FF70E961113 address of myStruct: 0000009260CFF6F8
address of myStruct.pFunc: 0000009260CFF700 value of myStruct.pFunc: 00007FF70E961113
```

Structure Methods

```
Structure Methods

struct MyStruct
{
      int field;
      PF  pFunc;
      int method (int i);
} myStruct {0, foo};

int MyStruct::method(int i) { return i; }

myStruct.pFunc(0);
myStruct.method(0);
```


C++ introduced structure or class methods. They can be defined either inside the structure definition (next slide) or outside with the structure name qualification.

Classic C++

```
typedef int (*PF)(int);

struct MyStruct
{
    int field;
    PF  pFunc;
    int method(int i);
} myStruct = { 0, foo };

int MyStruct::method(int i)
{
    return i;
}

std::cout << "--- Structure Methods ---" << std::endl;
{
    // std::cout interprets &MyStruct::method as a pointer to member instead (1)
    printf("address of myStruct: %p address of MyStruct::method: %p \n",
        &myStruct, &MyStruct::method);
```

```
    myStruct.pFunc(0);
    myStruct.method(0);
}
```

Output

```
--- Structure Methods ---
address of myStruct: 00007FF795D05000 address of MyStruct::method: 00007FF795CF11FE
```

Structure Methods (Inlined)

Structure Methods (Inlined)

```
struct MyStruct
{
      int field;
      PF  pFunc;
      int method (int i) { return i; }
} myStruct {0, foo};

myStruct.pFunc(0);
myStruct.method(0);
```


This is an alternative way to define short functions, although it exposes users to implementation details.

Classic C++

```
typedef int (*PF)(int);

std::cout << "--- Structure Methods (Inlined) ---" << std::endl;
{
    struct MyStruct
    {
        int field;
        PF  pFunc;
        int method(int i) { return i; }
    } myStruct = { 0, foo };

    // std::cout interprets &MyStruct::method as a pointer to member instead (1)
    printf("address of myStruct: %p address of MyStruct::method: %p \n",
        &myStruct, &MyStruct::method);

    myStruct.pFunc(0);
    myStruct.method(0);
}
```

Output

```
--- Structure Methods (Inlined) ---
address of myStruct: 0000002BC331ED28 address of MyStruct::method: 00007FF795CF4170
```

Structure Methods (Inheritance)

Structure Methods (Inheritance)

```
struct Base
{
      int method (int i) { return i; }
};

struct Derived : Base
{
      int method (int i) { return ++i; }
} myDerived;

myDerived.method(0);
myDerived.Base::method(0);

Base* pMyBase = &myDerived;
pMyBase->method(0);
```


In the case of inheritance, like with fields, the derived structure methods hide methods with the same name in the base type unless explicit base type name qualification is used. However, when we have a pointer to a base type, then the base type method is called even if the actual object belongs to a derived type:

Classic C++

```
std::cout << "--- Structure Methods (Inheritance) ---" << std::endl;
{
    struct Base
    {
        int method(int i)
        {
            std::cout << "Base::method called" << std::endl;
            return i;
        }
    };

    struct Derived : Base
    {
        int method(int i)
        {
            std::cout << "Derived::method called" << std::endl;
            return ++i;
        }
    } myDerived;

    std::cout << "myDerived.method(0): ";
    myDerived.method(0);
```

```
    std::cout << "myDerived.Base::method(0): ";
    myDerived.Base::method(0);

    std::cout << "---" << std::endl;

    Base* pMyBase = &myDerived;
    std::cout << "pMyBase->method(0): ";
    pMyBase->method(0);
}
```

Output

```
--- Structure Methods (Inheritance) ---
myDerived.method(0): Derived::method called
myDerived.Base::method(0): Base::method called
---
pMyBase->method(0): Base::method called
```

Structure Virtual Methods

Structure Virtual Methods

```
struct Base
{
        int method (int i) { return i; }
        virtual int vmethod (int i) { return i; }
};

struct Derived : Base
{
        int method (int i) { return ++i; }
        virtual int vmethod (int i) override { return ++i; }
} myDerived;

Base* pMyBase = &myDerived;
pMyBase->method(0);
pMyBase->vmethod(0);
pMyBase->Base::vmethod(0);
```


This previous slide problem is solved by introducing type-independent call virtual methods. In this case, the method of derived type is called when we have a pointer of a base type to it. The `override` specifier guarantees that we override the correct base method instead of introducing the new one by mistake.

Classic C++

```
std::cout << "--- Structure Virtual Methods ---" << std::endl;
{
    struct Base
    {
        int method(int i)
        {
            std::cout << "Base::method called" << std::endl;
            return i;
        }
```

```
        virtual int vmethod(int i)
        {
            std::cout << "Base::vmethod called" << std::endl;
            return i;
        }
    };

    struct Derived : Base
    {
        int method(int i)
        {
            std::cout << "Derived::method called" << std::endl;
            return ++i;
        }

        virtual int vmethod(int i)
        {
            std::cout << "Derived::vmethod called" << std::endl;
            return ++i;
        }
    } myDerived;

    Base* pMyBase = &myDerived;
    std::cout << "pMyBase->method(0): ";
    pMyBase->method(0);
    std::cout << "pMyBase->vmethod(0): ";
    pMyBase->vmethod(0);
    std::cout << "pMyBase->Base::vmethod(0): ";
    pMyBase->Base::vmethod(0);
}
```

Output

```
--- Structure Virtual Methods ---
pMyBase->method(0): Base::method called
pMyBase->vmethod(0): Derived::vmethod called
pMyBase->Base::vmethod(0): Base::vmethod called
```

Modern C++

```
std::println("--- Structure Virtual Methods ---");
{
    struct Base
    {
        int method(int i)
        {
            std::println("Base::method called");
            return i;
        }

        int method2(int i)
        {
            std::println("Base::method2 called");
            return i;
        }

        virtual int vmethod(int i)
        {
            std::println("Base::vmethod called");
            return i;
        }
```

```
    };

    struct Derived : Base
    {
        int method(int i)
        {
            std::println("Derived::method called");
            return ++i;
        }

        virtual int method2(int i) // override // error
        {
            std::println("Derived::method2 called");
            return i;
        }

        virtual int vmethod(int i) override // overrride is C++11
        {
            std::println("Derived::vmethod called");
            return ++i;
        }
    } myDerived;

    Base* pMyBase = &myDerived;
    std::print("pMyBase->method(0): ");
    pMyBase->method(0);
    std::print("pMyBase->vmethod(0): ");
    pMyBase->vmethod(0);
    std::print("pMyBase->method2(0): ");
    pMyBase->method2(0);
    std::print("pMyBase->Base::vmethod(0): ");
    pMyBase->Base::vmethod(0);
}
```

Output

```
--- Structure Virtual Methods ---
pMyBase->method(0): Base::method called
pMyBase->vmethod(0): Derived::vmethod called
pMyBase->method2(0): Base::method2 called
pMyBase->Base::vmethod(0): Base::vmethod called
```

Structure Pure Virtual Methods

Structure Pure Virtual Methods

```
struct Base
{
        int method (int i) { return i; }
        virtual int vmethod (int i) = 0;
};

struct Derived : Base
{
        int method (int i) { return ++i; }
        virtual int vmethod (int i) override { return ++i; }
} myDerived;

Base* pMyBase = &myDerived;
pMyBase->vmethod(0);
```


If we want to make sure we never define objects of the base type and make sure we override all **pure** virtual methods in the derived type, we can make the virtual function pure by using `= 0`.

Classic C++

```
std::cout << "--- Structure Pure Virtual Methods ---" << std::endl;
{
    struct Base
    {
        int method(int i)
        {
            std::cout << "Base::method called" << std::endl;
            return i;
        }

        virtual int vmethod(int i) = 0;
    };

    struct Derived : Base
    {
        int method(int i)
        {
            std::cout << "Derived::method called" << std::endl;
            return ++i;
        }

        virtual int vmethod(int i)
        {
            std::cout << "Derived::vmethod called" << std::endl;
            return ++i;
        }
    } myDerived;

    // Base base; // error
    Base* pMyBase = &myDerived;
    std::cout << "pMyBase->vmethod(0): ";
```

```
    pMyBase->vmethod(0);
}
```

Modern C++

```
std::println("--- Structure Pure Virtual Methods ---");
{
    struct Base
    {
        int method(int i)
        {
            std::println("Base::method called");
            return i;
        }

        virtual int vmethod(int i) = 0;
    };

    struct Derived : Base
    {
        int method(int i)
        {
            std::println("Derived::method called");
            return ++i;
        }

        virtual int vmethod(int i) override
        {
            std::println("Derived::vmethod called");
            return ++i;
        }
    } myDerived;

    // Base base; // error
    Base* pMyBase = &myDerived;
    std::print("pMyBase->vmethod(0): ");
    pMyBase->vmethod(0);
}
```

Output

```
--- Structure Pure Virtual Methods ---
pMyBase->vmethod(0): Derived::vmethod called
```

Structure as Interface

Structure as Interface

```
struct Interface
{
        virtual int vmethod1 (int i) = 0;
        virtual int vmethod2 (int i) = 0;
};

struct Implementer : Interface
{
        virtual int vmethod1 (int i) override { return ++i; }
        virtual int vmethod2 (int i) override { return ++++i; }

} myObject;

Interface* pIface = &myObject;
pIface->vmethod1(0);
```


Pure virtual functions allow specifying abstract interfaces the derived types have to implement.

Classic C++

```
std::cout << "--- Structure as Interface ---" << std::endl;
{
    struct Interface
    {
        virtual int vmethod1(int i) = 0;
        virtual int vmethod2(int i) = 0;
    };

    struct Implementer : Interface
    {
        virtual int vmethod1(int i)
        {
            std::cout << "Implementer::vmethod1 called" << std::endl;
            return ++i;
        }

        virtual int vmethod2(int i)
        {
            std::cout << "Implementer::vmethod2 called" << std::endl;
            return ++++i;
        }
    } myObject;

    Interface* pIface = &myObject;
    std::cout << "pIface->vmethod1(0): ";
    pIface->vmethod1(0);
}
```

Modern C++

```
std::println("--- Structure as Interface ---");
{
    struct Interface
    {
        virtual int vmethod1(int i) = 0;
        virtual int vmethod2(int i) = 0;
    };

    struct Implementer : Interface
    {
        virtual int vmethod1(int i) override
        {
            std::println("Implementer::vmethod1 called");
            return ++i;
        }

        virtual int vmethod2(int i) override
        {
            std::println("Implementer::vmethod2 called");
            return ++++i;
        }
    } myObject;

    Interface* pIface = &myObject;
    std::print("pIface->vmethod1(0): ");
    pIface->vmethod1(0);
}
```

Output

```
--- Structure as Interface ---
pIface->vmethod1(0): Implementer::vmethod1 called
```

Function Structure

```
Function Structure

struct MyFunction
{
    int field{1};
    int operator()() { return field; }
} myFunction;

myFunction();
```


Functions may also encapsulate state. The best way to do it is via structures that implement function call operators.

Classic C++

```
std::cout << "--- Function Structure ---" << std::endl;
{
    struct MyFunction
    {
        int field;

        int operator()()
        {
            return field;
        }
    } myFunction = { 1 };

    std::cout << "myFunction() return value: " << myFunction() << std::endl;
}
```

Modern C++

```
std::println("--- Function Structure ---");
{
    struct MyFunction
    {
        int field{1};

        int operator()()
        {
            return field;
        }
    } myFunction;
```

```
    std::println("myFunction() return value: {}",
        myFunction());
}
```

Output

```
--- Function Structure ---
myFunction() return value: 1
```

Structure Constructors

Structure Constructors

```
struct MyFunction
{
      MyFunction(): field{1} { }
      MyFunction(int _field): field{_field} { }
      int field;
      int operator()() { return field; }
} myFunction, myFunction2(2);

myFunction();
myFunction2();
```

© 2024 Software Diagnostics Services

Now, we come to traditional OOP topics in classic C++. Constructors are methods with or without arguments for structure initialization with custom initialization logic inside, for example, acquiring required resources.

Classic C++

```
std::cout << "--- Structure Constructors ---" << std::endl;
{
    struct MyFunction
    {
        MyFunction() : field(1)
        {
            std::cout << "MyFunction::MyFunction() called" << std::endl;
        }

        MyFunction(int _field) : field(_field)
        {
            std::cout << "MyFunction::MyFunction(int _field) called" << std::endl;
        }

        int field;

        int operator()()
        {
```

```
            return field;
        }
    } myFunction, myFunction2(2);

    std::cout << "myFunction() return value: " << myFunction() << std::endl;
    std::cout << "myFunction2() return value: " << myFunction2() << std::endl;
}
```

Output

```
--- Structure Constructors ---
MyFunction::MyFunction() called
MyFunction::MyFunction(int _field) called
myFunction() return value: 1
myFunction2() return value: 2
```

Structure Converting Constructors

Structure Converting Constructors

```
struct MyFunction
{
    MyFunction(): field{1} { }
    explicit MyFunction(int _field):
                field{_field} { }
    MyFunction(bool flag): field(flag) { }
    int field;
    int operator()() { return field; }
};

MyFunction myFunction = false;
MyFunction myFunction2 = 2;
MyFunction myFunction3(3);
```

© 2024 Software Diagnostics Services

Constructors with one parameter are called converting constructors. If you don't want them to be called inadvertently during assignments, you can mark them `explicit` to be only called in their constructor form.

Classic C++

```
std::cout << "--- Structure Converting Constructors ---" << std::endl;
{
    struct MyFunction
    {
        MyFunction() : field(1)
        {
            std::cout << "MyFunction::MyFunction() called" << std::endl;
        }

        explicit MyFunction(int _field) : field(_field)
        {
            std::cout << "MyFunction::MyFunction(int _field) called" << std::endl;
        }
```

```
        MyFunction(bool flag) : field(flag)
        {
            std::cout << "MyFunction::MyFunction(bool flag) called" << std::endl;
        }

        int field;

        int operator()()
        {
            return field;
        }
    };

    MyFunction myFunction = false;
    std::cout << "myFunction() return value: " << myFunction() << std::endl;

    MyFunction myFunction2 = 2; // truncation to bool warning
    std::cout << "myFunction2() return value: " << myFunction2() << std::endl;

    MyFunction myFunction3(3);
    std::cout << "myFunction3() return value: " << myFunction3() << std::endl;
}
```

Output

```
--- Structure Converting Constructors ---
MyFunction::MyFunction(bool flag) called
myFunction() return value: 0
MyFunction::MyFunction(bool flag) called
myFunction2() return value: 1
MyFunction::MyFunction(int _field) called
myFunction3() return value: 3
```

Structure Delegating Constructors

Structure Delegating Constructors

```
struct MyFunction
{
    MyFunction(): MyFunction(1) { }
    MyFunction(int _field): MyFunction(_field, 0) { }
    MyFunction(int _field, int _field2):
        field{_field}, field2{_field2} { }
    int field;
    int field2;
    int operator()() { return field; }
};

MyFunction myFunction;
MyFunction myFunction2(2);
MyFunction myFunction3(3, 3);
```


We can reduce error-prone duplicate initialization code in constructors by delegating such activity to other constuctors.

Modern C++

```
std::println("--- Structure Delegating Constructors ---");
{
    struct MyFunction
    {
        MyFunction() : MyFunction(1)
        {
            std::println("MyFunction::MyFunction() called");
        }

        MyFunction(int _field) : MyFunction(_field, 0)
        {
            std::println("MyFunction::MyFunction(int _field) called");
        }

        MyFunction(int _field, int _field2) : field{_field}, field2{_field2}
        {
            std::println("MyFunction::MyFunction(int _field, int _field2) called");
        }

        int field;
        int field2;

        int operator()()
        {
            return field;
        }
    };

    MyFunction myFunction;
    std::println("myFunction() return value: {}",
        myFunction());

    MyFunction myFunction2(2);
    std::println("myFunction2() return value: {}",
        myFunction2());

    MyFunction myFunction3(3, 3);
    std::println("myFunction3() return value: {}",
        myFunction3());
}
```

Output

```
--- Structure Delegating Constructors ---
MyFunction::MyFunction(int _field, int _field2) called
MyFunction::MyFunction(int _field) called
MyFunction::MyFunction() called
myFunction() return value: 1
MyFunction::MyFunction(int _field, int _field2) called
MyFunction::MyFunction(int _field) called
myFunction2() return value: 2
MyFunction::MyFunction(int _field, int _field2) called
myFunction3() return value: 3
```

Structure Member Initialization

Structure Member Initialization

```
struct MyFunction
{
      MyFunction():
            index(0), field(++index), field2(++index)

      int index;  // 0
      int field2; // 1
      int field;  // 2

      int operator()() { return field; }
} myFunction;

assert(1 == myFunction());
```


Structure fields are initialized in the order of their definition in the structure definition body, not in the order of their initialization in the constructor.

Classic C++

```
std::cout << "--- Structure Member Initialization ---" << std::endl;
{
    struct MyFunction
    {
        MyFunction() : index(0), field(++index), field2(++index)
        {
            std::cout << "MyFunction::MyFunction() called" << std::endl;
        }

        int index;
        int field2;
        int field;

        int operator()()
        {
            return field;
        }
    } myFunction;

    std::cout << "myFunction() return value: " << myFunction() << std::endl;

    // assert(1 == myFunction()); // fails
}
```

Output

```
--- Structure Member Initialization ---
MyFunction::MyFunction() called
myFunction() return value: 2
```

Structure Copy Constructor

Structure Copy Constructor

```
struct MyFunction
{
      MyFunction(): field{1} { }
      MyFunction(int _field): field{_field} { }
      MyFunction(const MyFunction& src):
            field{src.field} { }
      int field;
      int operator()() { return field; }
} myFunction;

MyFunction myFunction2(myFunction);
MyFunction myFunction3 = myFunction;
```


When we copy objects but need complex copying logic or nontrivial memory management copy constructor methods are quite handy. We pass the source object reference as const if we don't plan to modify it.

Classic C++

```
std::cout << "--- Structure Copy Constructor ---" << std::endl;
{
    struct MyFunction
    {
        MyFunction() : field(1) { }
        MyFunction(int _field) : field(_field) { }
        MyFunction(const MyFunction& src) : field(src.field)
        {
            std::cout << "MyFunction(const MyFunction& src) called" << std::endl;
        }

        int field;

        int operator()()
        {
            return field;
        }
    } myFunction;

    MyFunction myFunction2(myFunction);
    MyFunction myFunction3 = myFunction;
}
```

Output

```
--- Structure Copy Constructor ---
MyFunction(const MyFunction& src) called
MyFunction(const MyFunction& src) called
```

Copy vs. Move Semantics

Copy vs. Move Semantics

- Copy leaves source unaffected
- Move resets the source to its default state

Example: a valid pointer → nullptr

The main difference between copy and move semantics is that moves reset sources to their default value, for example, to `nullptr` in case of pointer fields or default-initialized integer fields.

Structure Move Constructors

Structure Move Constructors

```
struct MyFunction
{
       MyFunction(): field{1} { }
       MyFunction(int _field): field{_field} { }
       MyFunction(const MyFunction& src):
             field{src.field} { }
       MyFunction(MyFunction&& src):
             field{src.field} { src.field = 1; }
       int field;
       int operator()() { field; }
} myFunction;

myFunction();
MyFunction myFunction2(std::move(myFunction));
MyFunction myFunction3 = std::move(myFunction2);
```


We use move constructors when we don't want to copy the structure contents but move its values to another location. Such constructors reset source fields to their default values.

Modern C++

```
std::println("--- Structure Move Constructors ---");
{
    struct MyFunction
    {
        MyFunction() : field{1} { }
        MyFunction(int _field) : field{_field} { }
        MyFunction(const MyFunction& src) : field{src.field} { }
        MyFunction(MyFunction&& src) noexcept : field{src.field}
        {
            std::println("MyFunction(MyFunction&& src) called");
            src.field = 1;
        }

        int field;

        void use() { ++field; }
        int operator()() { return field; }
    } myFunction;

    myFunction.use();
    std::println("myFunction() return value: {}",
        myFunction());

    MyFunction myFunction2(std::move(myFunction));
    std::println("myFunction() return value: {}",
        myFunction());
    std::println("myFunction2() return value: {}",
        myFunction2());

    MyFunction myFunction3 = std::move(myFunction2);
    std::println("myFunction2() return value: {}",
        myFunction2());
    std::println("myFunction3() return value: {}",
        myFunction3());
}
```

Output

```
--- Structure Move Constructors ---
myFunction() return value: 2
MyFunction(MyFunction&& src) called
myFunction() return value: 1
myFunction2() return value: 2
MyFunction(MyFunction&& src) called
myFunction2() return value: 1
myFunction3() return value: 2
```

Structure Copy Assignment

Structure Copy Assignment

```
struct MyFunction
{
      MyFunction(): field{1} { }
      MyFunction(int _field): field{_field} { }
      MyFunction(const MyFunction& src):
            field{src.field} { }
      // ...
      MyFunction& operator=(const MyFunction& src)
            { if (this != &src) { field = src.field; }
              return *this; }
      int field;
      int operator()() { return field; }
} myFunction;

MyFunction myFunction2;
myFunction2 = myFunction;
```


In the case of nontrivial assignments, we can implement an assignment operator. We, however, should be careful not to copy to itself (`this`), and we return the non-const reference to itself (`*this`) to allow chained copies.

Classic C++

```
std::cout << "--- Structure Copy Assignment ---" << std::endl;
{
    struct MyFunction
    {
        MyFunction() : field(1) { }
        MyFunction(int _field) : field(_field) { }
        MyFunction(const MyFunction& src) : field(src.field) { }
        MyFunction& operator=(const MyFunction& src)
        {
            if (this != &src)
            {
                std::cout << "MyFunction& operator=(const MyFunction& src) called" << std::endl;
                field = src.field;
            }
            return *this;
        }

        int field;

        void use() { ++field; }
        int operator()() { return field; }
    } myFunction;

    myFunction.use();
    std::cout << "myFunction() return value: " << myFunction() << std::endl;

    MyFunction myFunction2;
    std::cout << "myFunction2() return value: " << myFunction2() << std::endl;

    myFunction2 = myFunction;
    std::cout << "myFunction2() return value: " << myFunction2() << std::endl;
```

```
    MyFunction myFunction3;

    myFunction3 = myFunction2 = myFunction;
}
```

Output

```
--- Structure Copy Assignment ---
myFunction() return value: 2
myFunction2() return value: 1
MyFunction& operator=(const MyFunction& src) called
myFunction2() return value: 2
MyFunction& operator=(const MyFunction& src) called
MyFunction& operator=(const MyFunction& src) called
```

Structure Move Assignment

Structure Move Assignment

```
struct MyFunction
{
        MyFunction(): field{1} { }
        // ...
        MyFunction& operator=(const MyFunction& src)
              { if (this != &src) { field = src.field; }
                return *this; }
        MyFunction& operator=(MyFunction&& src)
              { if (this != &src)
                   { field = src.field; src.field = 1; }
                return *this; }
        int field;
        int operator()() { return field; }
} myFunction;

MyFunction myFunction2;
myFunction2 = std::move(myFunction);
```


If we want to move the structure contents instead of copying, we can implement the move assignment operator. However, we should be careful not to move to itself in the case of non-trivial semantics.

Modern C++

```
std::println("--- Structure Move Assignment ---");
{
    struct MyFunction
    {
        MyFunction() : field{1} { }
        MyFunction(int _field) : field{_field} { }
        MyFunction(const MyFunction& src) : field{src.field} { }
        MyFunction(MyFunction&& src) noexcept : field{src.field}
        {
            std::println("MyFunction(MyFunction&& src) called");
```

```
            src.field = 1;
        }
        MyFunction& operator=(const MyFunction& src)
        {
            std::println("MyFunction& operator=(const MyFunction& src) called");
            if (this != &src)
            {
                field = src.field;
            }
            return *this;
        }
        MyFunction& operator=(MyFunction&& src) noexcept
        {
            if (this != &src)
            {
                std::println("MyFunction& operator=(MyFunction&& src) called");
                field = src.field;
                src.field = 1;
            }
            return *this;
        }

        int field;

        void use() { ++field; }
        int operator()() { return field; }
    } myFunction;

    myFunction.use();
    std::println("myFunction() return value: {}",
        myFunction());

    MyFunction myFunction2;
    myFunction2 = std::move(myFunction);
    std::println("myFunction() return value: {}",
        myFunction());
    std::println("myFunction2() return value: {}",
        myFunction2());

    MyFunction myFunction3;

    myFunction3 = std::move(myFunction2) = std::move(myFunction);
}
```

Output

```
--- Structure Move Assignment ---
myFunction() return value: 2
MyFunction& operator=(MyFunction&& src) called
myFunction() return value: 1
myFunction2() return value: 2
MyFunction& operator=(MyFunction&& src) called
MyFunction& operator=(const MyFunction& src) called
```

Structure Destructor

Structure Destructor

```
struct MyFunction
{
        MyFunction(): field{1} { }
        ~MyFunction() { /* close resources */ }
        MyFunction(int _field): field{_field} { }
        MyFunction(const MyFunction& src):
              field(src.field) { field; }
        MyFunction& operator=(const MyFunction& src)
              { if (this != &src) { field = src.field; }
                return *this; }
        // ...
        int field;
        int operator()() { return field; }
};

{ MyFunction myFunction; }
```


What if we want some complex logic, for example, releasing resources when the local object goes out of scope, or we delete it? Destructor is a method that is called automatically in such a case.

Classic C++

```
std::cout << "--- Structure Destructor ---" << std::endl;
{
    struct MyFunction
    {
        MyFunction() : field(1) { }
        ~MyFunction()
        {
            std::cout << "~MyFunction() called" << std::endl;
        }
        MyFunction(int _field) : field(_field) { }
        MyFunction(const MyFunction& src) : field(src.field) { }
        MyFunction& operator=(const MyFunction& src)
        {
            if (this != &src)
            {
                std::cout << "MyFunction& operator=(const MyFunction& src) called" << std::endl;
                field = src.field;
            }
            return *this;
        }

        int field;

        void use() { ++field; }
        int operator()() { return field; }
    };

    {
        std::cout << "Before inner scope" << std::endl;
        {
            MyFunction myFunction;
```

```
        }
        std::cout << "After inner scope" << std::endl;
    }
}
```

Output

```
--- Structure Destructor ---
Before inner scope
~MyFunction() called
After inner scope
```

Structure Destructor Hierarchy

Conceptually, destructors are just like a normal method, so the wrong one may be called when we have a pointer of base type to an object of a derived type.

Classic C++

```
std::cout << "--- Structure Destructor Hierarchy ---" << std::endl;
{
    struct IFunction
    {
        ~IFunction()
        {
            std::cout << "IFunction::~IFunction() called" << std::endl;
        }
        virtual int operator()() = 0;
    };

    struct MyFunction : IFunction
    {
        ~MyFunction()
        {
```

```
            std::cout << "MyFunction::~MyFunction() called" << std::endl;
        }

        int field;

        int operator()() { return field; }
    };

    IFunction* pIFunction = new MyFunction;
    pIFunction->operator()();
    (*pIFunction)();
    delete pIFunction; // ~IFunction()

    MyFunction* pMyFunction = new MyFunction;
    pMyFunction->operator()();
    (*pMyFunction)();
    delete pMyFunction; // ~MyFunction(), ~IFunction()
}
```

Output

```
--- Structure Destructor Hierarchy ---
IFunction::~IFunction() called
MyFunction::~MyFunction() called
IFunction::~IFunction() called
```

Structure Virtual Destructor

Structure Virtual Destructor

```
struct IFunction
{
        virtual ~IFunction() { }
        virtual int operator()() = 0;
};

struct MyFunction : IFunction
{
        ~MyFunction() override { /* close resources */ }
        int field;
        int operator()() override { return field; }
};

IFunction* pIFunction = new MyFunction;
pIFunction->operator()();
(*pIFunction)();
delete pIFunction; // ~MyFunction()
```


To make sure that the correct destructors are called, it is recommended to make them virtual too.

Classic C++

```
std::cout << "--- Structure Virtual Destructor ---" << std::endl;
{
    struct IFunction
    {
        virtual ~IFunction()
        {
            std::cout << "IFunction::~IFunction() called" << std::endl;
        }
        virtual int operator()() = 0;
    };

    struct MyFunction : IFunction
    {
        ~MyFunction()
        {
            std::cout << "MyFunction::~MyFunction() called" << std::endl;
        }

        int field;

        int operator()() { return field; }
    };

    IFunction* pIFunction = new MyFunction;
    pIFunction->operator()();
    (*pIFunction)();
    delete pIFunction; // ~MyFunction()
}
```

Output

```
--- Structure Virtual Destructor ---
MyFunction::~MyFunction() called
IFunction::~IFunction() called
```

Structure Member Destruction

Structure members are destructed in the opposite order of their initialization.

Classic C++

```
std::cout << "--- Structure Member Destruction ---" << std::endl;
{
    struct MyFunction
    {
        MyFunction() : field(1) { }
        ~MyFunction()
        {
            std::cout << "~MyFunction() called. Value of field: " << field << std::endl;
        }
        MyFunction(int _field) : field(_field) { }
        MyFunction(const MyFunction& src) : field(src.field) { }
        MyFunction& operator=(const MyFunction& src)
        {
            if (this != &src)
            {
                std::cout << "MyFunction& operator=(const MyFunction& src) called" << std::endl;
                field = src.field;
            }
            return *this;
        }

        int field;

        void use() { ++field; }
        int operator()() { return field; }
    };

    struct MyFunctionContainer
    {
        MyFunctionContainer() : myFunction1(1), myFunction2(2), myFunction3(3) { }
```

```
        MyFunction myFunction1;
        MyFunction myFunction2;
        MyFunction myFunction3;
    } myFunctionContainer;
}
```

Output

```
--- Structure Destructor Hierarchy ---
~MyFunction() called. Value of field: 3
~MyFunction() called. Value of field: 2
~MyFunction() called. Value of field: 1
```

Destructor as a Method

Destructor as a Method

```
struct Resource
{
        Resource() { /* acquire */ }
        ~Resource() { /* release */ }
private:
        int m_hData;
};

char buf[sizeof(Resource)];
Resource* pResource = new(buf) Resource();
// ...
pResource->~Resource();
```


Since a destructor is also a method, it is possible to call it directly in cases where we should not use standard delete methods, for example, when objects are allocated using placement **new**:

Classic C++

```
std::cout << "--- Destructor as a Method ---" << std::endl;
{
    struct Resource
    {
        Resource() : m_hData(0x1234)
        {
            std::cout << "Resource() called" << std::endl;
        }
        ~Resource()
        {
            std::cout << "~Resource() called" << std::endl;
```

```
        }
    private:
        int m_hData;
    };

    char buf[sizeof(Resource)];
    Resource* pResource = new(buf) Resource();
    // ...
    pResource->~Resource();
}
```

Output

```
--- Destructor as a Method ---
Resource() called
~Resource() called
```

Structure Default Operations

If you define certain operations, you must define others as well. You can define their default implementation instead of writing the default code yourself.

Modern C++

```
std::println("--- Structure Default Operations ---");
{
    struct MyFunction
    {
        MyFunction(int _field) { }
        MyFunction(MyFunction&& src) noexcept : field{src.field}
        {
            std::println("MyFunction(MyFunction&& src) called");
            src.field = 1;
```

```
        }

        MyFunction() = default;
        MyFunction& operator=(const MyFunction& src) = default;
        ~MyFunction() = default;

        int field{1};

        void use() { ++field; }
        int operator()() { return field; }
    };

    MyFunction myFunction, myFunction2;
    myFunction.use();
    std::println("myFunction() return value: {}",
        myFunction());
    myFunction2 = myFunction;
    std::println("myFunction2() return value: {}",
        myFunction2());
}
```

Output

```
--- Structure Default Operations ---
myFunction() return value: 2
myFunction2() return value: 2
```

Structure Deleted Operations

Structure Deleted Operations

```
struct MyFunction
{
        MyFunction() { }

        ~MyFunction() = delete;

        int field{1};

        void cleanup() { /* do cleanup */ }
};

MyFunction myFunction;
MyFunction* myFunction = new MyFunction;
delete myFunction;
myFunction->cleanup();
```


If you want to prevent behavior, for example, the ability to create objects on the stack, you can delete the destructor from the set of available operations.

Modern C++

```
std::println("--- Structure Deleted Operations ---");
{
    struct MyFunction
    {
        MyFunction()
        {
            std::println("MyFunction() called");
        }

        ~MyFunction() = delete;

        int field{1};

        void cleanup()
        {
            std::println("cleanup() called");
        };
    };

    // MyFunction myFunction; // error

    MyFunction* myFunction = new MyFunction;

    // delete myFunction; // error

    myFunction->cleanup();
}
```

Output

```
--- Structure Deleted Operations ---
MyFunction() called
cleanup() called
```

Conversion Operators

Conversion Operators

```
struct A
{
        unsigned int u1;
        unsigned int u2;
};

struct B
{
        unsigned long long ull;
        operator A()
        {
           return A
              {
                 static_cast<unsigned int>(ull & 0xFFFFFFFF),
                 static_cast<unsigned int>(ull >> 32)
              };
        }
} b;

A a = b;
```


Destinations for copy constructors and copy assignment operators are of the same type. What if we want to assign to a different structure type? We can define custom conversion operators (it is also possible to use a "conversion" constructor).

Classic C++

```
std::cout << "--- Conversion Operators ---" << std::endl;
{
    struct A
    {
        A(unsigned int _u1, unsigned int _u2) :
            u1(_u1), u2(_u2) { }

        A(const A& src) : u1(src.u1), u2(src.u2)
        {
            std::cout << "A(const A& src) called" << std::endl;
        }

        unsigned int u1;
        unsigned int u2;
    };

    struct B
    {
        unsigned long long ull;

        operator A()
        {
            std::cout << "operator A() called" << std::endl;

            return A
            (
                static_cast<unsigned int>(ull & 0xFFFFFFFF),
                static_cast<unsigned int>(ull >> 32)
            );
        }
    } b = { 0x0123456789abcdef };
```

```
    std::cout << "value of b: " << std::hex << b.ull << std::endl;

    A a = b; // no copy constructor is called

    std::cout << "value of a: { " << std::hex << a.u1 << ", " << a.u2 << " }" << std::endl;
}
```

Output

```
--- Conversion Operators ---
value of b: 123456789abcdef
operator A() called
value of a: { 89abcdef, 1234567 }
```

Parameters by Value

Parameters by Value

- Original value doesn't change
- Inefficient/efficient (basic types)
- Slicing (passing derived as base)
- Copy constructor/destructor

```
void func(MyStruct ms)
{ ms.field = 0; }

func(myStruct);
```

```
void func(int i)
{ i = 0; }

func(1);
```


When we pass parameters by values, any modifications inside functions are lost once we return. Passing basic types by value is efficient, but passing structures are not unless they are very simple: various functions may be called, for example, copy constructors and destructors unless optimized by a compiler. There is also a possibility of slicing when inheritance is used.

C

```
void func(int i)
{
    printf("func: address of i: %p value of i: %x \n", &i, i);

    i = 0;
}

struct MyStruct
{
    int field;
};
```

```
void func2(struct MyStruct ms)
{
    printf("func2: address of ms: %p value of ms.field: %x \n", &ms, ms.field);

    ms.field = 0;

    printf("func2: value of ms.field: %x \n", ms.field);
}

puts("--- Parameters by Value ---");
{
    func(1);

    struct MyStruct ms = { 1 };

    printf("main: address of ms: %p value of ms.field: %x \n", &ms, ms.field);

    func2(ms);

    printf("main: address of ms: %p value of ms.field: %x \n", &ms, ms.field);
}
```

C++ as a better C

```
void func(int i)
{
    printf("func: address of i: %p value of i: %x \n", &i, i);

    i = 0;
}

struct MyStruct
{
    int field;
};

void func2(MyStruct ms)
{
    printf("func2: address of ms: %p value of ms.field: %x \n", &ms, ms.field);

    ms.field = 0;

    printf("func2: value of ms.field: %x \n", ms.field);
}

puts("--- Parameters by Value ---");
{
    func(1);

    MyStruct ms = { 1 }; // struct keyword can be omitted

    printf("main: address of ms: %p value of ms.field: %x \n", &ms, ms.field);

    func2(ms);

    printf("main: address of ms: %p value of ms.field: %x \n", &ms, ms.field);
}
```

Output

```
--- Parameters by Value ---
func: address of i: 0000009260CFF680 value of i: 1
main: address of ms: 0000009260CFF724 value of ms.field: 1
func2: address of ms: 0000009260CFF680 value of ms.field: 1
func2: value of ms.field: 0
main: address of ms: 0000009260CFF724 value of ms.field: 1
```

Parameters by Pointer/Reference

Parameters by Pointer/Reference

- Original value may change
- Efficient/inefficient (basic types)
- Pointer/reference is passed by value
- Pointer by pointer (by pointer)

```
void func(MyStruct* pms)
{ pms->field = 0; }

func(&myStruct);
```

```
void func(int& ri)
{ ri = 0; }

int i{1};
func(i);
```


If we want efficiency for structures and also preserve changes to original values, we need to pass by reference. Again, this may be inefficient for basic types.

C

```
struct MyStruct
{
    int field;
};

void func3(struct MyStruct* pms)
{
    printf("func3: address of pms: %p value of pms: %p value of pms->field: %x \n", &pms, pms, pms-
>field);

    pms->field = 0;

    printf("func3: value of pms->field: %x \n", pms->field);
}
```

```
puts("--- Parameters by Pointer ---");
{
    struct MyStruct ms = { 1 };

    printf("main: address of ms: %p value of ms.field: %x \n", &ms, ms.field);

    func3(&ms);

    printf("main: address of ms: %p value of ms.field: %x \n", &ms, ms.field);
}
```

C++ as a better C

```
struct MyStruct
{
    int field;
};

void func3(MyStruct* pms)
{
    printf("func3: address of pms: %p value of pms: %p value of pms->field: %x \n", &pms, pms, pms-
>field);

    pms->field = 0;

    printf("func3: value of pms->field: %x \n", pms->field);
}

puts("--- Parameters by Pointer ---");
{
    MyStruct ms = { 1 };

    printf("main: address of ms: %p value of ms.field: %x \n", &ms, ms.field);

    func3(&ms);

    printf("main: address of ms: %p value of ms.field: %x \n", &ms, ms.field);
}
```

Output

```
--- Parameters by Pointer ---
main: address of ms: 0000009260CFF744 value of ms.field: 1
func3: address of pms: 0000009260CFF680 value of pms: 0000009260CFF744 value of pms->field: 1
func3: value of pms->field: 0
main: address of ms: 0000009260CFF744 value of ms.field: 0
```

Classic C++

```
void func4(int& ri)
{
    std::cout << "func4: address of ri: " << &ri << " value of ri: " << ri << std::endl;

    ri = 0;

    std::cout << "func4: value of ri: " << ri << std::endl;
}

std::cout << "--- Parameters by Reference ---" << std::endl;
{
    int i = 1;
```

```
    std::cout << "main: address of i: " << &i << " value of i: " << i << std::endl;

    func4(i);

    std::cout << "main: value of i: " << i << std::endl;
}
```

Output

```
--- Parameters by Reference ---
main: address of i: 0000002BC331F114 value of i: 1
func4: address of ri: 0000002BC331F114 value of ri: 1
func4: value of ri: 0
main: value of i: 0
```

Parameters by Ptr/Ref to Const

Parameters by Ptr/Ref to const

- Original value doesn't change
- Efficient/inefficient (basic types)
- Pointer/reference is passed by value
- Can pass temporary values and constants

```
void func(const MyStruct* pms)
{ pms->field = 0; }

func(&myStruct);
```

```
void func(const int& ri)
{ ri = 0; }

func(1);
```


If we only want efficiency for structures, we need to pass by reference to `const`. In such a case, we also cannot modify the original values.

C

```
struct MyStruct
{
    int field;
};

void func5(const struct MyStruct* pms)
{
    printf("func5: address of pms: %p value of pms: %p value of pms->field: %x \n", &pms, pms, pms->field);

    // pms->field = 0; error
```

```
}

puts("--- Parameters by Ptr to const ---");
{
    struct MyStruct ms = { 1 };

    printf("main: address of ms: %p value of ms.field: %x \n", &ms, ms.field);

    func5(&ms);

    printf("main: address of ms: %p value of ms.field: %x \n", &ms, ms.field);
}
```

C++ as a better C

```
struct MyStruct
{
    int field;
};
void func5(const MyStruct* pms)
{
    printf("func5: address of pms: %p value of pms: %p value of pms->field: %x \n", &pms, pms, pms->field);

    // pms->field = 0; error
}
puts("--- Parameters by Ptr to const ---");
{
    MyStruct ms = { 1 };

    printf("main: address of ms: %p value of ms.field: %x \n", &ms, ms.field);

    func5(&ms);

    printf("main: address of ms: %p value of ms.field: %x \n", &ms, ms.field);
}
```

Output

```
--- Parameters by Ptr to const ---
main: address of ms: 0000009260CFF764 value of ms.field: 1
func5: address of pms: 0000009260CFF680 value of pms: 0000009260CFF764 value of pms->field: 1
main: address of ms: 0000009260CFF764 value of ms.field: 1
```

Classic C++

```
void func6(const int& ri)
{
    std::cout << "func6: address of ri: " << &ri << " value of ri: " << ri << std::endl;

    // ri = 0; // error
}

std::cout << "--- Parameters by Ref to const ---" << std::endl;
{
    func6(1);
}
```

Output

```
--- Parameters by Ref to const ---
func6: address of ri: 0000002BC331F5B4 value of ri: 1
```

Parameters by Ref to Rvalue

Parameters by Ref to Rvalue

- For temporary values and constants
- You can change values inside the function

```
void func(int&& ri)
{ ri = 0; }

func(1);
```


Modern C++ added the possibility to explicitly pass references to temporary values. Since inside the function the values they refer to are backed by memory you can freely change the values inside the function.

Modern C++

```
void func7(int&& ri)
{
    std::println("func7: address of ri: {:016X} value of ri: {}",
        reinterpret_cast<uintptr_t>(&ri), ri);

    ri = 0;

    std::println("func7: value of ri: {}", ri);
}

std::println("--- Parameters by Ref to Rvalue ---");
{
    func7(1);
}
```

Output

```
--- Parameters by Ref to Rvalue ---
func7: address of ri: 000000776CBBF654 value of ri: 1
func7: value of ri: 0
```

Possible Mistake

Possible Mistake

- Original value doesn't change …
- … but you want to make sure
- You used languages with implicit references
- You should use const& instead

```
void func(const MyStruct ms)
{ ms.field = 0; }

func(myStruct);
```

```
void func(const MyStruct& ms)
{ ms.field = 0; }

func(myStruct);
```

© 2024 Software Diagnostics Services

Function Overloading

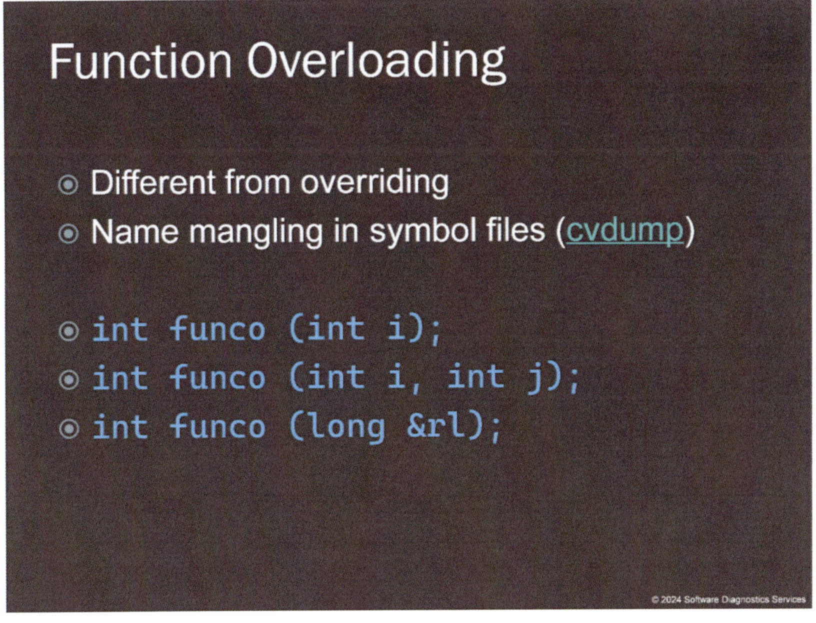

Function overloading allows reusing the same function names for functions with different numbers and types of parameters.

cvdump
https://github.com/microsoft/microsoft-pdb

Default Arguments

Default Arguments

- Help avoid overloading

- int funco (int i); // j == 0
- int funco (int i, int j);

- int funco (int i, int j = 0);

Default function arguments may help in avoiding the proliferation of overloaded functions.

Classic C++

```
int funco(int i, int j = 0)
{
    std::cout << "value of i: " << i << " value of j: " << j << std::endl;

    return i + j;
}

std::cout << "--- Default Arguments ---" << std::endl;
{
    funco(1);
    funco(1, 2);
}
```

Output

```
--- Default Arguments ---
value of i: 1 value of j: 0
value of i: 1 value of j: 2
```

Variadic Functions

Variadic Functions

- int varfunc (int numargs, ...);
- varfunc (3, 1.0, 2.0, 3.0);
- varfunc (4, 1.0, 2.0, 3.0, 4.0);
- varfunc (3, 1.0, 2.0, 3);

Variadic functions have a variable number of parameters. But they have undefined behavior when the number of the remaining parameters does not match the value for the number of arguments and their types are different.

C C++ as a better C

```
puts("--- Variadic Functions ---");
{
    printf("product: %f \n", varfunc(3, 1.0, 2.0, 3.0));

    assert(6.0 == varfunc(3, 1.0, 2.0, 3.0));

    printf("product: %f \n", varfunc(5, 1.0, 2.0, 3.0, 4.0));

    // assert(24.0 == varfunc(5, 1.0, 2.0, 3.0, 4.0)); // fails

    printf("product: %f \n", varfunc(3, 1.0, 2.0, 3));

    // assert(6.0 == varfunc(3, 1.0, 2.0, 3)); // fails
}
```

Output

```
--- Variadic Functions ---
product: 6.000000
product: 0.000000
product: 0.000000
```

Immutable Objects

Immutable Objects

```
struct MyStruct
{
      MyStruct(int _field) : field{_field} { }
      int  get() const { return field; }
      void set(int newval) { field = newval; }
private:
      int field;
} myStruct(1);

const MyStruct& myCStruct{myStruct};

myCStruct.get();

myCStruct.set(2);
```


If you have `const` objects, you are only allowed to call methods that have the `const` specifier in their definition.

Classic C++

```
std::cout << "--- Immutable Objects ---" << std::endl;
{
    struct MyStruct
    {
        MyStruct(int _field) : field(_field) { }
        int  get() const { return field; }
        void set(int newval) { field = newval; }
    private:
        int field;
    } myStruct(1);

    const MyStruct& myCStruct{ myStruct };

    myCStruct.get();

    // myCStruct.set(2); // error
}
```

Static Structure Functions

Static structure functions are only allowed to access static structure fields shared among objects.

Classic C++

```
// multithreading issues are ignored here
struct MyStructS
{
    MyStructS(int _field) : field(_field) { ++count; }
    int  get() const { return field; }
    void set(int newval) { field = newval; }
    static auto get_count()
    {
        // field++; error
        return count;
    };
private:
    int field;
    static unsigned count;
};

unsigned MyStructS::count = 0;

std::cout << "--- Static Structure Functions ---" << std::endl;
{
    MyStructS myStruct1(1), myStruct2(2);

    std::cout << "count of objects: " << MyStructS::get_count() << std::endl;

    assert(myStruct1.get_count() == myStruct2.get_count());
}
```

Output

```
--- Static Structure Functions ---
count of objects: 2
```

Lambdas

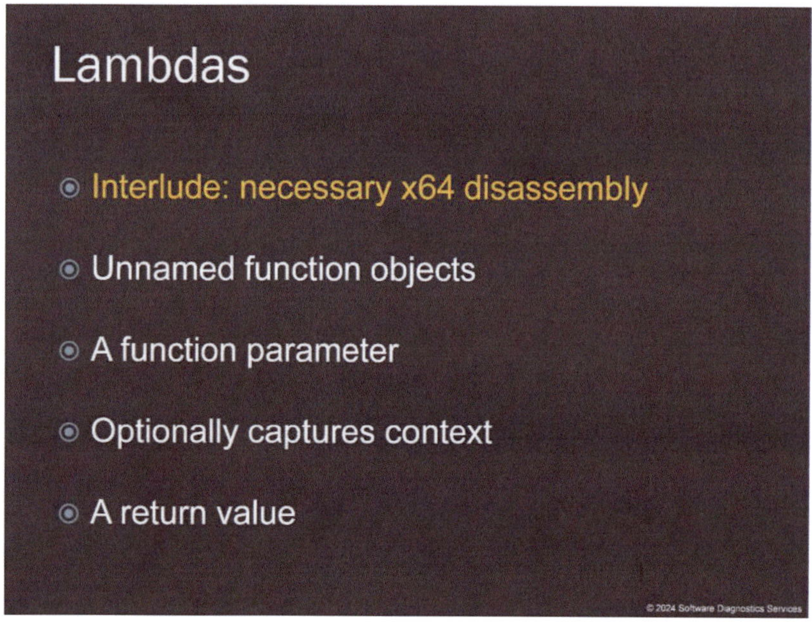

Before discussing lambdas introduced in C++11 and their internals, we take a brief tour around basic x64 disassembly.

x64 CPU Registers

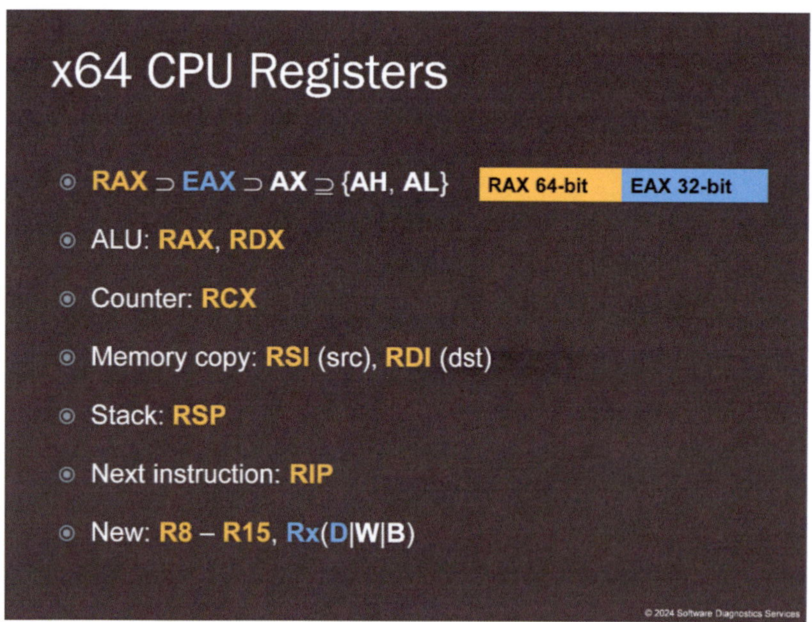

There are familiar 32-bit CPU register names, such as **EAX,** that are extended to 64-bit names, such as **RAX**. Most of them are traditionally specialized, such as ALU, counter, and memory copy registers. Although, now they all can be used as general-purpose registers. There is, of course, a stack pointer, **RSP**, and it also takes the role of a frame pointer, which is also used to address local variables and saved parameters. It can be used for stack reconstruction. In Microsoft compiler code generation implementtations, **RBP** is also used as a general-purpose register. An instruction pointer **RIP** is saved in the stack memory region with every function call, then restored on return from the called function. In addition, the x64 platform features another eight general-purpose registers, from **R8** to **R15**.

Instructions and Registers

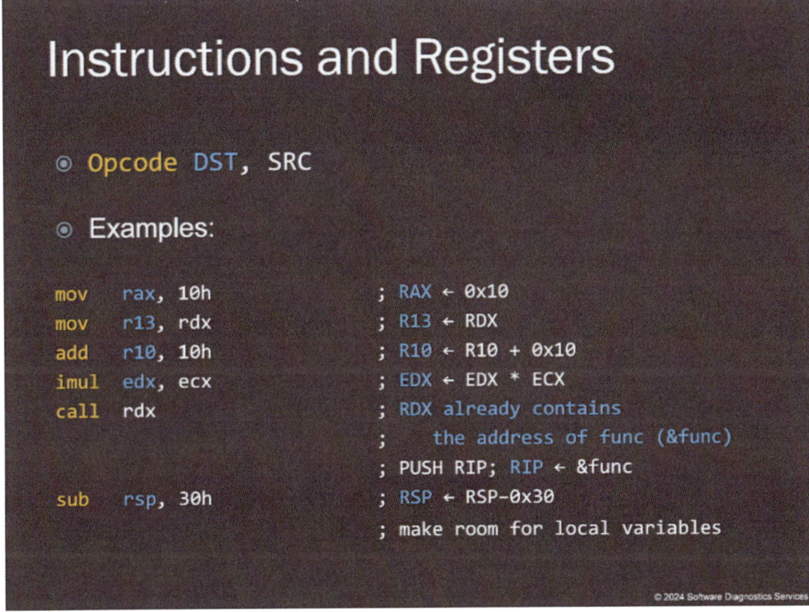

This slide shows a few examples of CPU instructions involving operations with registers, such as moving a value and doing arithmetic. The direction of operands is opposite to the AT&T x64 disassembly flavor if you are accustomed to default GDB disassembly on Linux.

Memory and Stack Addressing

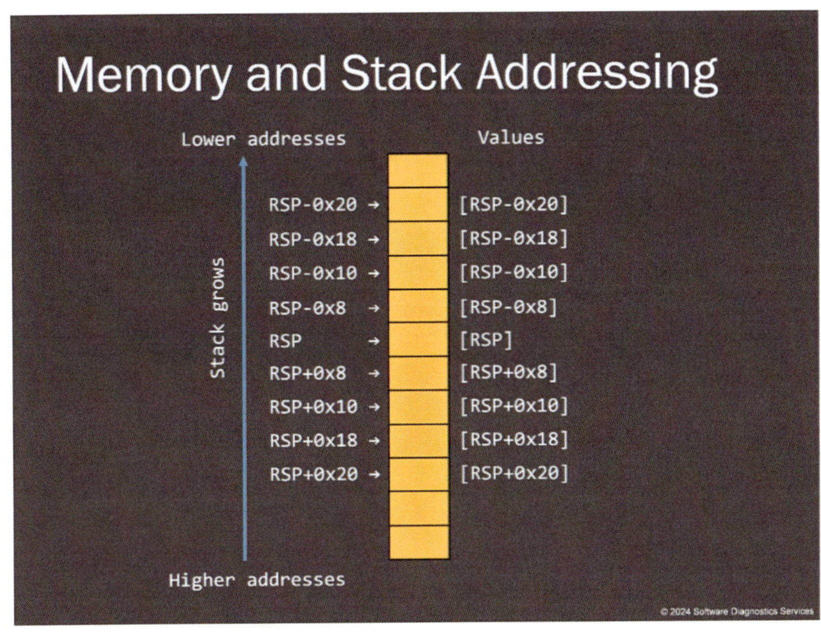

Before we look at operations with memory, let's look at a graphical representation of memory addressing where, for simplicity, I use 64-bit (or 8-byte) memory cells. A thread stack is just any other memory region, so instead of **RSP,** any other register can be used. Please note that the stack grows towards lower addresses, so to access the previously pushed values, you need to use positive offsets from **RSP**.

Memory Cell Sizes

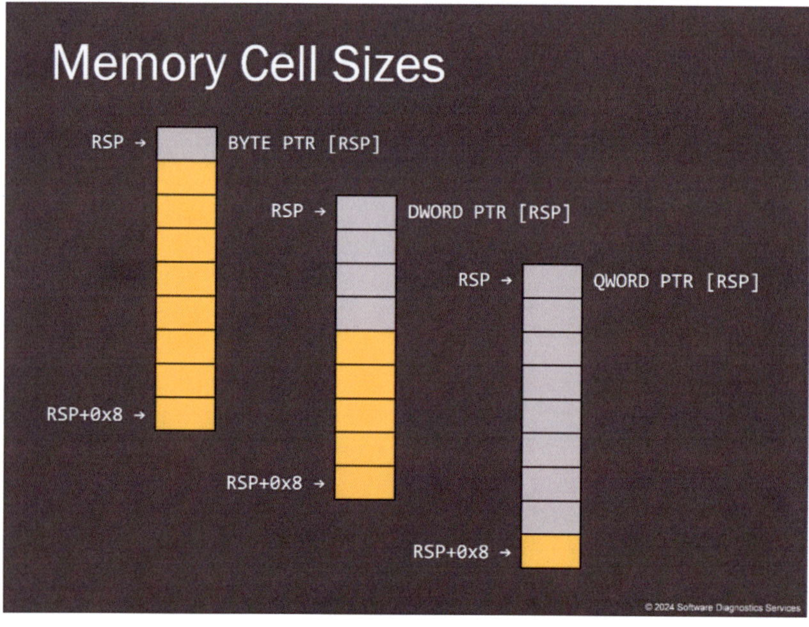

Here, each memory cell is 8-bit (or one byte). When we have a register pointing to memory, and we want to work with the value at that address, we need to specify the size of memory cells to work with, for example, **BYTE PTR** if we want to work with a byte, **DWORD PTR** if we want to work with 32-bit double words, and **QWORD PTR** if we want to work with 64-bit quad words. There's also **WORD PTR** for 16-bit values. This notation is different from Linux GDB, where we have bytes, half-words, words, and double words.

Memory Load Instructions

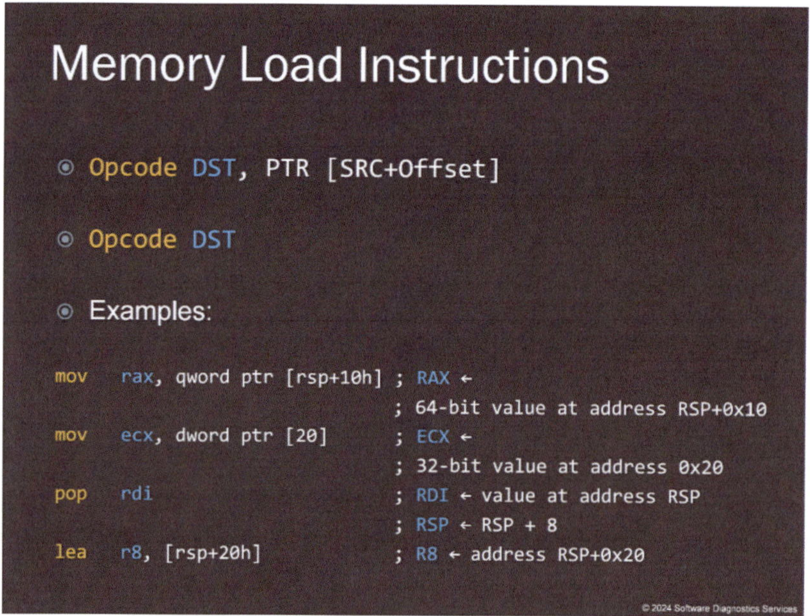

Constants are encoded in instructions, but if we need arbitrary values, we must get them from memory. Square brackets show memory access relative to an address stored in some register.

Memory Store Instructions

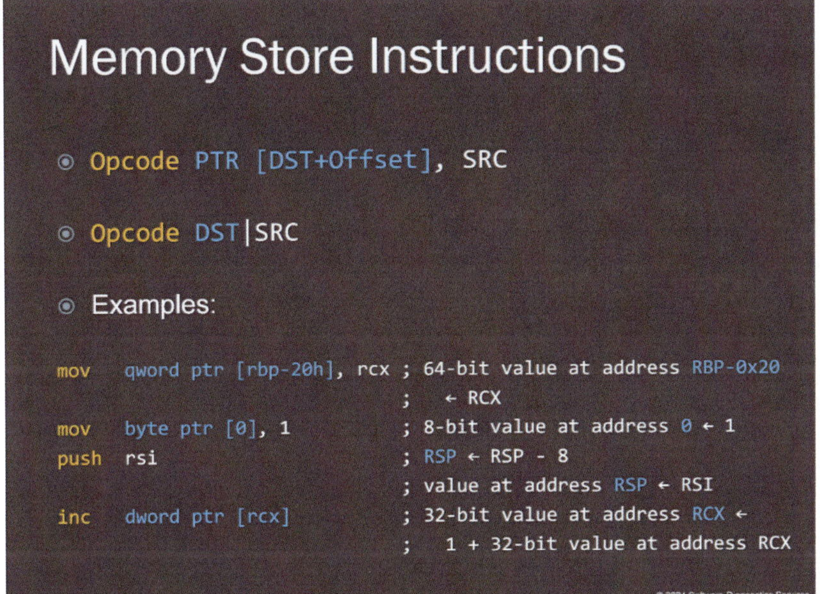

Storing is similar to loading.

Flow Instructions

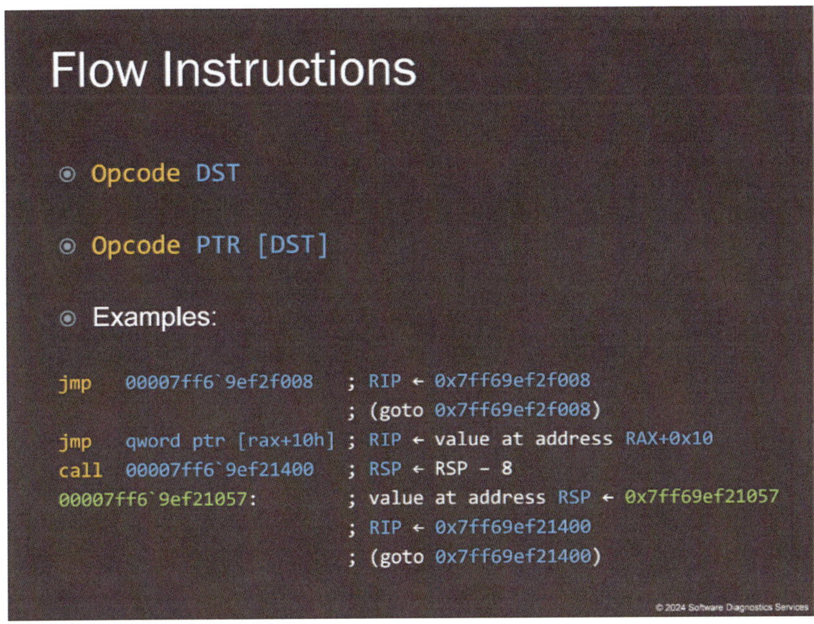

Goto (an unconditional jump) is implemented via the **JMP** instruction. Function calls are implemented via **CALL** instruction. For conditional branches, please look at the official Intel documentation. We don't use these instructions in our exercises.

Function Parameters

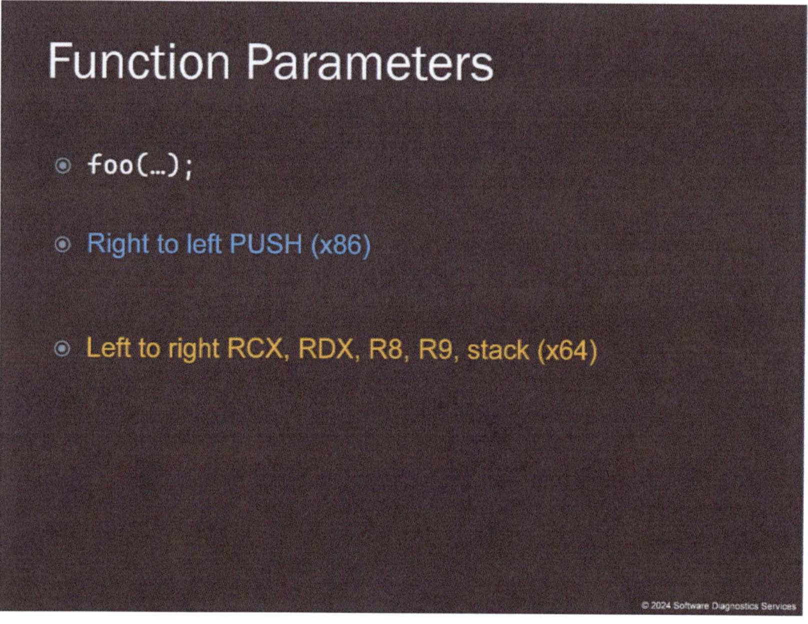

On the x86 32-bit platform, C and C++ function parameters are pushed from right to left to stack. On the x64 platform, the first four parameters from left to right are moved to CPU registers, and the rest are passed via stack locations.

Struct Function Parameters

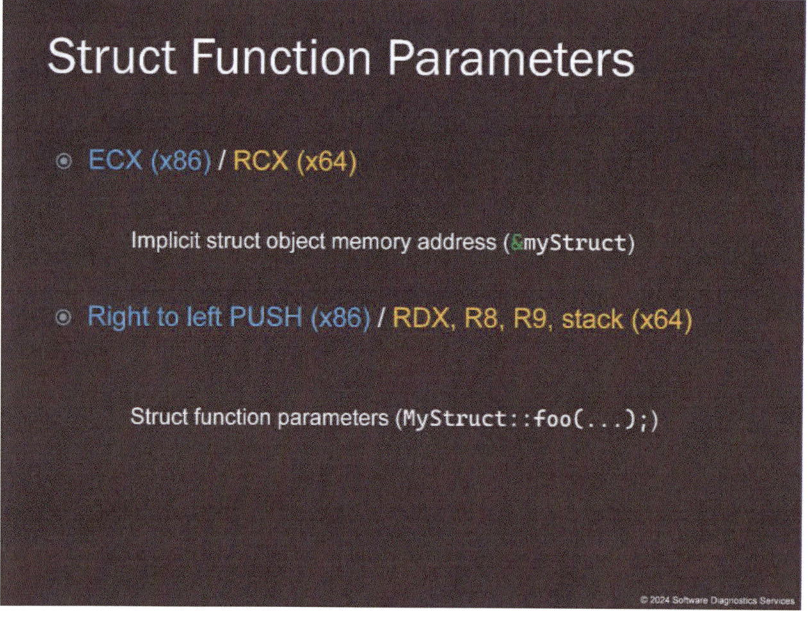

When an object struct nonstatic member function is called, the first parameter is implicit. It is an object address to help methods differentiate between objects of the same structure type and reference correct fields' memory. The rest of the parameters are passed as usual.

this

this

```
struct MyStruct
{
    int a;
    int foo(int i);
    MyStruct* myAddress() { return this; }
} myStruct;

// myStruct.myAddress() == &myStruct

int MyStruct::foo(/* myStruct* this, */ int i)
{
    return a + i + this->a + (*this).a;
}

// myStruct.foo(1) ≈ MyStruct::foo(&myStruct, 1)
```


The address of the current object is contained in `this` pointer inside C++ source code. It can be used to refer to the current object fields and methods and can also be dereferenced.

Classic C++

```
std::cout << "--- this ---" << std::endl;
{
    struct MyStruct
    {
        int a;
        int foo(/* myStruct* this, */ int i)
        {
            return a + i + this->a + (*this).a;
        }
        MyStruct* myAddress() { return this; }
    } myStruct;

    std::cout << "result of myStruct.myAddress(): " << myStruct.myAddress() <<
        " address of myStruct: " << &myStruct << std::endl;

    assert(myStruct.myAddress() == &myStruct);

    myStruct.foo(/* &myStruct, */ 1);
}
```

Output

```
--- this ---
result of myStruct.myAddress(): 0000002BC331F1F4 address of myStruct: 0000002BC331F1F4
```

Function Objects vs. Lambdas

Function Objects vs. Lambdas

```
struct lambda_1
{
    auto operator()(int x) { return -x; }
} negate;

// int negate(int)
auto negate = [](int x) { return -x; };
negate(10);

[](int x) { return -x; }(10);

// mov  edx,0Ah
// lea  rcx,[rsp+130h] ; &negate
// call <lambda_1>::operator()
```


Lambdas are internally implemented as function objects.

Modern C++

```
std::println("--- Function Objects vs. Lambdas ---");
{
    // struct lambda_1
    // {
    //     auto operator()(int x) { return -x; }
    // } negate;

    // int negate(int)
    auto negate = [](int x) { return -x; };
    negate(10);

    [](int x) { return -x; }(10);
}
```

Captures and Closures

Captures and Closures

```
{
    int b{0};

    auto negate1 = [](int x) { return b - x; };
    auto negate2 = [b](int x) { return b - x; };
    auto negate4 = [&b](int x) { return b - x; };
    auto negate5 = [=](int x) { return b - x; };
    auto negate6 = [&](int x) { return b - x; };
}
```

```
// [=]
struct lambda_5 {
    int b;
    lambda_5(int& _rb) : b(_rb) {}
    auto operator()(int x) { return b-x; }
} negate5;

lambda_5::lambda_5:
mov     qword ptr [rsp+10h],rdx
mov     qword ptr [rsp+8],rcx
mov     rax,qword ptr [rsp+8]
mov     rcx,qword ptr [rsp+10h]
mov     ecx,dword ptr [rcx]
mov     dword ptr [rax],ecx
mov     rax,qword ptr [rsp+8]
ret
```

```
// [&]
struct lambda_6 {
    int& rb;
    lambda_6(int& _rb) : rb(_rb) {}
    auto operator()(int x) { return rb-x; }
} negate6;

lambda_6::lambda_6:
mov     qword ptr [rsp+10h],rdx
mov     qword ptr [rsp+8],rcx
mov     rax,qword ptr [rsp+8]
mov     rcx,qword ptr [rsp+10h]
mov     qword ptr [rax],rcx
mov     rax,qword ptr [rsp+8]
ret
```


Inside lambda code, it is possible to use local objects from the outer scope either by copy or by reference. This mechanism is internally implemented by lambda function objects.

Modern C++

```
std::println("--- Captures and Closures ---");
{
    int b{ 0 };

    // auto negate1 = [](int x) { return b - x; }; // error
    auto negate2 = [b](int x) { return b - x; };
    auto negate4 = [&b](int x) { return b - x; };
    auto negate5 = [=](int x) { return b - x; };
    auto negate6 = [&](int x) { return b - x; };
}
```

Lambdas as Parameters

Lambdas as Parameters

```
auto negate = [](int x) { return -x; };

int apply(int arg, int (*pf)(int)) {
    return pf(arg);
}

int apply2(int arg, decltype(negate) f) {
    return f(arg);
}

void foo() {
  // apply(100, negate::<lambda>::lambda_invoker_cdecl)
  apply(100, negate);            apply2(102, negate);
}
```

```
apply:
mov     qword ptr [rsp+10h],rdx
mov     dword ptr [rsp+8],ecx
sub     rsp,38h
mov     rax,qword ptr [rsp+48h]
mov     qword ptr [rsp+20h],rax
mov     ecx,dword ptr [rsp+40h]
call    qword ptr [rsp+20h]
add     rsp,38h
ret
```

```
apply2:
mov     byte ptr [rsp+10h],dl // sizeof(negate) == 1
mov     dword ptr [rsp+8],ecx
sub     rsp,28h
mov     edx,dword ptr [rsp+38h]
lea     rcx,[rsp+38h]
call    negate::<lambda>::operator()
add     rsp,28h
ret
```


Lambdas can be passed as function parameters. We can use `decltype` to specify their type. If a normal function pointer is expected, then a special invoker function is internally called that takes care of the call. If the lambda type parameter is expected, the lambda function object `operator()` is called.

Modern C++

```
// --- Lambdas as Parameters ---

auto negate = [](int x) { return -x; };

int apply(int arg, int (*pf)(int)) {
    return pf(arg);
}

int apply2(int arg, decltype(negate) f) {
    return f(arg);
}

void fooP() {
    // apply(100, negate::<lambda>::lambda_invoker_cdecl)
    apply(100, negate);

    apply2(102, negate);
}
```

Lambda Parameter Optimization

Lambda Parameter Optimization

```
auto negate = [](int x) { return -x; };

int apply3(int arg, const decltype(negate)& crf)
{
    return crf(arg);
}

void bar()
{
    apply3(103, negate);
}
```

```
apply3:
mov     qword ptr [rsp+10h],rdx
mov     dword ptr [rsp+8],ecx
sub     rsp,28h
mov     edx,dword ptr [rsp+30h]
mov     rcx,qword ptr [rsp+38h]
call    negate::<lambda>::operator()
add     rsp,28h
ret
```


If you pass lambdas by reference, there is no function object copy.

In the disassembly, we see the function object address passed via RDX that later becomes an implicit RCX parameter for the `operator()`:

Modern C++

```
// --- Lambda Parameter Optimization ---

auto negate = [](int x) { return -x; };

int apply3(int arg, const decltype(negate)& crf)
{
    return crf(arg);
}

void bar()
{
    apply3(103, negate);
}
```

Lambdas as Unnamed Functions

Lambdas as Unnamed Functions

```
int apply(int arg, int (*pf)(int))
{
    return pf(arg);
}

void foo()
{
    int b{0};
    apply(100, [](int x) -> int { return -x-4; });
    apply(100, [=](int x) { return -x-b; });
}

lea     rdx,['2'::<lambda_1>::<lambda_invoker_cdecl>]
mov     ecx,64h
call    apply
...

lambda_invoker_cdecl:
mov     dword ptr [rsp+8],ecx
sub     rsp,38h
mov     edx,dword ptr [rsp+40h]
lea     rcx,[rsp+20h]
call    '2'::<lambda_1>::operator()
add     rsp,38h
ret
```


However, the most common usage of lambdas is unnamed functions in a local context. In such a case, a temporary function object is created. However, no context capture is allowed if lambdas are passed where function pointers are expected.

Modern C++

```
// --- Lambdas as Unnamed Functions ---

int apply(int arg, int (*pf)(int)) {
    return pf(arg);
}

void foo()
{
    int b{0};
    apply(100, [](int x) -> int { return -x - 4; });
    // apply(100, [=](int x) { return -x - b; }); // error
}
```

std::function Lambda Parameters

std::function Lambda Parameters

```
int apply4(int arg, std::function<int(int)> f) {
    return f(arg);
}

void foo4() {
    int b{0};

    apply4(100, [=](int x) -> int { return -x-b; });
}
```

```
mov     dword ptr [rsp+19Ch],0
lea     rax,[rsp+148h]
mov     qword ptr [rsp+0B0h],rax
lea     rdx,[rsp+19Ch]
lea     rcx,[rsp+70h]
call    `2'::<lambda_1>::<lambda_1> (00007ff6`39b41de0)
mov     rdx,rax
mov     rcx,qword ptr [rsp+0B0h]
call    std::function<int __cdecl(int)>::function<int __cdecl(int)><`2'::<lambda_1>,0>
mov     qword ptr [rsp+0B8h],rax
mov     rdx,qword ptr [rsp+0B8h]
mov     ecx,64h
call    apply4
```


To allow passing lambdas to capture context, we can use `std::function`.

In disassembly, we see the function object constructor that captures the context.

Modern C++

```
// --- std::function Lambda Parameters ---

#include <functional>

int apply4(int arg, std::function<int(int)> f) {
    return f(arg);
}

void foo4() {
    int b{0};

    apply4(100, [=](int x) -> int { return -x - b; });
}
```

auto Lambda Parameters

auto Lambda Parameters

```
int apply5(int arg, const auto& f) {
    return f(arg);
}

void foo5() {
    int b{0};

    apply5(100, [=](int x) -> int { return -x-b; });
}

mov     dword ptr [rsp+154h],0
lea     rdx,[rsp+154h]
lea     rcx,[rsp+88h]
call    '2'::<lambda_1>::<lambda_1>
mov     rdx,rax
mov     ecx,64h
call    apply5<'2'::<lambda_1> >
...
apply5<'2'::<lambda_1> >:
mov     dword ptr [rsp+10h],rdx
mov     dword ptr [rsp+8],ecx
sub     rsp,28h
mov     edx,dword ptr [rsp+30h]
mov     rcx,qword ptr [rsp+38h]
call    '2'::<lambda_1>::operator()
add     rsp,28h
ret
```


To capture the context and allow more flexibility and efficiency, the modern way is to use `auto`.

In disassembly, we see all necessary functions are generated automatically.

Modern C++

```
// --- auto Lambda Parameters ---

int apply5(int arg, const auto& f) {
    return f(arg);
}

void foo5() {
    int b{0};

    apply5(100, [=](int x) -> int { return -x - b; });
}
```

Lambdas as Return Values

Lambdas as Return Values

```
auto getFunc(int par) {
    return [par](int x) { return -x - par; };
}

void foo6() {
    getFunc(200)(16);
}

mov     edx,0C8h
lea     rcx,[rsp+70h]
call    getFunc
mov     qword ptr [rsp+0B8h],rax
mov     edx,10h
mov     rcx,qword ptr [rsp+0B8h]
call    `getFunc'::`2'::<lambda_1>::operator()
...
getFunc:
mov     dword ptr [rsp+10h],edx
mov     qword ptr [rsp+8],rcx
sub     rsp,28h
lea     rdx,[rsp+38h]
mov     rcx,qword ptr [rsp+30h]
call    `getFunc'::`2'::<lambda_1>::<lambda_1>
mov     rax,qword ptr [rsp+30h]
add     rsp,28h
ret
```


It is possible to return lambdas and thus mimic the so-called currying feature of functional programming.

When **`getFunc`** is called, the `par` parameter value is passed via `edx` because the first parameter in `rcx` is the implicit address of memory where to construct the returned lambda function object. When structures are returned from a function, the address to store them is passed implicitly via RCX because it is impossible to return the temporary local stack location, which can be invalid after the function return.

Modern C++

```
// -- Lambdas as Return Values ---

auto getFunc(int par) {
    return [par](int x) { return -x - par; };
}

void foo6() {
    getFunc(200)(16);
}
```

Virtual Function Call

This section provides an overview of virtual function calls in C++.

The `virtual_function_call` project:

- `virtual_function_call_classic_cpp` Classic C++

can be found in the archive[15]. In the following slide descriptions, we only show relevant code snippets and their output.

[15] https://www.patterndiagnostics.com/Training/ACPPWD/ACPPWD.zip

VTBL Memory Layout

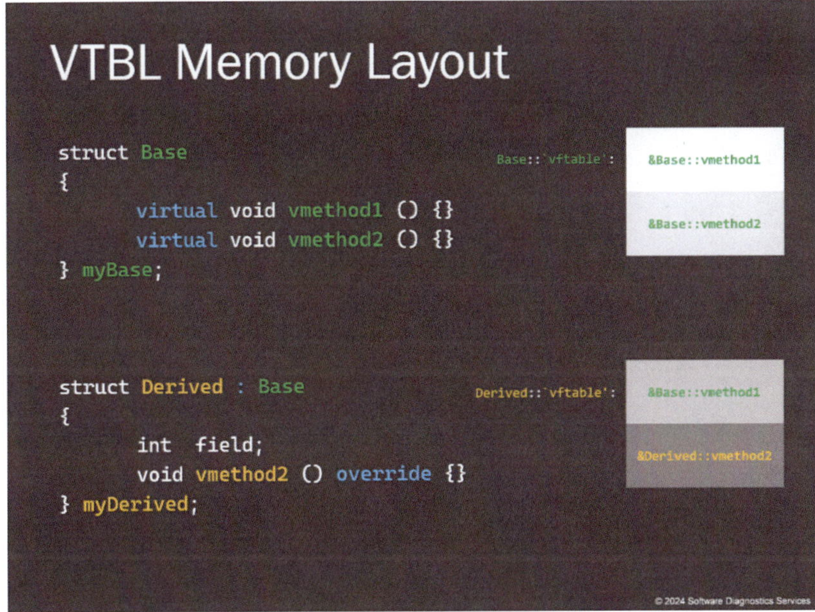

These virtual function calls are implemented uniformly by having a specific virtual function table (VTBL) for each structure where the addresses of the base structure methods are replaced with those of the derived structure methods, if any.

VPTR and Struct Memory Layout

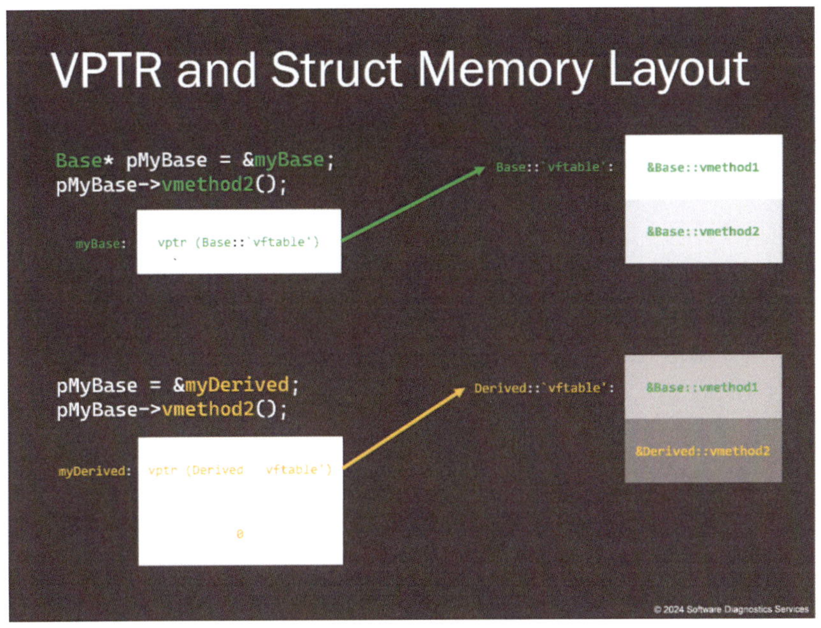

Every object, whose structure has virtual methods, has an implicit virtual function table pointer (VPTR) as its first member containing an address of the corresponding structure virtual functions table. Therefore, each virtual function call from a base structure pointer is a type-independent call where the target function address is easily calculated based on the address of the virtual function table and virtual function offset.

Classic C++

```
struct Base
{
        virtual void vmethod1() {}
        virtual void vmethod2() {}
} myBase;

struct Derived : Base
{
        int  field;
        void vmethod2() {}
} myDerived;

int main()
{
        Base* pMyBase = &myBase;
        pMyBase->vmethod2();

        pMyBase = &myDerived;
        pMyBase->vmethod2();

    return 0;
}
```

Templates: A Planck-length Introduction

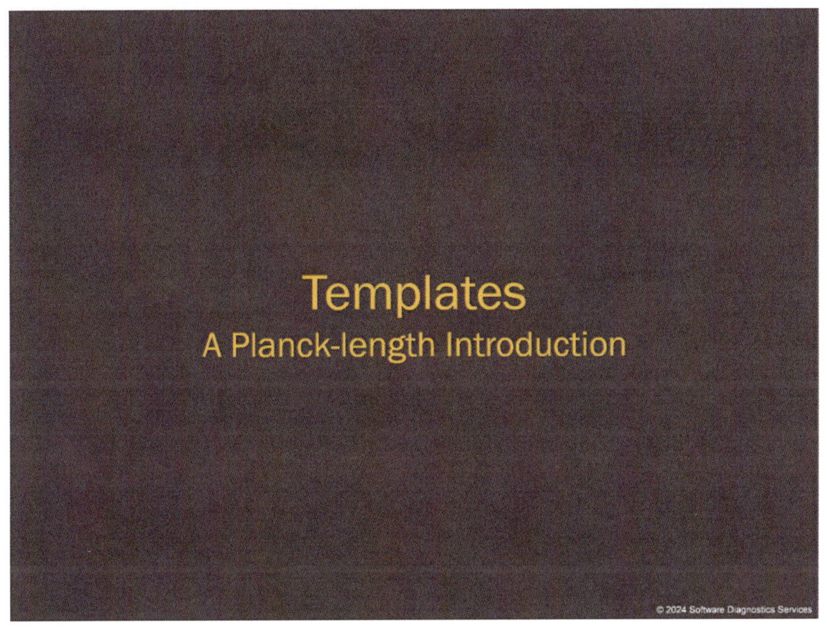

C++ templates and template meta-programming are a vast universe. We only cover a Planck-length distance in this introduction.

The `templates` project:

- `templates_modern_cpp` Modern C++

can be found in the archive[16]. In the following slide descriptions, we only show relevant code snippets and their output.

[16] https://www.patterndiagnostics.com/Training/ACPPWD/ACPPWD.zip

Why Templates?

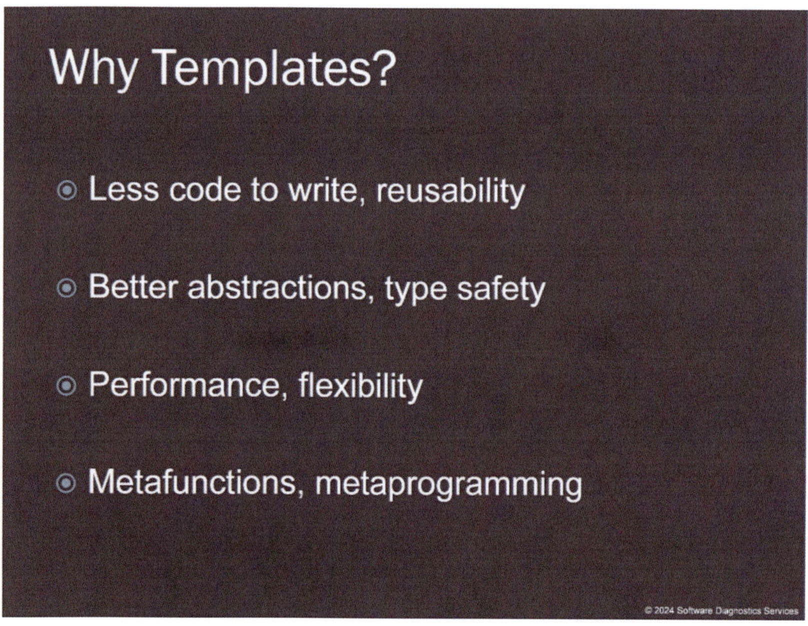

In the following slides, we briefly cover various "why" aspects.

Reusability

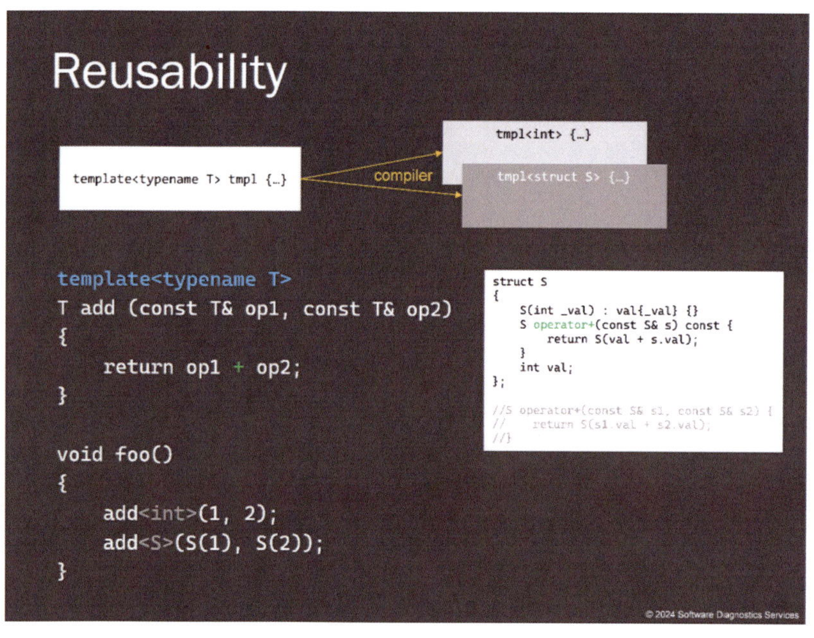

Templates allow us to write less code with higher abstractions, delegating implementation details to a compiler. The compiler checks that template arguments are compatible, for example, that they implement the required operations and methods.

Modern C++

```
template<typename T>
T add(const T& op1, const T& op2)
{
    return op1 + op2;
}

std::println("--- Reusability ---");
{
    struct S
    {
        S(int _val) : val{ _val } {}
        S operator+(const S& s) const
        {
            return S(val + s.val);
        }
        int val;
    };

    // or:
    //
    // S operator+(const S& s1, const S& s2)
    // {
    //     return S(s1.val + s2.val);
    // }

    add<int>(1, 2);
    add<S>(S(1), S(2));
}
```

Types of Templates

Types of Templates

- Struct templates

```
template <typename T> struct TStruct { T data; };
TStruct<int> ts{0};
```

- Function templates

```
struct FStruct {
    template <typename T> T zero() { return T(0); }
} fs;
fs.zero<int>();
```

- Variable templates

```
template <typename T> T zero{0};
auto z = zero<int>;
```


The following code provides examples for struct, function, and (recent) variable template categories.

Modern C++

```
template <typename T> struct TStruct { T data; };

struct FStruct
{
    template <typename T> T zero() { return T(0); }
};

template <typename T> T zero{0};

std::println("--- Types of Templates ---");
{
    TStruct<int> ts{0};

    FStruct fs;
    fs.zero<int>();

    auto z = zero<int>;
}
```

Types of Template Parameters

Types of Template Parameters

- Type parameters

```
template <typename T> ...
```

- Non-type parameters

```
template <int c> decltype(c) constant() { return c; }
constant<1>();


// call constant<1>
// ...
// constant<1>:
//   mov     eax,1
//   ret
```


There are two categories of template parameters: type and non-type.

Non-type template parameters allow the generation of very compact code with a distinct purpose.

Modern C++

```
template <int c> decltype(c) constant() { return c; }

std::println("--- Types of Template Parameters ---");
{
    constant<1>();
}
```

Type Safety

Type Safety

```
template <typename T>
T add (const T& op1, const T& op2)
{
    return op1 + op2;
}

void foo()
{
    add(M(1), M(2));
}
```

```
struct S
{
    S(int _val) : val{_val} {}
    S operator+(const S& s) const {
        return S(val + s.val);
    }
    int val;
};

struct M
{
    M(int _val) : val{_val} {}
    int val;
};
```


Compared to pointer casting, the general template code enforces type safety by checking the required operations and compatible types.

Modern C++

```
template<typename T>
T add(const T& op1, const T& op2)
{
    return op1 + op2;

}

std::println("--- Type Safety ---");
{
    struct S
    {
        S(int _val) : val{_val} {}
        S operator+(const S& s) const
        {
            return S(val + s.val);
        }
        int val;
    };

    struct M
    {
        M(int _val) : val{_val} {}
        int val;
    };

    add(S(1), S(2));
    // add(M(1), M(2)); // error
}
```

Flexibility

Flexibility

```
template<>
M add<M> (const M& op1, const M& op2)
{
    return op1.val + op2.val;
}

void foo()
{
    add<M>(M(1), M(2));
}

template<>
decltype(13) constant<13>() { return 14; }
```


It is also possible to specialize template definitions for specific types for performance and other reasons.

Modern C++

```
template<typename T>
T add(const T& op1, const T& op2)
{
    return op1 + op2;
}

struct M
{
    M(int _val) : val{_val} {}
    int val;
};

template<>
M add<M>(const M& op1, const M& op2)
{
    return op1.val + op2.val;
}

template<>
decltype(13) constant<13>() { return 14; }

std::println("--- Flexibility ---");
{
    add(M(1), struct M(2));
}
```

Metafunctions

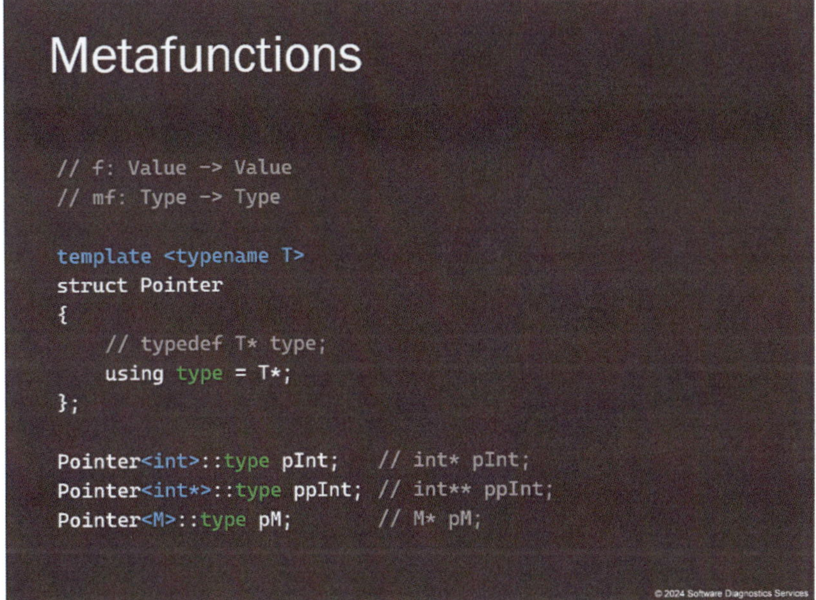

Metafunctions transform type: they take types as parameters and return types as output.

Modern C++

```
template <typename T>
struct Pointer
{
    using type = T*;
};

std::println("--- Metafunctions ---");
{
    // see above

    Pointer<int>::type pInt{};     // int* pInt;
    Pointer<int*>::type ppInt{};   // int** ppInt;
    Pointer<M>::type pM{};         // M* pM;
}
```

Variadic Templates

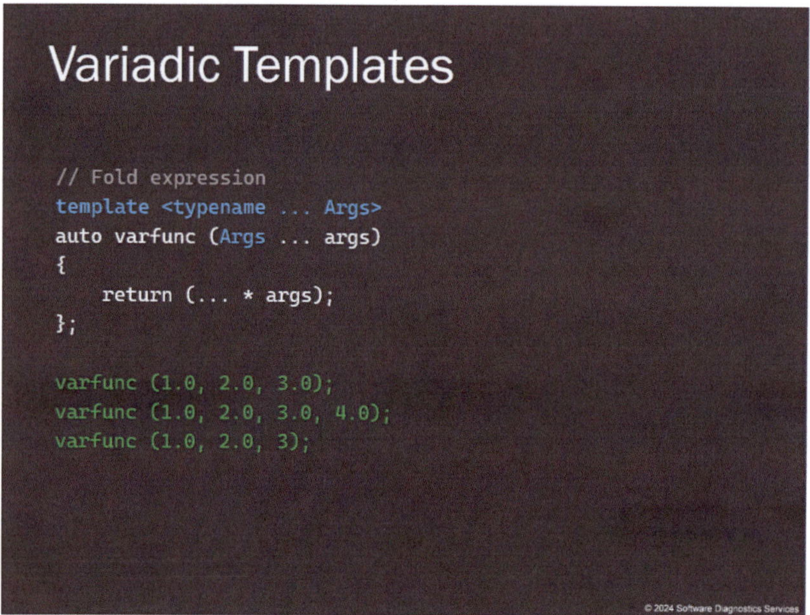

Using variadic templates solves all problems with old-style variadic functions.

Modern C++

```
template <typename ... Args>
auto varfunc(Args ... args)
{
    return (... * args);

};

std::println("--- Variadic Templates ---");
{
    // see above

    std::println("result: {}", varfunc(1.0, 2.0, 3.0));
    std::println("result: {}", varfunc(1.0, 2.0, 3.0, 4.0));
    std::println("result: {}", varfunc(1.0, 2.0, 3));

}
```

Output

```
--- Variadic Templates ---
result: 6
result: 24
result: 6
```

Iterators as Pointers

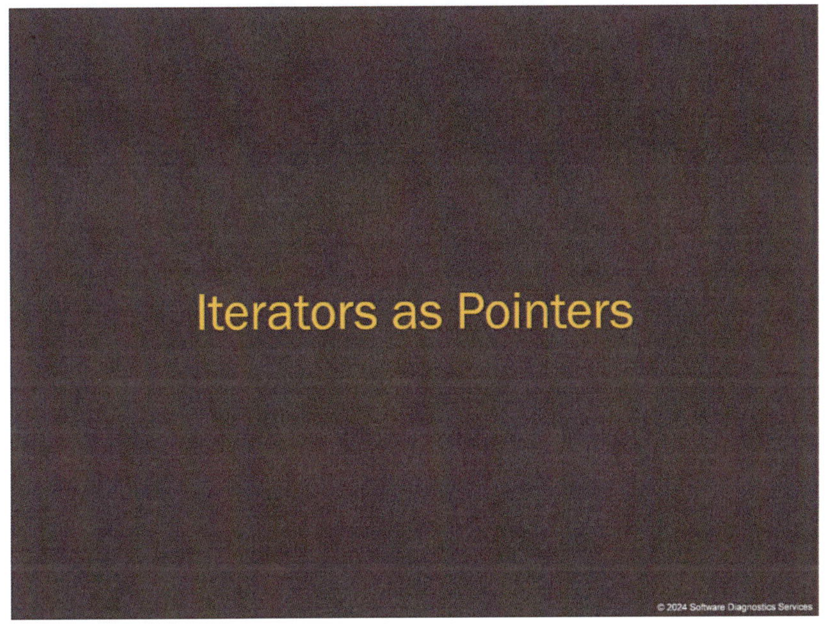

Now, we take a bird's eye view of standard library containers, iterators, and algorithms from a pointer perspective.

The `iterators_as_pointers` project:

- `iterators_as_pointers_modern_cpp` Modern C++

can be found in the archive[17]. In the following slide descriptions, we only show relevant code snippets and their output.

[17] https://www.patterndiagnostics.com/Training/ACPPWD/ACPPWD.zip

Containers

There are many container types in the standard C++ library (formerly called STL, Standard Template Library). In this course edition, we don't delve into their specifics. We hope the names intuitively suggest their semantics.

Iterators


```
std::vector<int> v{1, 2, 3, 4, 5};
std::vector<int>::iterator it = v.begin();

while (it != v.end())
{
        std::cout << *it;
        ++it;
}

int a[5]{1, 2, 3, 4, 5};
int* pa = &a[0];

while (pa != &a[5])
{
        std::cout << *pa;
        ++pa;
}
```


An iterator is a pointer abstraction. You can move it (depending on container semantics) like a pointer increment/decrement, and you can dereference it like a pointer to get a value.

Modern C++

```
std::println("--- Iterators ---");
{
	std::vector<int> v{1, 2, 3, 4, 5};
	std::vector<int>::iterator it = v.begin();

	while (it != v.end())
	{
		std::print("{} ", *it);
		++it;
	}

	std::println("");

	int a[5]{1, 2, 3, 4, 5};
	int* pa = &a[0];

	while (pa != &a[5])
	{
		std::print("{} ", *pa);
		++pa;
	}

	std::println("");
}
```

Output

```
--- Iterators ---
1 2 3 4 5
1 2 3 4 5
```

Constant Iterators

Constant Iterators

```
std::vector<int> v{1, 2, 3, 4, 5};
std::vector<int>::const_iterator cit = v.cbegin();

while (cit != v.cend())
{
	std::cout << *cit;
	++cit;
}

int a[5]{1, 2, 3, 4, 5};
const int* cpa = &a[0];

while (cpa != &a[5])
{
	std::cout << *cpa;
	++cpa;
}
```


Like a pointer to constant values, there are constant iterators.

Modern C++

```
std::println("--- Constant Iterators ---");
{
        std::vector<int> v{1, 2, 3, 4, 5};
        std::vector<int>::const_iterator cit = v.cbegin();

        while (cit != v.cend())
        {
                std::print("{} ", *cit);
                ++cit;
        }

        std::println("");

        int a[5]{1, 2, 3, 4, 5};
        const int* cpa = &a[0];

        while (cpa != &a[5])
        {
                std::print("{} ", *cpa);
                ++cpa;
        }

        std::println("");
}
```

Output

```
--- Constant Iterators ---
1 2 3 4 5
1 2 3 4 5
```

Pointers as Iterators

Pointers as Iterators

```
int arr[5]{1, 2, 3, 4, 5};
int* itarr = std::begin(arr);

// auto itarr = std::begin(arr);

while (itarr != std::end(arr))
{
        std::cout << *itarr;
        ++itarr;
}

const int* citarr = std::cbegin(arr);

while (citarr != std::cend(arr))
{
        std::cout << *citarr;
        ++citarr;
}
```


Pointers can also be considered as iterators.

Modern C++

```
std::println("--- Pointers as Iterators ---");
{
        int arr[5]{1, 2, 3, 4, 5};
        int* itarr = std::begin(arr);

        // auto itarr = std::begin(arr);

        while (itarr != std::end(arr))
        {
                std::print("{} ", *itarr);
                ++itarr;
        }

        std::println("");

        const int* citarr = std::cbegin(arr);

        while (citarr != std::cend(arr))
        {
                std::print("{} ", *citarr);
                ++citarr;
        }

        std::println("");
}
```

Output

```
--- Pointers as Iterators ---
1 2 3 4 5
1 2 3 4 5
```

Algorithms

Algorithms

```
std::vector<int> vec{2, 1, 3, 5, 4};

std::sort(vec.begin(), vec.end());


int arr[5]{2, 1, 3, 5, 4};

std::sort(std::begin(arr), std::end(arr));
```


Both iterators and containers and pointers as iterators and arrays can be used with the C++ standard library algorithms.

Modern C++

```
std::println("--- Algorithms ---");
{
	std::vector<int> vec{2, 1, 3, 5, 4};

	for (auto const& val : vec)
	{
		std::print("{} ", val);
	}
	std::println("");

	std::sort(vec.begin(), vec.end());

	std::for_each(vec.cbegin(), vec.cend(),
		[](auto const& val) { std::print("{} ", val); });
	std::println("");

	int arr[5]{20, 10, 30, 50, 40};

	for (auto const& val : arr)
	{
		std::print("{} ", val);
	}
	std::println("");

	std::sort(std::begin(arr), std::end(arr));

	std::for_each(std::cbegin(arr), std::cend(arr),
		[](auto const& val) { std::print("{} ", val); });
	std::println("");
}
```

Output

```
--- Algorithms ---
2 1 3 5 4
1 2 3 4 5
20 10 30 50 40
10 20 30 40 50
```

Memory Ownership

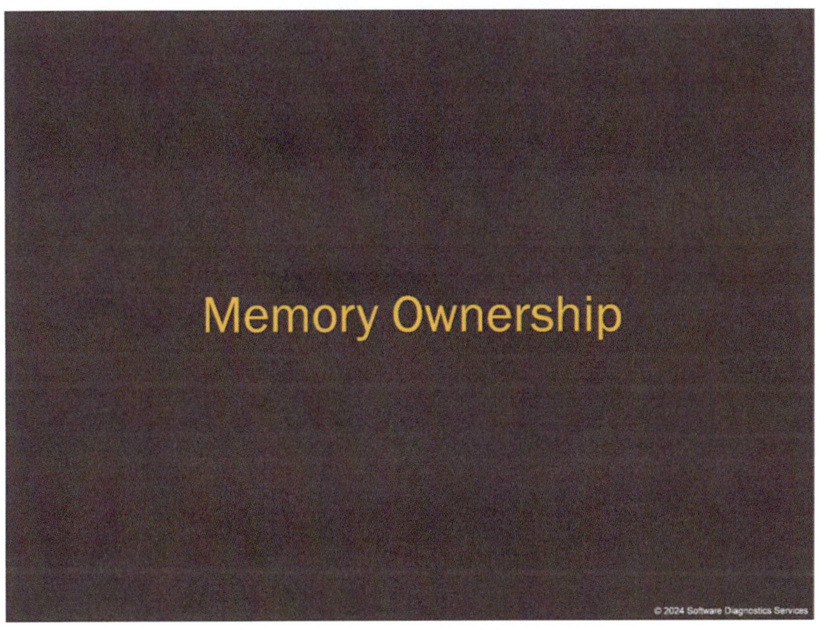

We now look at common memory ownership problems and see how they are resolved in modern C++.

Pointers as Owners

Pointers as Owners

- Ownership of dynamic memory after allocation
- Contain the address of allocated memory
- Can try Read/Write/Execute/Release

Pointers can be considered owners of dynamically allocated memory since they contain the address, and that memory can be accessed through them.

Problems with Pointer Owners

Problems with Pointer Owners

- Shared ownership after copying a pointer content
- Leak: overwriting the previous address without release
- Multiple release
- Dangling pointers pointing to already released memory
- Leak: no release before going out of scope

However, manual pointer usage is prone to multiple errors due to possible shared ownership, crashes due to possible multiple releases, and memory leaks due to dangling pointers and going out of scope.

Smart Pointers

To solve memory ownership problems, modern C++ included several kinds of smart pointers in its standard library.

The `smart_pointers` project:

- `smart_pointers_modern_cpp` Modern C++

can be found in the archive[18]. In the following slide descriptions, we only show relevant code snippets and their output.

[18] https://www.patterndiagnostics.com/Training/ACPPWD/ACPPWD.zip

Basic Design

A smart pointer should include functionality similar to raw pointers for seamless use during the refactoring of legacy code and simultaneously eliminate most, if not all, problems with raw pointer usage.

Unique Pointers

Unique Pointers

```
std::unique_ptr<int> fooU(std::unique_ptr<int> pIntPar)
{
    std::unique_ptr<int> pInt{pIntPar.release()};
    assert(pIntPar == nullptr);
    if (pInt)
        int n = *pInt; // *pInt.get();
    return pInt;
}

void barU()
{
    std::unique_ptr<int> pIntPar{new int(0)};
    std::unique_ptr<int> pIntRes{};
    assert(pIntRes == nullptr);
    pIntRes = fooU(std::move(pIntPar));
    assert(pIntPar == nullptr && pIntRes != nullptr);
}
```


For smart pointers without sharing functionality, the `unique_ptr` should be used. Copying must transfer ownership, making the source `nullptr`.

Modern C++

```
std::unique_ptr<int> fooU(std::unique_ptr<int> pIntPar)
{
    std::unique_ptr<int> pInt{pIntPar.release()};
    assert(pIntPar == nullptr);

    if (pInt)
        int n = *pInt; // *pInt.get();

    return pInt;
}

void barU()
{
    std::unique_ptr<int> pIntPar{new int(0)};
    std::unique_ptr<int> pIntRes{};
    assert(pIntRes == nullptr);

    pIntRes = fooU(std::move(pIntPar));
    assert(pIntPar == nullptr && pIntRes != nullptr);
}

std::println("--- Unique Pointers ---");
{
    barU();

}
```

Handles as Unique Pointers

Handles as Unique Pointers

```
// HANDLE hXXX{CreateXXX(...);}
// CloseHandle(hXXX);

auto hDeleter{
    [](auto ph)
    {
        if (ph && (*ph != INVALID_HANDLE_VALUE))
            ::CloseHandle(*ph);
    }};

using Handle = std::unique_ptr<HANDLE, decltype(hDeleter)>;
```


Resource handles are good candidates for unique pointers, but they should be supplied with a custom deletion mechanism.

Modern C++

```
std::println("--- Handles as Unique Pointers ---");
{
    auto hDeleter{
        [](auto ph)
        {
            if (ph && (*ph != INVALID_HANDLE_VALUE))
                ::CloseHandle(*ph);
        }};

    using Handle = std::unique_ptr<HANDLE, decltype(hDeleter)>;
}
```

Shared Pointers

Shared Pointers

```
std::shared_ptr<int> fooS(std::shared_ptr<int> pIntPar)
{
    std::shared_ptr<int> pInt{pIntPar};
    assert(pIntPar != nullptr &&
           pInt.use_count() == 3 && pIntPar.use_count() == 3);
    if (pInt)
        int n = *pInt;
    return pInt;
}

void barS()
{
    std::shared_ptr<int> pIntPar{new int(0)};
    std::shared_ptr<int> pIntRes{};
    assert(pIntRes == nullptr &&
           pIntRes.use_count() == 0 && pIntPar.use_count() == 1);
    pIntRes = fooS(pIntPar);
    assert(pIntPar != nullptr && pIntRes != nullptr &&
           pIntRes.use_count() == 2 && pIntPar.use_count() == 2);
}
```


If we want to freely copy pointers around with all new copies pointing to the same memory, then our choice is `shared_ptr`.

Modern C++

```
std::shared_ptr<int> fooS(std::shared_ptr<int> pIntPar)
{
    std::shared_ptr<int> pInt{pIntPar};

    std::println("fooS: pInt.use_count(): {} pIntPar.use_count(): {}",
        pInt.use_count(), pIntPar.use_count());
    assert(pIntPar != nullptr &&
        pInt.use_count() == 3 && pIntPar.use_count() == 3);

    if (pInt)
        int n = *pInt;

    return pInt;
}
```

```
void barS()
{
    std::shared_ptr<int> pIntPar{new int(0)};
    std::shared_ptr<int> pIntRes{};

    std::println("barS: pIntRes.use_count(): {} pIntPar.use_count(): {}",
        pIntRes.use_count(), pIntPar.use_count());
    assert(pIntRes == nullptr &&
        pIntRes.use_count() == 0 && pIntPar.use_count() == 1);

    pIntRes = fooS(pIntPar);

    std::println("barS: pIntRes.use_count(): {} pIntPar.use_count(): {}",
        pIntRes.use_count(), pIntPar.use_count());
    assert(pIntPar != nullptr && pIntRes != nullptr &&
        pIntRes.use_count() == 2 && pIntPar.use_count() == 2);
}

std::println("--- Shared Pointers ---");
{
    barS();
}
```

Output

```
--- Shared Pointers ---
barS: pIntRes.use_count(): 0 pIntPar.use_count(): 1
fooS: pInt.use_count(): 3 pIntPar.use_count(): 3
barS: pIntRes.use_count(): 2 pIntPar.use_count(): 2
```

RAII

Finally, the **RAII** idiom is specifically about managing resources, including memory.

The `raii` project:

- `raii_modern_cpp` Modern C++

can be found in the archive[19]. In the following slide descriptions, we only show relevant code snippets and their output.

[19] https://www.patterndiagnostics.com/Training/ACPPWD/ACPPWD.zip

RAII Definition

RAII Definition

```
struct Resource
{
```

- Resource Acquisition Is Initialization

```
    Resource()
    {
        // acquire resource, e.g., new
        // initialize resource, e.g., set memory values to 0
    }
```

- Includes resource release

```
    ~Resource()
    {
        // release resource, e.g., delete
    }
};
```


An RAII structure encapsulates simultaneous "atomic" resource acquisition and initialization in its constructors and includes resource release logic in its destructor.

RAII Advantages

RAII Advantages

- Resource safety

```
void foo() { Resource r{}; }
```

- Resource life-cycle predictability
- Exception safety

```
try
{
    Resource r{};
    throw -1;
}
catch (...)
{
}
```


There are several advantages to using the RAII idiom. When going out of scope, it automatically releases a resource due to a called destructor.

In the presence of exceptions, the destructor releases the acquired resource automatically. All these contribute to the predictable resource life cycle.

Handle RAII

Handle RAII

```
struct RAII_HANDLE : Handle
{
    RAII_HANDLE(HANDLE _h) : Handle(&h, hDeleter), h{_h} {};
    void operator= (HANDLE _h) { Handle::reset(); h = _h;
                                 Handle::reset(&h); }
    operator HANDLE() const { return h; }
private:
    HANDLE h;
};

int foo ()
{
    RAII_HANDLE hFile{::CreateFile(...)};

    if (hFile == INVALID_HANDLE_VALUE)
        return -1;
    // ...
    return 0;
}
```


The code example of encapsulating Windows handles using the RAII idiom. We reuse the **Handle** type from the previous *Handles as Unique Pointers* slide:

Modern C++

```
auto hDeleter{
    [](auto ph)
    {
        if (ph && (*ph != INVALID_HANDLE_VALUE))
        {
            std::println("File handle has been closed.");
            ::CloseHandle(*ph);
        }
    }};

using Handle = std::unique_ptr<HANDLE, decltype(hDeleter)>;

struct RAII_HANDLE : Handle
{
    RAII_HANDLE(HANDLE _h) : Handle(&h, hDeleter), h{_h} {};
    void operator= (HANDLE _h) {
        Handle::reset(); h = _h;
        Handle::reset(&h);
    }
    operator HANDLE() const { return h; }
private:
    HANDLE h;
};
```

```
int main()
{
    {
        RAII_HANDLE hFile{::CreateFile(L"test.txt",
            GENERIC_READ,
            0,
            NULL,
            CREATE_ALWAYS,
            FILE_ATTRIBUTE_NORMAL,
            NULL)};

        if (hFile == INVALID_HANDLE_VALUE)
        {
            std::println("File has not been created successfully.");
            return -1;
        }

        std::println("File has been created successfully.");
    }

    {
        RAII_HANDLE hFileFail{::CreateFile(L"C:/",
            GENERIC_READ,
            0,
            NULL,
            CREATE_ALWAYS,
            FILE_ATTRIBUTE_NORMAL,
            NULL)};

        if (hFileFail == INVALID_HANDLE_VALUE)
        {
            std::println("File has not been created successfully.");
            return -1;
        }

        std::println("File has been created successfully.");
    }

}
```

Output

```
File has been created successfully.
File handle has been closed.
File has not been created successfully.
```

Threads and Synchronization

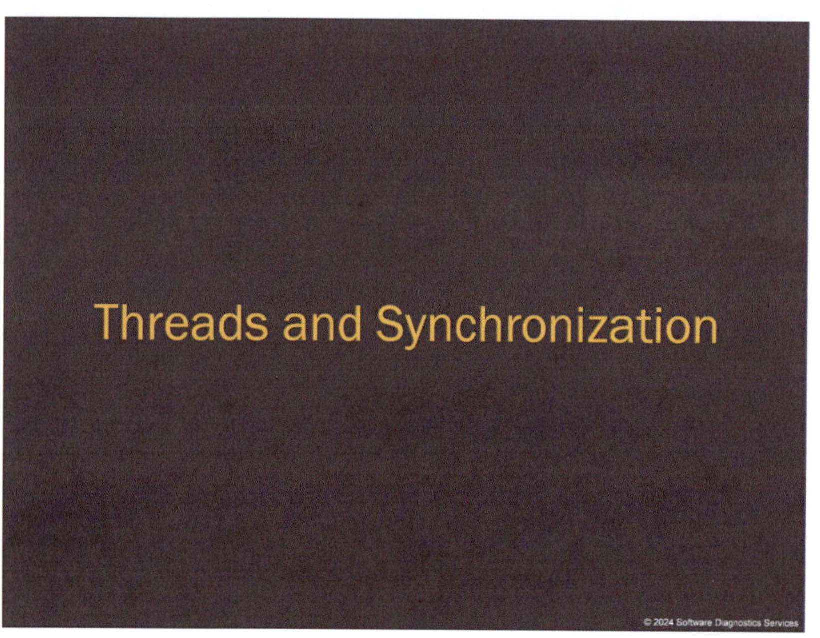

Our final section in this edition is about threads and synchronization in C++.

The **threads_synchronization** project:

- `threads_synchronization_modern_cpp` Modern C++

can be found in the archive[20]. In the following slide descriptions, we only show relevant code snippets and their output.

[20] https://www.patterndiagnostics.com/Training/ACPPWD/ACPPWD.zip

Threads in C/C++

Threads in C and Classic C++

```
// typedef DWORD (WINAPI *PTHREAD_START_ROUTINE)(
//     LPVOID lpThreadParameter
//     );
// typedef PTHREAD_START_ROUTINE LPTHREAD_START_ROUTINE;

DWORD WINAPI threadProc (void* param)
{
    Sleep((int)param * 1000);
    return 0;
}

void foo()
{
    CreateThread(NULL, 0, threadProc, (void*)5, 0, NULL);
}
```


Traditional C/C++ threading using raw Windows API is limited. Passing any parameter type and casting it is error-prone.

Modern C++

```
DWORD WINAPI threadProc(void* param)
{
    std::println("threadProc started");
    Sleep(static_cast<DWORD>(reinterpret_cast<ULONG64>(param)) * 1000);
    std::println("threadProc finished");
    return 0;

}

std::println("--- Threads in C and Classic C++ ---");
{
    HANDLE hThread{::CreateThread(NULL, 0, threadProc, (void*)5, 0, NULL)};
    if (hThread)
    {
        ::WaitForSingleObject(hThread, INFINITE);
    }

}
```

Threads in C++ Proper

Threads in C++ Proper

```
// functions, function objects, lambdas
void threadProcCpp(int param, std::wstring msg)
{
    ::Sleep(param * 1000);
    ::MessageBox(NULL,
        (L"New Thread Created! " + msg).c_str(),
        L"Thread Check", MB_OK | MB_SETFOREGROUND);
}

void foo()
{
    std::thread threadCpp(threadProcCpp, 6, L"Hello");
    //...
    threadCpp.join();
    // std::jthread threadCpp(threadProcCpp, 6, L"Hello");
}
```


The proper C++ standard library `thread` allows the utilization of the power of modern C++ abstractions. Please also note the existence of `jthread` that combines both thread creation and `join`.

Modern C++

```
void threadProcCpp(int param, std::wstring msg)
{
    ::Sleep(param * 1000);
    ::MessageBox(NULL,
        (L"New Thread Created! " + msg).c_str(),
        L"Thread Check", MB_OK | MB_SETFOREGROUND);

}

std::println("--- Threads in C++ Proper ---");
{
    std::jthread threadCpp(threadProcCpp, 6, L"Hello");
}
```

Synchronization Problems

Synchronization Problems

```
long long counter{0};

void threadProcCpp(std::wstring msg)
{
    while (true)
    {
        std::wcout << msg << L": " << ++counter << std::endl;
    }
}

void foo()
{
    std::jthread thread1(threadProcCpp, L"Hello1");
    std::jthread thread2(threadProcCpp, L"Hello2");
}

// Hello2: 1694
// : 1695
```


In the code example, the output from << operators from different threads is mixed and looks like garbage.

Modern C++

```
long long counter{0};

void threadProcCppProblem(std::wstring msg)
{
    int num{1000};

    while (num--)
    {
        std::wcout << msg << L": " << ++counter << std::endl;
    }
}

std::println("--- Synchronization Problems ---");
{
    std::jthread thread1(threadProcCppProblem, L"Hello1");
    std::jthread thread2(threadProcCppProblem, L"Hello2");
}
```

Synchronization Solution

Synchronization Solution

```
std::atomic<long long> counter{0};

std::mutex m;

void threadProcCpp(std::wstring msg)
{
    while (true)
    {
        std::scoped_lock lock {m};
        std::wcout << msg << L": " << ++counter << std::endl;
    }
}

void foo()
{
    std::jthread thread1(threadProcCpp, L"Hello1");
    std::jthread thread2(threadProcCpp, L"Hello2");
}
```


The following code example solves the data race problem by guarding access via `scoped_lock` that is implemented using `mutex`:

Modern C++

```
std::atomic<long long> counterAtomic{0};

std::mutex m;

void threadProcCppSolution(std::wstring msg)
{
    int num{1000};

    while (num--)
    {
        std::scoped_lock lock{m};
        std::wcout << msg << L": " << ++counterAtomic << std::endl;
    }

}

std::println("--- Synchronization Solution ---");
{
    std::jthread thread1(threadProcCppSolution, L"Hello1");
    std::jthread thread2(threadProcCppSolution, L"Hello2");

}
```

Memory-safe C++ Development

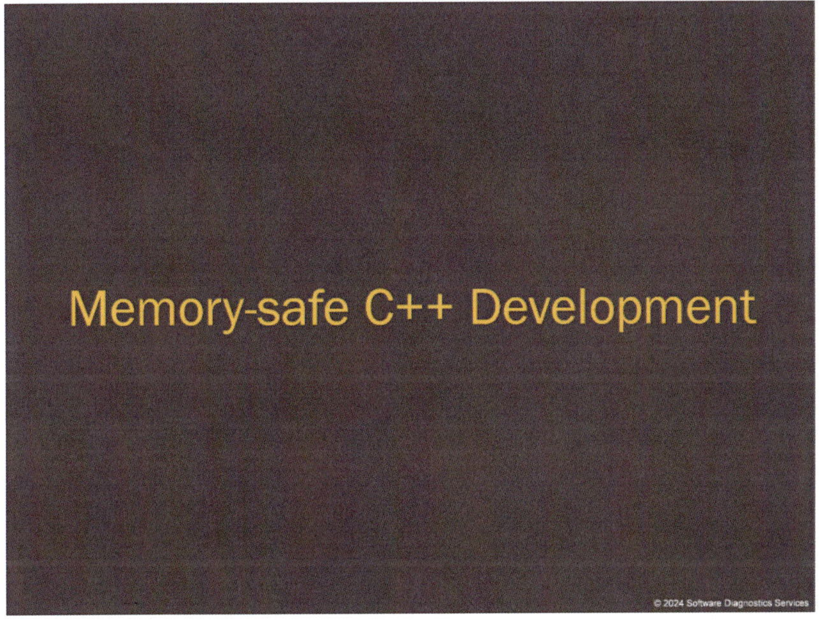

Here I share with you my own recommendation based on more than two decades of classic and modern C++ development experience.

URSS Principle

URSS Principle

- Uniform initialization
- References
- Smart pointers
- Standard containers

When writing in C++, I use two classic and two modern features that allow me to write memory-safe code that never has memory leaks or crashes. These are **U**niform initialization, **R**eferences, **S**mart pointers, and **S**tandard Containers (**URSS**). Although I also use standard library algorithms, I didn't include them in the set because they help eliminate another class of bugs – logic bugs.

Resources

Now, I have a few slides about references and resources for further reading.

C and C++

C and C++

- My Road to Modern C++
- A Tour of C++, Third Edition
- Embracing Modern C++ Safely
- C++ Core Guidelines Explained
- cppreference

My reading list up to C++17:

My Road to Modern C++
https://www.linkedin.com/pulse/my-road-modern-c-dmitry-vostokov/

cppreference
https://en.cppreference.com/w/

Three recent books are also recommended:

- A Tour of C++, Third Edition
- Embracing Modern C++ Safely
- C++ Core Guidelines Explained

Reading Windows-based Code

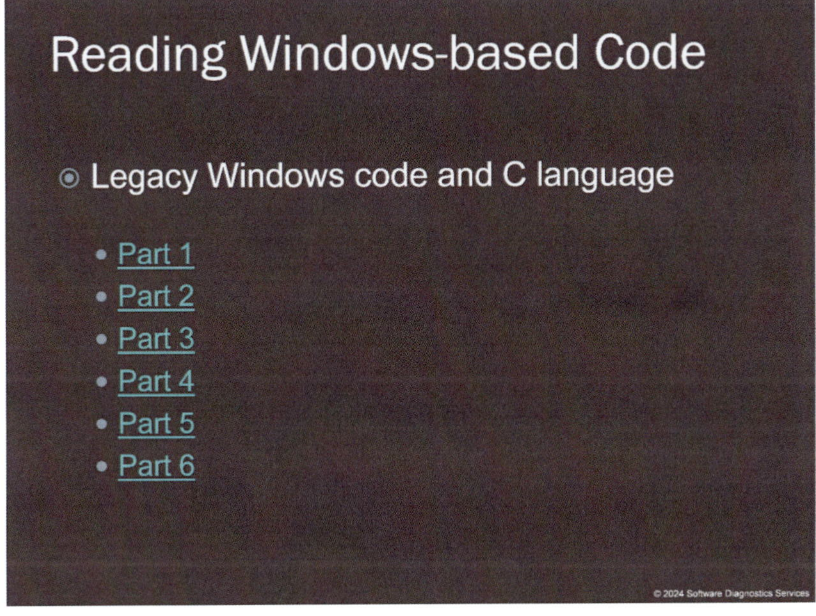

In 2004, I developed training sessions for reading Windows-based code. It combines Windows-specific types with required C language knowledge to follow basic SDK samples.

Part 1
https://patterndiagnostics.com/Training/Reading-Windows-based-Code-Part1.pdf

Part 2
https://patterndiagnostics.com/Training/Reading-Windows-based-Code-Part2.pdf

Part 3
https://patterndiagnostics.com/Training/Reading-Windows-based-Code-Part3.pdf

Part 4
https://patterndiagnostics.com/Training/Reading-Windows-based-Code-Part4.pdf

Part 5
https://patterndiagnostics.com/Training/Reading-Windows-based-Code-Part5.pdf

Part 6
https://patterndiagnostics.com/Training/Reading-Windows-based-Code-Part6.pdf

Windows (C and C++)

Windows (C and C++)

- Programming Windows, 5th Edition
- ATL Internals
- Windows Graphics Programming: Win32 GDI and DirectDraw
- Introduction to 3D Game Programming with DirectX 12
- Windows via C/C++
- Introducing Windows 7 for Developers
- Mastering Windows 8 C++ App Development
- Windows System Programming, 4th Edition
- Windows 10 System Programming
- Windows Kernel Programming, 2nd Edition
- Concurrent Programming on Windows
- The Old New Thing
- Fundamentals of Audio & Video Programming for Games
- Software Application Development: A Visual C++, MFC, and STL Tutorial
- Dump2Picture

The Old New Thing
https://devblogs.microsoft.com/oldnewthing/

The following project illustrates idioms like RAII in the context of Windows API:

Dump2Picture
https://bitbucket.org/softwarediagnostics/dump2picture

The following Windows C and C++ books are recommended:

Programming Windows, 5th Edition
ATL Internals
Windows Graphics Programming: Win32 GDI and DirectDraw
Introduction to 3D Game Programming with DirectX 12
Windows via C/C++
Introducing Windows 7 for Developers
Mastering Windows 8 C++ App Development
Windows System Programming, 4th Edition
Windows 10 System Programming
Windows Kernel Programming, 2nd Edition
Concurrent Programming on Windows
Fundamentals of Audio & Video Programming for Games
Software Application Development: A Visual C++, MFC, and STL Tutorial

Training (Windows C and C++)

Training (Windows C and C++)

- Practical Foundations of Windows Debugging, Disassembling, Reversing, Second Edition
- Accelerated Windows Memory Dump Analysis, Sixth Edition
- Accelerated Windows Debugging^4, Fourth Edition
- Accelerated Disassembly, Reconstruction and Reversing, Third Edition
- Accelerated Windows API for Software Diagnostics
- Extended Windows Memory Dump Analysis

Additional training courses that use Windows C and C++:

Practical Foundations of Windows Debugging, Disassembling, Reversing, Second Edition
https://www.patterndiagnostics.com/practical-foundations-windows-debugging-disassembling-reversing

Accelerated Windows Memory Dump Analysis, Sixth Edition
https://www.patterndiagnostics.com/accelerated-windows-memory-dump-analysis-book

Accelerated Windows Debugging^4, Fourth Edition
https://www.patterndiagnostics.com/accelerated-windows-debugging-book

Accelerated Disassembly, Reconstruction and Reversing, Third Edition
https://www.patterndiagnostics.com/accelerated-disassembly-reconstruction-reversing-book

Accelerated Windows API for Software Diagnostics
https://www.patterndiagnostics.com/accelerated-windows-api-book

Extended Windows Memory Dump Analysis
https://www.patterndiagnostics.com/extended-windows-memory-dump-analysis-book

www.ingramcontent.com/pod-product-compliance
Lightning Source LLC
Chambersburg PA
CBRC091940210326
41598CB00013B/872

* 9 7 8 1 9 1 2 6 3 6 6 1 7 *